The Governance Report 2017
Hertie School of Governance

OXFORD

The Governance Report 2017

OXFORD
UNIVERSITY PRESS

OXFORD
UNIVERSITY PRESS

Great Clarendon Street, Oxford, OX2 6DP,
United Kingdom

Oxford University Press is a department of the University of Oxford.
It furthers the University's objective of excellence in research, scholarship,
and education by publishing worldwide. Oxford is a registered trade mark of
Oxford University Press in the UK and in certain other countries.

© Hertie School of Governance 2017

The moral rights of the authors have been asserted

First Edition published in 2017

Impression: 1

British Library Cataloguing in Publication Data
Data available

Library of Congress Cataloging in Publication Data
Data available

ISBN 978-0-19-878732-7

Printed in Great Britain on acid-free paper
by Clays Ltd, St Ives plc

Managing Editor: Regina A. List
Associate Editor: Sonja Kaufmann
Book design: Plural | Severin Wucher
Cover illustration: Emilia Birlo
Information graphics: Plural | Kilian Krug
Typeset in Publico and TheSans

Table of Contents

Preface

In January 2017, Donald Trump took office as President of the United States. While a change of administration would normally not seem so dramatic, in times of rising populism and distrust of political institutions, increasing illiberalism, continuing threats of terrorism, and changing power relations, it serves as an urgent signal of the need for responsible steward-ship of democratic values, principles, and institutions. This edition of the Governance Report, highlighting and assessing democratic innovations, could therefore not be more timely.

The Governance Report 2017 is the fifth in an annual series about the changing conditions of governance, the challenges and opportunities involved, and the implications and recommendations that present them-selves to analysts and policy-makers.

The Governance Report is an interdisciplinary effort to examine state-of-the-art governance. In doing so, it enlists experts from the Hertie School of Governance in Berlin as well as from other institutions. Special attention is paid to institutional designs and approaches, changes, and innovations that both state and non-state actors have adopted in response to shifts that have been occurring–and, in this year's edition, in relation to innovations intended to manage and care for democracy.

The results are available in an annual series that includes this compact report and a companion edited volume, both published by Oxford University Press, and a dedicated website at www.governancereport.org. Together, these outputs and outlets are designed to provide both policy-makers and analysts with ideas, knowledge, and tools to consider and implement poli-cies and programmes that lead to better solutions to public problems.

Launched in February 2013, the first edition examines the challenges of financial and fiscal governance, and proposes a new paradigm of responsi-ble sovereignty for tackling global issues. In the 2014 edition, the focus turns to the administrative capacity of public administrations, whereas in 2015, the Report examines the governance of the European Union and assesses the status of the European integration project, highlighting the practical and political dilemmas involved. The 2016 edition, a collaborative effort with the OECD, puts focus on the governance of infrastructure by emphasising the complexity and trade-offs faced by decision-makers, project managers, busi-nesses, and the population at large in setting priorities, choosing projects, and implementing them.

For this 2017 edition, we asked a group of scholars to explore what is being done today to counteract the democratic malaise experienced in many countries and shed light on how to manage and care for democracy itself. *The Governance Report 2017* emphasises solutions geared toward enhancing citizen participation and improving institutions in various contexts. Going beyond identifying best practices, the Report also examines the trade-offs these solutions entail and how policy-makers can make sense of them.

Finally, the Governance Report series seeks to provide evidence to support decision-making processes by developing a new generation of indicators. The dashboards, presenting data on variables either taken from existing sources or collected by our indicators team, provide a wealth of information for policy-makers and researchers that can be extracted and analysed according to the issue or question at hand. The 2017 edition of the compact report assembles data on the availability of types of democratic innovations around the world. The dashboards and analytical tools described in the Report are also available at www.governancereport.org.

Typically the Report's companion edited volume examines the same topic as that year's compact report. The 2017 edition of the edited volume departs from this tradition in order to look back on how the field of governance indicators has developed since the first Report was published and then look forward to suggest ways such indicators can be even better used for policy-making and research.

Future editions of the Report will focus on the governance of the United Nations, the metropolis, digitalisation, energy, and security. We invite your comments and suggestions at governance.report@hertie-school.org.

Helmut K. Anheier and Regina A. List
Berlin, February 2017

Acknowledgements

Many people have been involved in developing this edition of *The Governance Report*, in addition to the authors of the various chapters.

We are grateful to Claus Offe and Alina Mungiu-Pippidi for providing valuable input to Helmut K. Anheier's introductory chapter 'Democracy Challenged' and to Larry Diamond, Frank Fukuyama, and Ira Katznelson for their feedback on it. Wolfgang Merkel offers thanks to Seongcheol Kim for his invaluable linguistic support in preparing Chapter VIII 'The Limits of Democratic Innovations in Established Democracies'.

We also appreciate the ideas and constructive criticism provided by members of the Hertie School community, especially faculty. This Report could not have come together without the work of the core Hertie School Governance Report team, which, in addition to authors Matthias Haber, Sonja Kaufmann, Olga Kononykhina, and Regina List, includes Jessica Leong Cohen and Christopher (CJ) Yetman. Hertie School staff members Ines Andre-Schulze, Zora Chan, Magriet Cruywagen, Doroteja Enčeva, Faye Freyschmidt, Cristina Gonzalez, Charlotte Koyro, Regine Kreitz, and Ellen Thalman supported the team in innumerable ways.

We also wish to thank the Board of the Hertie School of Governance for encouraging this Report, and for providing critical feedback and direction. In addition, we would like to mention the members of the Report's International Advisory Committee: Craig Calhoun (Berggruen Institute), William Roberts Clark (Texas A&M), John Coatsworth (Columbia University), Ann Florini (Singapore Management University and Brookings Institution), Geoffrey Garrett (University of Pennsylvania), Mary Kaldor (London School of Economics), Edmund J. Malesky (Duke University), Henrietta Moore (University College London), Woody Powell (Stanford University), Bo Rothstein (University of Oxford), Shanker Satyanath (New York University), James Vreeland (Georgetown University), Kent Weaver (Georgetown University), Arne Westad (Harvard University), and Michael Zürn (Wissenschaftszentrum Berlin).

At Oxford University Press, we thank Dominic Byatt for seeing the promise in this enterprise and to Olivia Wells for guiding us through.

For the Report's look we are grateful to the team of Severin Wucher and Kilian Krug at Plural in Berlin, and to Emilia Birlo for the cover art. We also thank Jaina Hirai for her very careful proofreading.

Finally, we are especially grateful to the Hertie Foundation for its support, to Evonik and Stiftelsen Riksbankens Jubileumsfond for their support in launching the Report series, and to the Berggruen Institute for providing a part of the financial resources that made this Report's development and production possible.

List of Figures, Tables, and Boxes

List of Abbreviations

AfD	Alternative for Germany
AVR	automatic voter registration
CETA	Comprehensive Economic Trade Agreement
CSO	civil society organisation
CSR	corporate social responsibility
DANS	State National Security Agency (Bulgaria)
DMV	Department of Motor Vehicles (US)
EIU	Economist Intelligence Unit
EU	European Union
FISA	Foreign Intelligence Surveillance Act (US)
FISC	United States Foreign Surveillance Court (US)
GJM	Global Justice Movement
ID	identification
LGBTQ	lesbian, gay, bisexual, transgender, and queer
NATO	North Atlantic Treaty Organization
NGO	non-governmental organisation
OECD	Organisation for Economic Co-operation and Development
OPEN	Online Progressive Engagement Network
PB	participatory budgeting
Pegida	Patriotic Europeans Against the Islamisation of the West
PiS	Law and Justice Party (Poland)
R&D	research and development
SVP	Swiss People's Party
TTIP	Transatlantic Trade and Investment Partnership
WSF	World Social Forum

I. Democracy Challenged

HELMUT K. ANHEIER

Current debates on the problems of democracy have disproportionately focused on familiar sets of shortcomings and emerging deficiencies, be they issues associated with democratic rollback (see Anheier 2015) or the rise of populism (Müller 2016). By contrast and with few exceptions[1], there has been less attention paid to assessing the numerous efforts and innovations taking place at the local, national, and international levels that seek to remedy backsliding and subversion, that contribute to resilience and consolidation, and that assist in the expansion of democracy in an era of limited sovereignty and, often, statehood. Especially where illiberalism is emerging and populism threatens, potentially innovative reactions and counter-actions in the democracies affected tend to receive less attention.

This is where *The Governance Report 2017* comes in. The Report and its accompanying website (http://www.governancereport.org) focus on those policies, programmes, projects, and initiatives meant to address the causes of democracy subversion, to stimulate democratic resilience, and to foster the consolidation and development of democratic regimes. The Report's ambition, reflecting its evidence-based approach, is to shed light on how to manage and care for democracy itself.[2] Specifically, the Report will emphasise solutions, enriched by a comparative empirical overview and case studies of innovations and best practices, and, in a final chapter, will offer a tableau of innovations and suggestions to policy-makers.

Caring for Democracy

From a global perspective, three major trends characterise current debates on democracy: low-key malaise mostly among the consolidated democracies of western Europe, the United States, and Australia, which remained seemingly dormant for years and now threatens to develop into a fuller crisis[3]; democratic resilience amidst sometimes serious threats and uneven performances in former communist countries, Latin America, Southeast Asia, and parts of Africa; and various forms of rejecting western democracy in favour of some version of authoritarian, technocratic forms of governance, with Russia, China, and Singapore as prime exemplars.

Leaving the latter aside, the main factors associated with the trends affecting democratic regimes are:

- Political, such as changing party systems (Alonso, Keane, and Merkel 2011; Katz and Mair 1994; Lindner, Aichholzer, and Hennen 2016), institutional voids and closures (Mair 2013), and inclusion and exclusion of key constituencies (Burden 2007; Lublin 1999);
- Social, such as changing demographics or the role of elites (Weßels 2015);
- Economic, such as rising inequalities (Atkinson 2015; Bartels 2008) and opportunities (Fukuyama 2012) or recession and growth (Haggard and Kaufman 1995);
- Cultural, such as participation patterns, erosion of trust, and identity (Inglehart and Norris 2016; McLaren 2017; Parvin 2015);
- Legal and regulatory, such as rule of law, public sector performance, and corruption (Mungiu-Pippidi 2015b);
- Communication, such as the rise of new communication technologies and profound changes in the role of the media through social networking sites and fake news (McCombs 2004; Placek 2016).

The strengths of these factors, typically in some combination or another, help explain why some democracies are doing better than others and why governance performance among democratic states varies–both subjectively in the eyes of constituencies as well as based on objective indicators. It is one of the main tenets of political science that the legitimacy of the democratic order depends on performance, both actual and assumed, and the capacity to master governance requirements. We hasten to add the fundamental insight that longer-term performance and the challenges encountered are closely related to the promises made and the constraints present when a democratic regime is founded (Linz and Stepan 1996; Seibel 2016).

Three Scenarios

*T*he Economist opened its 'The World in 2015' Leaders piece with the statement: 'Of all the predictions to be made about 2015, none seems safer than the idea that across the great democracies people will feel deeply let down by those who lead them' (Micklethwait 2014). The *Financial Times* called 2016 'the year of the demagogue' (Barber 2016). Indeed, 2015 and 2016 witnessed the rise of populist candidates, parties, and movements challenging those in power–perhaps most dramatically illustrated by the Brexit vote in the United Kingdom; the election of Donald Trump in the US; the strong showing of populist right-wing parties in France, Austria, the Netherlands, Poland, and Hungary; and movements of dramatically different political agendas like Podemos in Spain, Syriza in Greece, and Pegida in

Germany that draw their strength from voter dissatisfaction with the way contemporary politics work.

Evidence from Europe and the US seems sobering. Since the beginning of the 2008-9 economic crisis, citizens across western democracies have lost confidence in key institutions: political parties are on average now trusted by only 19 per cent of Europeans, governments and national parliaments by about 29 per cent (Mungiu-Pippidi 2015a). For over a decade, a clear majority of Americans have claimed to be dissatisfied with the way they are governed, with the share of those unhappy reaching over 80 per cent, higher than during the Watergate era (Gallup 2016a, 2017). Using data from parlgov.org, Inglehart and Norris (2016: 2) report that across Europe, the average share of populist parties in legislative bodies has risen from 5.1 per cent to 13.2 per cent since the 1960s.

On top of the growing sentiment that elections and traditional parties do not provide a sufficient redress mechanism are profound changes in the public sphere: the media, traditionally a major factor of democratic polities and open societies, are facing many challenges themselves, including resurgent threats to media freedom in a growing number of countries.[4] At the same time, in many places the media's authoritative role in holding democratic systems accountable is being put to the test as some political leaders–typically populists–accuse journalists and news outlets of disseminating falsehoods, leaving the populace wondering what news is real and what is fake. The vast amount of information and opinions now available via the internet and social media comes as both an opportunity for enabling an informed citizenry and a threat of either overwhelming the citizen or spreading disinformation more broadly and more rapidly.

The public spheres of informed and engaged citizens seem to be weakening across countries, even in those with well-functioning media landscapes and relatively high levels of political awareness and participation. In the US, for example, interest in running for political office is at an all-time low, and there are concerns about how to fill some 520,000 elected offices given an increasingly under-informed and less engaged public (Lawless and Fox 2015). Such trends are paralleled by fears of perceived corruption of the political class, which in turn feed the success of new populist movements threatening to destabilise democracy even further with promises impossible to keep (Kriesi 2014b).

Concurrently, neo-populism is on the rise (Chwalisz 2015; Grabbe and Lehne 2016; Inglehart and Norris 2016; Müller 2016). Irrespective of its many varieties, Abromeit et al. (2016: xiv) identify several key constitutive elements of populism: a belief in the sovereignty of 'the people' as the harbour of moral virtue, exploited by elites; anti-pluralist notions of stark friend-enemy distinctions, not of negotiated compromises; and nativist beliefs that suggest overly simplistic solutions for perceived crises. Pointing out that populism can be either pro-state or anti-state, an urban as well as a rural

Box 1 Workplace democracy

Workplaces are usually situated in hierarchical organisations with clear lines of command. Workplace democracy refers to procedures and institutions that allow workers to have a say in the fundamental rules and regulations governing their workplaces and their employment relationships. These procedures and institutions can take many different forms, from autonomous trade union representation in the workplace and workers' councils rooted in legislation to voluntary management instruments such as employee surveys and independent teams. Collective action by workers, such as forming trade unions and organising collective bargaining and strikes, is a fundamental right enshrined in International Labour Organization conventions and part of the fundamental responsibilities of business.

The key issue of workplace democracy is to ensure the right to representation, collective bargaining, strike action, and participation in the workplace for all workers. In many parts of the world, workplace democracy is not recognised—either in law or in practice—and management exercises unilateral control over all aspects of the workplace. Authoritarian regimes still prosecute and intimidate trade union activists and oppress freedom of speech in firms. Even in modern workplaces, management often actively discourages workplace democracy.

Innovation in workplace democracy has occurred over the last few decades in several ways: first, diversity has become an increasingly important issue; second, communication has profoundly changed; and third, companies have addressed workplace issues more explicitly through corporate social responsibility (CSR) strategies.

As women have entered the workforce and in many countries the workforce has become more heterogeneous through immigration, themes of workplace democracy have widened. While they used to centre around pay and working conditions, discrimination and work–life balance have become important themes.

Second, new technology, social media, and digitalisation have changed workplaces tremendously. Digitalisation and data sharing can increase the control of employers over employees. For example, Amazon tracks all movements of its logistic workers, including bathroom breaks. At the same time, workers' representatives use communication platforms to share information about working conditions and to mobilise collectively.

Third, large global companies have adopted CSR management strategies that include ethical approaches towards fundamental labour rights. At a policy level, these companies encourage collective representation within their supply chains. For instance, Nike has eradicated child labour in its manufacturing of shoes and other garments. However, the effectiveness of these approaches is not proven and often only amounts to lip service.

While on the one hand, trade unions and workers' representation are declining, the issue of fair treatment and work and the expectation to have a voice in workplace matters are still on the agenda. Companies have not found alternative ways of reflecting employees' perspectives, even though highly productive firms experiment with feedback processes (e.g. 360-degree feedback) or quality circles. There is some evidence that job satisfaction is related to unionisation and workplace democracy. In the vast majority of firms, employee participation and workplace democracy remain underdeveloped and underused, leading to low levels of job satisfaction across the western world.

Anke Hassel and Nicole Helmerich

phenomenon, and ideologically corporatist, Keynesian, and even neoliberal, Abromeit et al. (2016) distinguish progressive from reactionary populism.

On the one hand, what is progressive or reactionary is both ultimately a normative question and depends on one's historical perspective. On the other, political scientists suggest that populism rarely benefits democracy in the medium to long terms and is more likely to lead to failure and breakdown rather than renewal (Müller 2016). Populist movements are inherently opportunistic, and because of their often rather eclectic programmes and organisational setup, they can be a source of unexpected developments and perhaps even innovation, if not change, by challenging the establishment.

Could it be that the populism label, having risen to new prominence in just a few years, is too easily applied to new forms of activism that established parties cannot control and that may not even find a political home in social movements? Kaldor and Selchow (2015) point to a new kind of 'subterranean politics', transcending established left and right categorisations and driven by concerns about social justice and by political entrepreneurs seeking opportunities in a changing public sphere and media landscape.

Contrasting the western scenario of low-key malaise and backsliding are large parts of Latin America and Southeast Asia, in particular Indonesia, as well as India that have reached a certain level of democratic stability. Such countries not only managed to adjust western models of democracy to their societies (see Lehmann 2014) but have also coped successfully with the international economic crisis. As a result, and the western malaise notwithstanding, the world actually contains more democratic regimes than ever before (Center for Systemic Peace 2016; Rosner 2016); it has also turned into a vast laboratory in which new solutions to chronic or acute challenges are identified and implemented. Indeed, the world today offers a rich tapestry of democratic models, patterns, and experiences that can be examined for what works—and what does not work—under given and changing circumstances.

Yet there is also a third scenario: failure and breakdown. Whereas western models were adapted rather successfully in the regions mentioned in the previous paragraph, western-sponsored models of democracy and political modernisation failed to take root in countries in the Middle East, Africa, and Central Asia as well as in Belarus and Russia. While the circumstances leading to failure may well be specific, there are commonalities such as political apathy, identity threats, corruptible political elites, and disregard of rule of law as well as infringements on human rights and freedom of speech. Of course, problem-solving in democracies is bound to be a more tedious affair than in autocracies and will encounter collective action problems more frequently, but many third wave democracies have endured and seem resilient.

Given these scenarios, the West seems far less of a benchmark than before, and for two reasons. First, caught in its own malaise, the West can no longer point easily to its successes; many of the countries showing resilience and even progress over time are either former communist and authoritarian regimes or economically underdeveloped with high levels of social and economic inequality. So if rich and developed countries seem to experience difficulties in democracy, why expect poor, less democratically consolidated countries to look to the West if they wish to do better?

Second, there is the rise of apparent alternative models, with China and Singapore as frequently heralded examples. High levels of political control combined with economic success propelled millions out of poverty and have created a system of technocratic governance that seems to rival the appeal of democratic modernisation—even among some western and international elites. And if US President Trump praises autocrats like Russia's Vladimir Putin for their capacity to control, it is no surprise that democracy promotion, a flourishing industry by the end of the twentieth century, seems to have lost some of its universal esteem and aspirations.

While consolidated democracies are unlikely to look for alternative forms of government, notwithstanding ideologies like Victor Orban's illiberalism in Hungary, there is an urgent need to examine cures to the pathologies of the democratic malaise in the West as well as look at the resourcefulness of resilient democracies. Even in the oldest democracies, some core democratic institutions need attention and care within both the state organisation as well as the societies themselves—societies that originally produced this political regime but have meanwhile undergone important changes. (See Box 1 for developments related to democracy in the workplace.)

What Works—And What Does Not

This Report examines policies, programmes, projects, and initiatives that are said to nurture and develop democracy under each of the three scenarios, with a special focus on democratic innovations. By innovations we mean novel rules and approaches that seek to address a deficit in democratic institutions and practices in order to bring about more effective and efficacious ways to achieving better outcomes and greater legitimacy (see Anheier and Korreck 2013). In so doing, the Report goes beyond but also builds on research and reports on existing attempts to address the democratic malaise, such as greater use of plebiscites and referendums; modes of deliberation, mini-publics, and assemblies; and e-democracy.

In exploring issues associated with democratic consolidation, resilience, and backsliding, the Report takes different perspectives in the search for innovations, including the dilemmas and trade-offs that each innovation entails. Not all innovations have positive outcomes for all groups in society; they typically change access to and participation in the political process, and hence power dynamics. Often, judging whether an innovation is seen as positive or negative rests on normative assumptions. For example, in some countries where electoral turnout had declined for some time, neo-populist parties have successfully mobilised non-voters, thereby increasing turnout. Normally, established parties would have welcomed such developments. Also, referendums, often used to make complex choices that governments themselves are unable or unwilling to make, can ultimately yield even more complex outcomes or undermine the legitimacy of those elected.

After addressing the nature of democratic innovation (Claus Offe), this Report continues in roughly three parts:

- The first chapters take on a geographic perspective and look at: developments in Eastern Europe after more than a quarter century of democratic experience (Daniel Smilov); the US and its long history of democratic development by addressing the question of why innovations in America seem less prominent and frequent today (Didi Kuo); innovations beyond the West, mostly in Latin America (Thamy Pogrebinschi); and, using various data sources, democratic innovations comparatively across a wide range of countries (Matthias Haber).
- The second set of chapters covers a series of analyses of particular issues and institutions: how democracy can be saved in times of emergencies and profound distress (Ewa Atanassow and Ira Katznelson); a critical assessment of the performance of direct democratic innovations as they play out in more established systems (Wolfgang Merkel); the role of social movements (Donatella Della Porta and Andrea Felicetti); and new forms of digital-based advocacy organisations (Nina Hall).
- The final two chapters present summary assessments: concluding reflections on the lessons learned and their wider implications (Claus Offe) and a systematic tableau of democratic innovations (Helmut K. Anheier, Sonja Kaufmann, and Regina A. List).

In addition, textboxes spread throughout the Report highlight further interesting places, situations, and opportunities where innovations are occurring or might be needed. Generally, this Report can only showcase and address a limited number of generic types and specific examples of democratic innovations, leaving out some potential actors, emerging practices, and innovation hotspots. However, the wealth of cases and analyses presented here point to potential opportunities (and risks) for meeting the challenges facing democracies today and into the future.

Endnotes

1   See for example the works from Smith (2009), Merkel (2015b), Geissel and Newton (2012), Goodwin (2011), Bermeo (2016), and Helms (2016).

2   Clearly, definitions of democracy differ, and many variants of democratic regimes exist. Some challenges pertain to any form and definition of democracy, while others are more specific. The same would, presumably, be the case for innovations. For this reason and as applicable in the specific context of each chapter, we will use minimalist (Schumpeterian, with a focus on the electoral system), intermediate (which includes civil society and citizen engagement), and maximal (which factors in state welfare functions and related) notions of democracy, as discussed, for example, by Merkel (2015b: 8–10).

3   Several articles have suggested that the concept of democracy is facing serious problems (for example Annan 2016 or Kelemen 2016). In their article, Foa and Mounk (2017) also see signs for democratic deconsolidation in many liberal democracies based on an early-warning system they developed.

4   According to the World Press Freedom Index, which measures the degree of freedom available to journalists in 180 countries, scores have declined on every continent, marking a 'deep and disturbing decline in respect for media freedom at both the global and regional levels' (Reporters Without Borders 2016). This finding is corroborated by Freedom House's Freedom of the Press Report (Dunham 2016).

II. On Democratic Innovations

CLAUS OFFE

Innovation is a name for the practices undertaken by identifiable actors to address challenges in novel ways (see Anheier and Korreck 2013). The concept has its roots in discourses on industrial production in which challenges to the economic viability of a firm are addressed through the adoption of new product lines, new technologies, new organisational patterns, or the opening up of new markets. Such adoption is driven by the expectation that it will result in increased productivity, competitiveness, and ultimately profitability. In modern societies, new products, production processes, and organisational practices are the fruits of systematic and specific research and development (R&D) activities–more so, probably, than the result of creative inspirations of those talented entrepreneurs that Schumpeter had in mind. R&D activities first result in discoveries or inventions that are then applied (innovation in the narrow sense) and eventually undergo a process of diffusion that transforms innovations into ubiquitous routines.

Innovation is thus an instrumental category, not something that is intrinsically valuable. To the contrary, innovation can be unwelcome and even painful to vested interests. It also refers to purposive agency, as opposed to novel phenomena that just happen.

> *Applied to social and political challenges, the concept of innovation has a metaphorical and slightly fuzzy ring to it.*

Applied to social and political challenges, the concept of innovation has a metaphorical and slightly fuzzy ring to it. Both the nature and even the presence of a challenge and the standards by which an innovative response can be judged as successful are typically contested to some extent. Social and political systems do not have unequivocal goals or objectives that can be assessed with the same degree of definiteness afforded by the yardstick of profitability as in the case of business firms. Individual government departments may be mandated to achieve solutions for specific policy problems, say the improvement of the quality of drinking water or the reduction of the high school dropout rate, according to predetermined standards of desired policy outcomes. Even such seemingly simple policy problems lead to questions, the answers to which cannot easily be found according to an instrumental, or means-ends, logic. For example, in the case of water, is a political coalition in place that allows for the effective (and for its member as well as eventually consumers, costly) regulation of waste disposal practices of industrial pig farmers? And in the case of dropouts, are there fiscal and institutional means available to train and recruit additional teaching staff and perhaps also social workers as might be needed in high schools? As a rule of thumb, one might say that inside even a seemingly trivial policy problem we discover, upon closer inspection, a problem of politics: a power contest over goals and means, competencies, and resources. Such realities tend to blur the simplistic managerial analogy that smart ideas about instrumental innovations are enough to solve any policy problem. What is needed, at least in addition, is control over necessary resources and decision-making powers. What is lacking, it seems, is not so much innovation but the requisite level of control.

When starting to consider democratic innovations, one needs to spell out what purpose they are supposed to serve. There are two ways of doing so. One consists of an answer to the question, how can the functioning of the machinery of the democratic state be further improved so as to make it more consistent with its own normative aspirations and promises? If a sense of idealistic arbitrariness is to be avoided, this approach requires that the normative postulates about the nature of those aspirations be made explicit and argued for as norms that are at least widely shared if not even cogently derived from universal principles or constitutional stipulations. For instance, innovations that aim at providing citizens with a maximum of institutional options to express their preferences more often, more directly, or on more subject matters than status quo conditions allow are neither self-evidently supported by the preferences of constituencies nor validated by compelling normative reasoning.

The other approach to designing innovations does not look for ways to improve the working of democracy but proposes ways to halt or even reverse its degradation and decay as empirically observable in many countries (some authors speak of 'crisis'). To be sure, this approach also makes use of norma-tive criteria. For instance, how do we discern an observed degradation from an entirely unproblematic process of change? But the implied normativity is less demanding: if we observe rampant political corruption, growing politi-cal disaffection, the unsanctioned disregard of legal and even constitutional rules on the part of political and economic elites, the fiscal incapacity of gov-ernments to provide social and civil protection, the corruption and perver-sion of popular will formation through media communication of the post-truth era, or large-scale successes of anti-democratic mobilisation, it is hard to disagree on the diagnosis of the democratic malaise.

It can be concluded from this rough comparison of the two approaches that innovation is primarily needed for the sake of defending and rescuing democracy; only after that task is accomplished can attempts be made to improve it.

As we know from Max Weber, the state has no inherent and universal ends (but only the means of its monopolistic control of physical force); the ends of public policy-making are contingent. The democratic state, however, establishes institutions and procedures designed to cope with that contingency and to continuously transform it into a (temporal) determinacy. Democratic governance is a continuous process of defining ends, the most abstract common feature of which is that they shape and affect the life chances of citizens. The institutional complexes that serve this purpose in liberal democracies are (a) popular sovereignty (spelled out in terms of equal political rights; independent professional media as a vehicle of political will formation; periodic elections; party competition; secure rights and fair opportunities available to opposition movements and parties; representative legislative bodies and functional modes of representation; and the accountability of governments) and (b) the rule of law (implemented through constitutions with bills of rights protecting the physical integrity and the religious, economic, and political autonomy of citizens; an independent judiciary within a system of division of powers; and enforceable legal claims to state-provided services and transfers).

Without oversimplifying the picture, one can thus say that there are two defining features of anything one would call a democracy. These are (a) collective self-determination based on popular sovereignty and (b) the rule of legal and constitutional norms in which such sovereignty is embedded. In an ideal world, these two relate to each other as a balance of content and form, or political substance and institutional shell. In such a world, there is no need for democratic innovation. Contrariwise, innovation is called for if and when these two constituent components of democracy conflict with or come to contradict each other.

Such dilemmas and contradictions can and do occur in a great variety of ways. A classical one, described by de Tocqueville and sometimes used as a diagnosis of today's populist movements and politics, is the case of 'tyranny of the majority', in which the popular will aims to break the institutional shell protecting constitutional liberties and procedures available to dissenters, resulting in what has been called illiberal democracy, or electoral authoritarianism. The inverse–the paradigmatic case of Marxian analyses–is that of economic elites being permitted, due to the economic liberties of property, contract, and mobility constitutionally granted to them, to deform and prevail over interests and values that can plausibly be taken to inform the will of the people–the case of (neo)liberal post-democracy. Here, the markets come to determine and rule over the possibility space of democratic politics in ways that amount to a structural veto power of capital. To the extent this is the case, democracy is paralysed in its capacity to shape life chances by the predominance of investors, employers, and creditors. The 'voice' of the people, as well as that of its representatives, is silenced by the 'exit' these agents can threaten (Hirschman 1970). Where this applies, the possibility of democratic self-determination is curtailed by an inverse power asymmetry: investors can pick the states offering conditions that are conducive for their business activities, yet states cannot pick the investors on which they critically depend for fiscal resources, employment, and credit. The more open economies are and the more they compete for investment and employment, the greater the impact of this power asymmetry.

There are thus two clear-cut reference problems, the solutions to which democratic innovations can contribute. They are mirror images of each other. One is that of illiberal democracy: can democratic politics be enriched in ways that enhance the responsiveness of the liberal democratic state within a consolidated framework of its main institutional features, such as equal civil and political rights of all citizens, representative government, and the checks and balances of constitutional government? It is these features that are in many capitalist democracies of the OECD world currently facing serious threats from the forces of rightist populist mobilisation with their manifest authoritarian implications. That is the 'by-the-people' question. The other reference problem for democratic innovators is the 'for-the-people' issue: can the performance (or policy output) of the democratic state, which is irreversibly inserted into a supranational environment of military, economic, political, and demographic forces, be enhanced so that the life chances of all of its citizens are effectively protected and opportunities are provided in ways that reasonably conform to prevailing normative standards of social justice? Without the need to elaborate here, the two questions are closely interrelated: if the answer to the second question is 'no', a condition emerges that precludes a positive answer to the first one, too. Instead, the will of the people will manifest itself in ways that much of the current political science literature describes with a litany of 'dis'-terms: widespread political disaffection, distrust of the establishment or the political class accused of corruption and dishonesty, dissatisfaction with policy outcomes and a state perceived as dysfunctional, disenchantment with democratic politics in their entirety, and patterns of conflict that are disruptive of institutional order, often violently so.

Contributors to this Report actually do address both of these questions, though issues having to do with the input side of the political process, including participation, movement politics, parties, media, and other 'by-the-people' aspects, are more often addressed than issues having to do with the output side, or the making of public policy and its repercussions on political attitudes and patterns of participatory behaviour. Enhancing 'voice' and curbing the constraining power of 'exit' over the making of public policies are the two equally challenging areas of democratic innovations intended to strengthen the robustness and resilience of democratic governance. Unless the latter is effectively addressed, proposals aiming at the former are in danger of yielding more populist noise instead of democratic voice.

III. Democratic Innovation and the Politics of Fear
Lessons from Eastern Europe

DANIEL SMILOV

D istrust and fear are the circumstances of contemporary politics around the world, it seems. Though the picture is not so dire everywhere, it has become a mundane observation that people do not have confidence in the most important institutions of representative democracy: political parties and parliaments. In most democracies–established and transitional–large majorities of citizens report declining levels of trust in key republican institutions. Significant numbers also do not believe that elections can change public policy for the better.

These are not novel attitudes. Distrust and dissatisfaction are integral to democratic politics, and moderate levels of distrust could be simple signs of a critical, attentive, and active public. Moreover, political parties and parliaments have always been targets of criticism: the Rousseauistic rejection of representation and the insistence on direct involvement of people in politics have always made mediators look awkward in the general democratic setup. Such mediators may either be seen as victims of capture by special interests and thus as distorting the general will, or they may be criticised as being too responsive to the whims of the public and thus as outlets of populism.

> *Distrust and dissatisfaction are integral to democratic politics, and moderate levels could be simple signs of an attentive public.*

Yet there are differences between the present circumstances and earlier periods in which parties, parliaments, and liberal democracy have been put to the test. Compared to the 1930s, today there is no consistent ideological alternative to liberal democracy. In Europe there may be pockets of resurgence of some radical ideologies–including fascism and communism–but they are marginal and enjoy only limited public support.[1] Within liberal democracy, ideological battles are still fought mostly over issues such as immigration, globalisation, multi-culturalism, minority rights, and supranationalism. Further, in comparison to the Cold War era, today there is no second, aggressive, non-democratic superpower challenging the dominance of the West.

Eastern Europe, referring here to the whole post-communist region and including Russia, demonstrates these circumstances of contemporary politics in terms of both widespread distrust and fears that existing political instru-

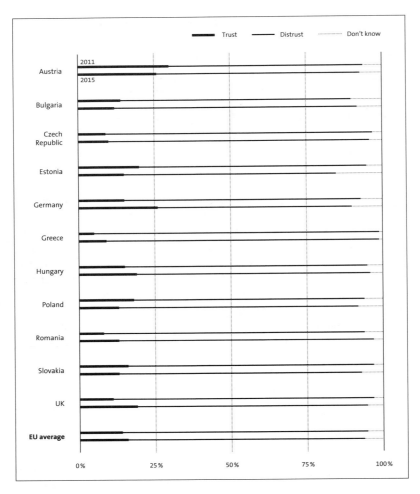

Figure 3.1 **Trust in parties in selected European countries**
Source: Eurobarometer (2015, 2011)

ments do not sufficiently protect the interests of the people. Confidence in institutions in the region is generally lower compared to that in western European countries (see Figures 3.1 and 3.2 comparing trust in parties and parliaments, respectively). Interestingly, these lower levels of trust often affect not only institutions that are political in nature (parties and parliaments) but also courts and prosecutors, especially in countries with systemic corruption-related problems, such as Bulgaria, Slovakia, Romania, and Macedonia.

These low levels of trust reflect a whole catalogue of fears and anxieties held by people in Eastern Europe (Smilov 2013). Fear, for the present purposes, is a popular negative attitude: a perception of threat and danger to the

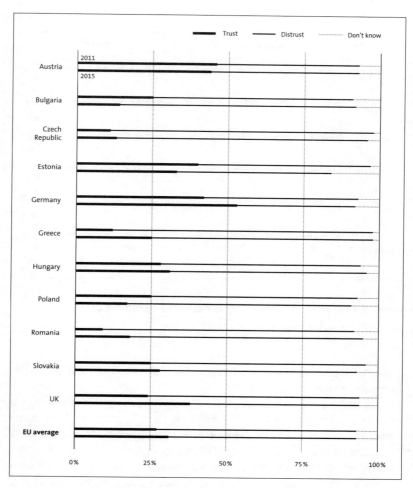

Figure 3.2 **Trust in parliaments in selected European countries**
Source: Eurobarometer (2015, 2011)

integrity and well-being of a polity. Fears come in a variety of forms, mainly differentiated by intensity. For the sake of brevity, more intense and acute fears will be referred to as paranoias and the least dramatic ones as anxieties.

From a political point of view, the most basic fear underlying the lack of trust in republican institutions is that collective, state action cannot improve the status of the majority but can only undermine it further. This is a background, non-hysterical fear: low in intensity, but constant and pervasive. In some countries it is more prominent than in others, and it fits well with popular perceptions of state capture and systemic, structural corruption. This fear betrays widespread perceptions, particularly in Eastern European

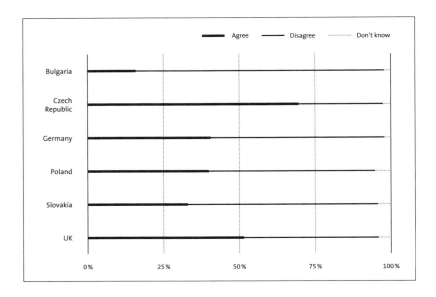

Figure 3.3 **Do you believe the state is run to the benefit of all?**
Source: Pew Research Center (2009)

countries such as Bulgaria and Slovakia, that the state is not working in the interest of all (see Figure 3.3.)

Apart from this 'master fear', Eastern Europe is riddled with a range of more specific anxieties and more intense negative attitudes. First, many Eastern European states see themselves as lagging behind in terms of modernisation as compared to the core countries in western Europe. Because of this fear of underperformance, the European Union (EU) is often seen as an instrument whose main utility is in allowing Eastern European countries to catch up through the receipt of benefits. Second, fear of treason by and corruption of national elites is widespread. People have the perception that elites have become more and more cosmopolitan: their children study abroad, their money is in foreign banks, and they have property in other states (Krastev 2017). Third, the population fears insecure borders and national identities–something that has been traditional for the region and only exacerbated after the Ukrainian crisis. A fourth is demography paranoia, strengthened by trends of declining and aging populations and emigration by young people: countries such as Latvia and Bulgaria are among the fastest shrinking countries in the world in terms of population. Furthermore, lingering Cold War as well as real war paranoias are spurred by developments in Ukraine as well as in Turkey and Syria. Last but not least, refugee influx paranoia, caused by the situation in the Middle East, is particularly striking because it affects countries that have no or very few migrants, like

Poland. Moreover, migrants see these countries mainly as a transit desti-
nation on their way to Germany or Sweden. This shows that fears are not
necessarily always based on hard facts and correct assessment of the situation but may be the result of deliberate attempts by political actors and the
media to create specific public perceptions.

The advent of social media has contributed to the manipulative generation of such anxieties and fears via two novel forms of freedom that social
media offers: the choice of authority and the choice of audience. Since
almost everyone seems to be on Facebook or Twitter, the average user
potentially has access to the views of the most prominent authorities on
most topics. Contesting the state's traditional role as possessor of immensely
greater expertise and therefore unquestioned authority, social networks
today provide an enormous pool of expert opinions from which citizens can
draw to criticise the positions of public bodies. In addition, social media also
offers speakers more freedom to choose their audiences. Since people tend
to communicate with like-minded people in social networks, the promise
of limitless access to all opinions and the best expertise is often narrowed
to access to the opinions of real and virtual 'friends' and friends of friends.
This feature of digital communication is argued to have aided ghettoisation
(Blank 2013) and radicalisation and to have created new opportunities for
manipulation. The abundance of likeable viral news–real or fake–has been
well-captured by Oxford Dictionaries' word of the year for 2016, 'post-truth',
which reflects the secondary importance of fact and authenticity in the
news: more essential is the potential to generate a response from the public
(in terms of clicks, likes, dislikes, and so on), which in turn generates influence (and in many cases also profit).

The Nature of Democratic Innovation in Eastern Europe

Against this background, Eastern European politics has recently featured a number of novelties or innovations in comparison to the
1990s and the first decade of the 2000s. At least four different, general features characterise these innovations.

Ad hoc experimentalism

As noted above, despite a sense of crisis of liberal democracy, no coherent
alternative to this ideology exists. Thus, innovation takes place broadly in
the framework of liberal democratic institutions and practices, some of
which are revised or removed. Quite apparent in Eastern Europe is the dis-

solution of the so-called liberal consensus of the 1990s, which consisted of the belief that European integration, the opening up of the economies to globalisation, market-oriented reforms, and political assistance from western democracies are of unquestionable value. Today, while many political players challenge one or all of these elements of the liberal consensus, it remains unclear what the alternative is.

President Vladimir Putin's Russia has attempted to conceptualise the alternative as 'sovereign democracy', but both the theory and especially its practice smack of outright authoritarianism (Sontag 2013). The restriction of civil society activities through the registration of so-called foreign agents, for instance, has eliminated the last traces of genuine political pluralism in Russia, bringing its 'managed democracy' to a whole new, markedly undemocratic level (Krastev 2012). In this sense, it is impossible to argue that Putinism presents a consistent alternative to liberal democracy.

Similar arguments could be applied to Hungarian Prime Minister Viktor Orban's claim of installing 'illiberal democracy'.[2] Most of his actions can be understood as self-entrenchment and limitation of competition within a system that has generally preserved its democratic character and many constitutional limitations on power. While both of these have been partly undermined, the whole exercise appears to be opportunistic experimentalism by an ambitious political operator.

Even more opportunistic and ad hoc experimentalist is the so-called conservative revolution taking place in countries such as Poland and Bulgaria. Here conservative national-populists have made significant gains in recent elections; in Poland they are in control of the government. Whether this is the same agenda as Orban's illiberal democracy is a matter of some dispute: PiS, Poland's Law and Justice Party, has given the distinct impression that it follows the Hungarian example by openly attacking the independent judiciary and media and endorsing Orban's hard stance on refugees. But is this an alternative to liberal democracy or just conservative experimentalism within it? In both Hungary and Poland it seems to be the latter.

Indeed, the protective umbrellas of the EU and North Atlantic Treaty Organization (NATO) have encouraged experimentalism by voters in Eastern Europe. They have started voting for new, unorthodox, and often irresponsible parties with the understanding that even if those parties come to power, major policies would hardly change. The EU's current troubles raise questions about what the impact on experimentalism will ultimately be. One hypothesis is that such experimentalism may diminish since people will understand the high price they may potentially pay for it. However, the power of path dependence and inertia should not be underestimated, since they favour ad hoc experimentalism.

Non-radicalism and non-extremism

New social movements, institutional designs, and practices in general have a non-radical nature in Eastern Europe. Mass protests, for instance, have happened in many countries but have been peaceful as a rule (with the partial exception of Maidan in Ukraine). Moreover, the demands of the protesters have almost never gone outside of the broad liberal democratic framework. In general, they have all claimed to be perfecting democracy rather than displacing it, as they have done for constitutionalism and the rule of law. In fact, in many countries protests have taken place precisely in the name of the rule of law.

Regarding the institutional imagination of the democratic innovators—be they political parties, social movements, or policy-makers—the lack of radicalism and novelty is also striking. The ideas that are presented have been part of democratic debates for centuries. Insistence on the value of referendums and other instruments of direct democracy falls in this category, as do proposals for the reduction of the number of legislative representatives, the elimination of public subsidies for political parties (as in Poland, Hungary, and Bulgaria), and so on. For the most part, the innovations could at best be understood as recombinations of familiar elements.

Virtual reality of participation and representation

The third general feature of democratic innovations in Eastern Europe is the virtual reality of citizen involvement in politics. Most measures are designed to enhance virtual rather than actual participation and representation. In general, innovations seek to lower the cost of citizen involvement in terms of both finances and time. Citizens are not asked to invest significant resources in politics but rather are given the opportunity to mobilise rapidly in order to make a point (see Hall's chapter in this Report for more on rapid-response digital advocacy). Whether it be a flash mob or an ad hoc electoral party or movement, the idea is to provide an opportunity for a brief and inexpensive moment of actual involvement, which will then become the basis of an inflated virtual reality of participation and representation. This virtual reality is a product of the media—both new and traditional—which will for a long time circulate images, slogans, and speeches from the event in the electronic realm. Thus, through minimum actual participation citizens will receive a maximum amount of lasting virtual representation.

Acceleration of change and the growing demand for change

The citizenry's discontent with the performance of public authorities has had a curious result: a constant pressure for reform. Reform has become a permanent condition of public bodies: the lack of reform is a sign of stagnation, corruption, and inefficiency. In such circumstances, most political players have presented considerable plans for reform, starting from the constitutional level, going through the workings of the electoral system, and ending up in the administrative maze of modern healthcare, education, and social insurance. Interestingly, continuity and consistency with former efforts are not seen as a condition *sine qua non*. Rather experimentalism–albeit non-radical–applies here as well. Therefore, in many countries in Eastern Europe major or minor revisions of the constitution have occurred in recent years (as has also occurred in several Latin American countries, as Pogrebinschi recounts in her Report chapter). Hungary adopted a whole new Fundamental Law in 2010, and others have followed suit, applying the logic that genuine reforms cannot be achieved without major constitutional change. A similar logic has been applied to electoral rules. For example, in Romania the proportional representation system was replaced by a mixed one in 2008, but the country went back to the proportional system in 2016.[3]

These developments have created a sense of transience of the basic rules of the political system. The paradox is that even after the end of the so-called transition in Eastern Europe, the perception of the transitional character of even fundamental rules remains strong, as do the expectations for accelerated change. These expectations have become even more important than the reality itself: even though the overall difference may in the end be negligible, as in the Romanian electoral case, the constant demand for change creates a lot of dynamism in the political process.

Before moving to the discussion of actual innovations, another common element should be noted. In the 1990s much of the democratic innovation in Eastern Europe was legitimised in terms of transplantation or importation from established western democracies (Dupré 2003). In the current situation transplantation has lost its popularity, and most political players prefer to go for 'authentic' domestic solutions to problems. This is hardly surprising when the EU and NATO are dealing with a variety of crises. Further, a number of weaknesses and susceptibility to the lures of populism have also emerged in the established democracies of the West. In this sense, as Anheier notes in the introduction to this Report, the soft power of the West has diminished, and transplantation and importation have given way to creation and innovation as legitimation strategies for the adoption of specific policies.

Democratic Innovations in Eastern Europe

The specific innovations highlighted here cover four fields–protests, parties, counter-democracy, and authority–that trace democracy as a process: from the formation of the will of the people by means of assembly and association to the translation of their preferences into authoritative decisions. 'Counter-democracy', a term borrowed from Rosanvallon (2008), refers to watchdog, monitoring, and feedback functions–also an important part of democracy that helps citizens hold their representatives accountable.

Innovation I: Mass protests and the bypass of the mediators

Mass protests have taken place in most Eastern European countries over the last several years. The most dramatic events took place in Kiev, Ukraine, where then-President Yanukovych was deposed as a result of the Maidan protests (2013-4), leading to violence and military interference–direct or indirect–by Russia. Governments have resigned as a result of protests in Bulgaria (2013 and partly in 2014) and in Romania (2014). Budapest and Warsaw have become regular sites of anti-government gatherings, and even Moscow saw impressive anti-Putin demonstrations (2012).

Protests are by no means an innovation in democracy: they constitute the expression of a well-entrenched basic civil right (Smilov 2009). Moreover, Eastern Europe has seen quite dramatic protests since 1989: after all, the fall of communism took place with memorable occasions of enormous assemblies of people in public spaces–non-violent in most cases.

The novelties compared to the mass protests of the 1990s are considerable. First, the established convention for years was that mass protests were justified only as a weapon of last resort, to be used in exceptional circumstances deemed existential for the polity. The dismantling of the communist regime was definitely a once-in-several-generations phenomenon. So were the removal of Milosevic's semi-authoritarian regime in Belgrade and the protests of Bulgarians in 1996-7 when the country's banking system collapsed and hyperinflation raged. Yet, none of the most recent mass protests has been triggered by such dramatic and existential events. Even in Ukraine's case, the stakes raised by its association agreement with the EU were by no means as high as in 1989. Instead mass protests have been triggered by (perception of) corrupt governments (Bulgaria, Macedonia, and Romania), authoritarian tendencies and manipulations of elections (Russia), or self-entrenchment by an aggressively majoritarian government (Hungary and Poland).

A second novelty of the new wave of mass protests is its markedly anti-party character. Many of these protests have been clearly against specific parties but not necessarily for any of the others. Protesters portrayed themselves as active citizens rather than as partisans. Some have actually harboured and fanned dangerous anti-party feelings, failing to realise that contemporary democracy at its heart is a competition among parties. Thus, in the February 2013 protests in Bulgaria a sizeable group of protesters demanded the limitation of the role of parties and the formation of citizens' councils in all major public authorities. Most commonly, public protests have difficulty translating their demands into support for a specific party (Krastev 2014). Therefore, it very often happens that the political party against which such mass protests have been held wins the next parliamentary or major election, as in Russia, Bulgaria, Hungary, Macedonia, and Romania. The reasons for these developments are of course more complex, but still it is quite curious that mass protests have become an instrument of routine opposition work rather than a device of radical transformation of the political system.

Their anti-elitist motivational force is a third novelty of today's mass protests. In many cases, the protesting public perceives the elite as corrupt, treacherous, and incompetent. In Hungary and Poland the protests have been against the self-entrenchment attempts of Fidesz and PiS, respectively, and their moves to dismantle fundamental checks on government power. The most distinctive feature of these protests is that they claim to represent the people as a whole: as a form of expression of the sovereignty of a nation, the protests are portrayed as an alternative channel of popular representation superior to political parties and other mediated forms of representation.

Thus, mass protests are gradually becoming a rather routine instrument of opposition, albeit not necessarily partisan opposition. The rise of social networks has contributed significantly to this development because it has made inexpensive and almost immediate coordination of angry and dissatisfied people possible. Such flash protests have become a routine instrument of saying 'no' to a proposed policy in a matter of hours after its announcement, as happened in Bulgaria in 2013. There, the government made a very unpopular appointment for head of the state security services in the morning, and by the afternoon more than 10,000 protesters gathered in front of its offices.

Innovation II: The party-media hybrid

Political parties, as the main mediators between citizens and the state, have tried to adapt to the new realities of widespread distrust in representatives and fears that the state does not operate in the interest of all. In order to tackle this challenge they have resorted to a number of techniques, among them the hybridisation between political parties and the media (Smilov and Smilova 2015). Strictly speaking, this is by no means an invention of Eastern Europe: in Italy, Silvio Berlusconi was probably the first significant example of this type, with United States President Donald Trump the most recent. These are politicians/media personalities who use their media exposure as political capital. What is more, once in office they continue to function

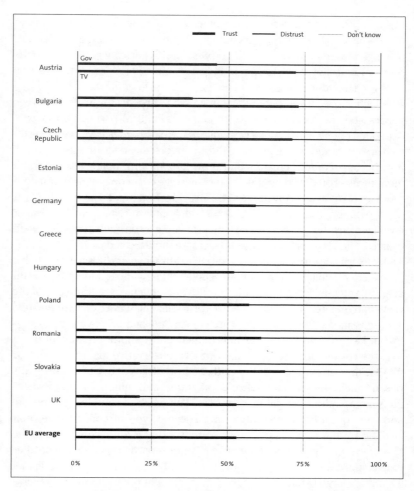

Figure 3.4 **Trust in government and television in selected European countries**
Source: Eurobarometer (2011)

partly as media outlets in terms of generating news and communicating with voters.

This hybridisation phenomenon is explained by the fact that while trust in political representatives is generally low, trust in the media–especially television–has been high (see Figure 3.4). Even in countries such as Bulgaria and Romania with minimal confidence in traditional political structures, trust in television is well above 60 per cent and within the EU on average 53 per cent, which is quite astonishing when compared to trust in government. Thus, political parties compensate for lack of trust by merging with popular media programmes or by building themselves around media personalities.

Bulgaria provides spectacular cases of television networks and programmes turned into political parties, including a regional network (SKAT) that has produced two nationalistic parties represented in parliament (Ataka and the National Front for the Salvation of Bulgaria) and a popular programme that organised a national referendum on the electoral system.

Such cases are not exceptional in Eastern Europe and the link between parties and the media is quite pronounced. Political parties have always depended on the media. However, while in the past parties have been the content providers and the media mere disseminators, the media themselves have now become content creators and providers. In turn, politicians today are more focused on the communication of messages than on their elaboration.

Two phenomena contribute to the hybridisation trend. The first concerns the rise of populism in Europe and beyond. Populism is a minimalist, default-level ideology that poses a homogeneous people against a corrupt and inefficient elite and is resorted to when other, more sophisticated political platforms such as social or Christian democracy fail to attract voters. It is a promise that its leaders will follow the will of the people as it is, without attempting to educate the voter. In essence, populist parties are a media–a re-translator of the views and preferences of other people–providing the service of dissemination and translation of these views and preferences into authoritative decisions.

In Eastern Europe, populism is influenced by another dominant narrative: the conservative revolution, in which conservative majorities are fearful that they are losing status, wealth, and privileges and are negatively disposed against newcomers, refugees, migrants, and minorities, all of whom are seen as a drain on public resources. The result of combining populism and the conservative revolution is a specific type of conservative, non-egalitarian, and non-emancipatory populism that is quite conducive to the hybridisation of parties and the media. Populist parties need to rely on alternative sources of mass mobilisation, normally the charisma of the leader, which to a large extent is a media construction in the contemporary world. Further, the generation of specific fears and anxieties is essential for voter mobilisation, and here the media are indeed indispensable.

The second phenomenon contributing to party-media hybridisation relates more to organisational opportunities than to ideology. Since the mid-1990s, the regulation of party and campaign finance has become much stricter, and Eastern Europe is one of the most regulated regions in the world in this regard. At the same time the financing of the media–especially private entities–is much less transparent. Thus, it may be more attractive to start a political project as a media outlet rather than as a political party. Further empirical work is needed to substantiate this hypothesis, but obviously freedom of speech protection as applied to the media provides much more confidentiality and room for financial manoeuvring than it does in the case of political parties and even non-governmental organisations (NGOs).

Innovation III: Counter-democracy and the rise of the new experts

Rosanvallon's (2008) concept of counter-democracy can be applied to the situation in Eastern Europe. Counter-democracy refers to a trend of providing additional non-electoral, non-parliamentary channels for the citizenry's representation. Such channels include non-elected expert bodies such as independent courts, central banks, and regulatory agencies as well as watchdog NGOs and other monitoring mechanisms that allow citizens to exercise greater control over their representatives and are essential for strengthening and caring for democracy. (See Box 2 on the role of citizens in fighting corruption.)

Although one might suppose that populist parties would do away with such independent bodies, the rise of conservative populism has actually not stopped or blocked the extension of counter-democracy. At first glance, what Orban in Hungary and PiS chief Jaroslaw Kaczynski in Poland have done might be interpreted in this majoritarian, populist fashion, but a few other developments should be taken into account before jumping to conclusions.

First, despite the conservative populism trend, powerful independent bodies have been institutionalised in many countries since the new century began. Central banks–especially for EU members and countries in the eurozone–are an obvious case in point. Moreover, Eastern European countries have signed up to the EU's Fiscal Compact and have accepted coordination of budgetary and fiscal policies. This has gone hand in hand with the establishment of fiscal councils at the national level, some of which, as in Hungary, have considerable prerogatives to block certain budget decisions.

Second, powerful independent judicial bodies have emerged, in Romania for example, to carry out 'clean hands' operations. The final assessment of the Romanian operation's effects is yet to come, but there is no doubt that Romania's anticorruption prosecutorial office has been a spectacular example of Rosanvallon's counter-democracy. Similar developments, though with less visible success, have resulted in the creation of a number of powerful independent agencies in Bulgaria, such as the state security agency DANS.

Third, trust in the EU is higher in Eastern Europe than in the rest of the Union and, more significantly, generally higher than trust in local and national elites. Thus many societies accept the EU's monitoring role over the functioning of national governments. In fact, this monitoring role helps the electorate to hold its national representatives more accountable. Curiously, instead of undermining popular sovereignty, the EU–as well as the Council of Europe, the European Court of Human Rights, and the Venice Commission, considered authoritative in most countries–may actually strengthen it by reinforcing representation via such accountability bodies and measures.

Fourth, the popularity of counter-democratic measures encourages some political parties to imitate independent monitoring institutions or even NGOs. The 'party of experts' model is probably the second most popu-

Box 2 Enlightened citizens, not mere elections, enable control of corruption

If one knows how many educated people a country had in 1900, controlling for its current literacy rate, its present state of corruption can be predicted with great accuracy. But this is not so much about education as it may seem at first sight, but about citizenship. One hundred years of informed and active citizenship, what Robert Dahl (1972) called enlightened participation, is what it takes to deliver good governance. The current rate of education matters far less: Spain and Italy, two highly educated countries, topped a recent YouGov poll on corruption in higher education (Milata KG 2016), and this is just one example.

What recent research teaches us is that control of corruption is a matter of constant and massive public scrutiny of government. Control of corruption is highly correlated with a number of closely interrelated factors: development controls, newspaper readership, access to internet, usage of e-government services by citizens, functioning executive constraints, freedom to organise on social media, number of civil society associations, and others

(Mungiu-Pippidi 2015b). Taken together, these factors translate into the existence of autonomous citizens able to act together and demand better government. Without this, control of corruption is not robustly correlated with the existence of elections.

If collusion or indifference takes over due to apathy, clientelism, or disempowerment of any kind, any unconstrained power establishment will spoil public resources for its own benefit. One should not make the mistake of believing that virtuous government is some inborn quality of the human species; rather, it is the result of strong and sustained demand for it. The longer an autonomous society can inflict constraints on its government, the better and less corrupt its governance will be. Otherwise, evidence from the many democracies from the third wave of democratisation would not indicate that the great majority remains systematically corrupt, while in older democracies corruption has been reduced to just an exception.

Alina Mungiu-Pippidi

---

lar after the party-media model. Drawing on distrust in parties, the expert model offers a fake alternative: the non-partisan party. Variations abound, but political formations built around specific experts can be found in almost all parliaments in Eastern Europe. The drama of the Hungarian left is that it is currently fragmented into a number of similar organisations–partly NGOs, partly expert councils. In Bulgaria, the Reformist Bloc emerged in 2014 by combining the significant presence of experts, the NGO model of horizontal organisation, and strong criticism of the political establishment. This Bulgarian party gained parliamentary representation, just as a similar Romanian party did in 2016, emerging as a spin-off of a prominent monitoring NGO.

Finally, consider the more troubling cases of Orban in Hungary and Kaczynski in Poland, who seem to go against the counter-democratic trend described above. Both seem determined to dismantle the independent institutions in their countries. However, this may be an overstatement since they are instead taking over these institutions by filling them with loyalists. Especially telling is the Hungarian example with its new constitution, which envisions numerous independent bodies having long mandates (Csink, Schanda, and Varga 2012; Venice Commission 2012). It is true that the current political leadership can appoint party loyalists to positions within these entities, but if the government changes, these bodies could serve in the future as a significant counter-majoritarian check. No matter how problematic the situation in Hungary and Poland, the levels of political pluralism, the viability of the opposition, and the overall chances for a change of the majority are still real there.

In sum, populism and counter-democracy are not mutually exclusive trends. The basic reason is that both are the product of significant distrust in the functioning of political representatives. In fact, the fanning of fears that representatives betray the people works to both boost populist players and strengthen counter-democratic measures.

Innovation IV: The non-authoritative authority

All these innovations are designed to compensate for the lack of trust in political parties and parliaments, which undermines their authority. Some of these bodies have decided to accept that they lack authority and thus to create something paradoxical–the non-authoritative authority. The main technique that makes this option possible is twofold. First, a political party sends the policy question on which it has to decide back to the people either via referendum or by turning the political party into a deliberative framework in which the people purportedly decide what course of action should be taken. Second, the party promises complete transparency in its manner of taking decisions–both organisationally and financially. These two measures intend to convince the public that it actually participates in decision-making. Notably, both the non-authoritative authority and the party-media hybrids discussed previously have the potential to transform politics into a reality television product.

Referendums have become quite popular in Eastern Europe. In 2016 at least two such major events occurred in the region: in Hungary (on refugees) and in Bulgaria (on electoral rules). Furthermore, the refugee crisis has provided fertile ground for numerous local referendums or threats of such. For instance, it is the strategy of national-populists in Bulgaria to threaten to stage local referendums wherever the government plans to situate a refugee camp.

The dominance of new digital media and social networks helps sustain the illusion that non-authoritative authorities are actually possible. As argued above, the internet could be seen as an endless source of expertise and self-organisation of large groups of people. Political players may offer to coordinate such efforts and to publicise the decisions reached by the citizenry through referendums, deliberative polls, intense structured discussions, and so on.

The effects of this phenomenon are the following. First, the underplaying of the capacity of politicians to determine the agenda and the content of policy decisions may actually strengthen their capacity to do so in hidden and partly manipulative ways. As the example of the local referendums in Bulgaria shows, it is clear that the agenda is driven by the nationalist-populist parties and that the referendums and public protests are just part of the strategy of these political players. In fact, there is hardly a referendum initiative in Europe that is not the result of a political party strategy. So, the draining of authority from politics should not be taken at face value: it may rather be seen as a manoeuvre by the parties that allows them to do what they have always done but this time in circumstances of low trust and high anxiety.

Second, the invention of the non-authoritative authority shifts some powers to other actors, which are bound to fill the authority vacuum. As noted previously, the most likely candidates are media outlets and the corporate interests behind them. Fears sell, and many among the commercial media have specialised in selling fears throughout Eastern Europe. When political players remove themselves from their responsibility to shape public discourse, educate the public, and take unpopular decisions, they shift authority to actors that excel in fanning fears for commercial purposes.

Conclusion

The innovations described in this chapter have a common function: they try to adapt democratic institutions to the circumstances of low and generally declining trust in parties and parliaments. Some of the innovations, such as regular mass protests, attempt to bypass these representative bodies. Others, such as the party-media hybrid and party of experts, are ways political parties adapt to conditions of low trust by attempting to exploit trust in other institutions (television or expert bodies, for instance). Further, political parties may decide to surrender their authority by deferring policy-making and all substantive decisions to the people via non-authoritative authorities. In this way the political party becomes merely an infrastructure for decision-making whose main characteristics are transparency and efficiency of coordination, something like a social network. Finally, the present conditions of low trust have proven a fertile ground for the emergence of counter-democratic (in Rosanvallon's sense) institutions such as NGOs, watchdogs, powerful courts, and independent agencies that are meant to monitor the exercise of democratic power and to bring a higher level of non-political expertise in decision-making. Though in most Eastern European countries the expansion of such bodies has been celebrated as strengthening of civil society, more recently some governments have attempted to start wars against NGOs and independent institutions.

All in all, these innovations have created a political system that is more sensitive to the moods of the people and less concerned with ideological coherence or long-term political strategies. Even very popular leaders such as Orban or Putin work on the assumption that the public mood could change very quickly, and they have taken extraordinary measures to entrench themselves and lessen the potential impact of changes of public attitude. Thus far this self-entrenchment has been rather the exception. The more general pattern has been the creation of political vehicles–parties, movements, and protest networks–capable of carrying a political actor on the wave of popular emotion. In such circumstances, negative emotions–fears of various sorts–have proven to be the favourite fuel of political ascent.

Many of these developments may be treated as rehearsals of themes that have been part of the history of democracy. Yet, one of the truly novel elements is that most of them are based on the unquestioned dominance of a noble fiction: the fiction of the citizen ready to contribute time, resources, and efforts to advance the public interest. Though long recognised by political theorists, this fiction has never been built to such an extent into the functioning of modern, representative democracy. The advent of digital social networks has strengthened the notion that virtually everyone could be informed about and participate in public decision-making. The dominance of this fiction has had an empowering effect for many people in terms of both public discourse and institutional imagination. The party-media hybrids, mass protests, referendums, and non-authoritative authorities are all based on the assumption that citizens are capable of autonomous and responsible decisions in which they put the public interest ahead of their self-interest. Compared to this fiction, all representative structures appear corrupt and egoistic, and trends of low trust have not been reversed through any of the innovations described in this chapter.

The dominance of the fiction of the noble citizen has other negative consequences as well. First, it does not prevent attempts by political actors to concentrate power or seek self-entrenchment, as in Russia and Hungary. Skilful political operators may use the myth to denigrate their opponents as corrupt elites and then grab arbitrary, unchecked powers. In some cases, the fiction of the noble citizen may be used to discredit all political players and the political system as a whole: with such widespread cynicism, those in power can continue to rule unopposed. Thus, the introduction of a fictional, too demanding ideal may contribute to the spread of cynicism in society.

Second, the fiction of the non-egoistic citizen may simply be too demanding. Citizens have their own fears and anxieties, whether real or imagined, and they do care first and foremost about themselves and their relatives in many, if not most situations. Populists have proven so successful because they have 'liberated' the median voter from the excessive demand to be an altruistic citizen. Populists both generate unreal fears and fan real ones to create conservative majorities afraid for their own rights and privileges. In some cases, these majorities are nothing more than a backlash against the fiction of the citizen.

Thus, although as yet the framework of liberal democracy is largely preserved in Eastern Europe (apart from Russia and the post-Soviet space where it was probably never fully installed but has markedly deteriorated in the last years), the pressures that are building are quite strong and significant. The innovations discussed in this chapter are partly a response to and partly a causal effect of these pressures.

Liberal democracy needs to be rethought on the basis of more realistic assumptions regarding the role of the citizens. After all, contemporary democracy is both representative and meritocratic. People not only want self-government but also desire good governance. Yet, two measures with the potential to radically transform democracy have never been seriously considered: the substitution of elections with lotteries (van Reybrouck 2016) and radical reduction of terms of office so that many citizens may have access to power (Manin 1997). The ancient Greeks operated their democracy in this way precisely because they thought that ex ante equality should be given preference to merit, competence, and qualification. Contemporary democracy tries to combine equality and merit, and most are not ready to part with either. In this sense, the lack of certain innovations tells us more about the character of present-day democracy than some of the above-mentioned novelties do.[4]

In conclusion, experiments may be successful even if they fail. The party-media hybrid for instance should not be treated as a model for all future parties. It only reveals a lot about the challenges and pressures that representative structures currently experience and suggests one possible way to deal with them. Even if none of these innovations remains a lasting feature of future democracies, their careful study may be instrumental and indeed indispensable for a better understanding of the functioning of liberal democracy.

Endnotes

1   For opposing arguments, see Krastev (2016) and Foa and Mounk (2017).

2   See the full text of Viktor Orbán's speech at Băile Tuşnad (Tusnádfürdő) on 26 July 2014 (available online at http://budapestbeacon.com/public-policy/full-text-of-viktor-orbans-speech-at-baile-tusnad-tusnadfurdo-of-26-july-2014/10592).

3   In both cases arguments about better representation of the people, greater links between representatives and the electorate, and the costs of the electoral system were taken into account. The major argument for going back to the proportional representation system in 2016 was that the mixed system proved to be costly and created more incentives for corruption during campaigns in single-member districts.

4   For an account of rather radical experimental democratic measures that have been tried in Eastern Europe, see Schmitter and Trechsel (2004).

IV. The Contradictions of Democratic Innovation in the United States

DIDI KUO

Rarely is democratisation a linear process. The history of contemporary democracies shows that the process of expanding representative institutions is punctuated by periods of rollback and plagued by ongoing tensions over citizenship and access. Nowhere is this more obvious than in the United States, where the democratic Constitution of 1789 limited suffrage to only 6 per cent of the population. Over the next 200 years, the franchise was extended to non-property-owning males, to African Americans, to women, to Native Americans, to people aged 18-21, and to citizens subject to discriminatory poll taxes, often after protracted and violent struggle.[1]

Although it may seem as though the basic democratic principle of enfranchisement is an antiquated concern, this chapter will focus on the promise– and challenges–of innovations in American electoral institutions. In the past decade, there have been paradoxical trends in democratic innovation. Understanding them requires examining the political motivations that drive reforms, rather than the normative reasons offered by politicians. In the US, 'innovations' are always justified through appeals to fairness and process, although they often serve explicitly political goals of ensuring partisan victories.

Decades of rising political polarisation and declining trust in government have produced a desire on the part of the two traditional political parties–the Republicans and the Democrats–to reform the electoral system. However, there is little political will to enact structural reforms on the national level. Instead, the two parties experiment with election rules at the state and local levels to address problems important to their electoral goals. Their diagnoses of the problems with democracy and the solutions they therefore seek differ completely. In general, the left (typically more aligned with the Democrats) wants to ensure that the greatest number of citizens who want to vote can actually vote, while the right (typically aligned with the Republicans) attempts to shape the electorate through restrictions–or at the very least, burdens–on the voting process.

This chapter discusses the contradictions of democratic innovation in the US. One set of democratic innovations is designed to be democracy enhancing and includes reforms such as automatic voter registration (AVR), top-two primaries, ranked-choice voting, and non-partisan redistricting. Some of these reforms try to decrease the time and complexity of voting, while others try to increase the likelihood that moderate candidates, as opposed to ideologically extreme candidates, are elected. In general, these innovations have been supported by Democrats at the state level, along with a coalition of reformers who believe that improving electoral institutions can expand democratic access and build momentum for greater, more systematic change.

The second set of democratic innovations, in tension with the first, targets the electoral process by placing stricter requirements on voters. As a result, these innovations are democracy restricting. They include voter identification (ID) requirements, voter registration cut-offs, and limits to alternatives to voting on Election Day, which is always a weekday. These laws have been supported and passed most often by Republican governors and legislatures and have the effect of limiting access to the polls. They disproportionately affect minority and poor voters, since they increase the difficulty and cost of voting.

Voting is the fundamental exercise of democracy; it is the most basic way citizens have a say in politics. And yet, voting remains contested in the US, which lacks centralised election administration. Elections are carried out by partisan elected officials who determine every aspect of voting: the boundaries and demographic composition of electoral constituencies, restrictions on suffrage,[2] and most importantly, the rules governing how voters access the polls. This entails widespread variation in the voting experience. It can also affect public trust in electoral institutions. In the presidential race between George W. Bush and Al Gore in 2000, Democrats questioned the ability of the Republican Secretary of State in Florida to administer the Florida recount in a politically neutral manner. More recently, President Donald Trump, warning of vote stealing, drummed up fears of a rigged election during the 2016 race.

As Anheier noted in the introduction to this Report, a host of democratic innovations seek to change access to and participation in the political process. Other Report chapters examining such practices as participatory budgeting, referendums, and online activism show that many democracies are devising ways to modernise institutions and enhance representation. However, most innovations in the US concern election administration and voting access.

This chapter explores the contradictions of democratic innovation in the US, where states and cities have implemented an array of reforms since 2000. It begins by providing background on election administration and explaining how federalism and decentralisation create a patchwork of election laws across the country. The following section describes the problems that democratic innovations seek to address, particularly political polarisation and unequal influence in politics. Two divergent sets of reforms are then discussed: those that aim to help more voters participate and to moderate politics, and those that instead place burdens on voters. Both sets of reforms explain the overall limited picture of democratic innovation in the US.

Federalism and Election Administration

The foremost reason we see diverging trends in American democratic innovation is the decentralisation of election administration. States are responsible for overseeing elections, and most states delegate a great deal of authority to counties and towns. Thus, there is a great deal of variation in the rules by which citizens elect candidates to office, and as many as 8,000 jurisdictions oversee elections (Bauer et al. 2014). These jurisdictions dictate all aspects of the voting process and determine the location and availability of polling stations, the hours each polling station is open, and the type of ballot or voting technology used. States also determine whether voters have alternatives to voting in person on Election Day.

Decentralisation of election administration plays a critical role in determining the cost of voting, which is already high in the US relative to other advanced democracies. Voters are not automatically registered to vote and must navigate a series of laws that govern how far in advance of Election Day they must register. For citizens who cannot find time to get to the polls on Election Day (polls may only be open during working hours, or may be located far away from a voter's residence), there may not be ready alternatives to cast a ballot, for example through absentee ballots or early voting. Americans also have many elections, including primary races, two-year election cycles for Congress, and in many jurisdictions the opportunity to vote for any number of offices, including judges, sheriffs, and school board members. The costliness and frequency of voting lend themselves to voter fatigue or abstention.

A few examples illustrate the differential experience of voting in the US. According to state law, a voter in Oregon is automatically registered to vote when requesting or renewing a driving licence with the Department of Motor Vehicles (DMV). She receives her ballot in the mail and can send it in advance of Election Day. She never has to show identification or worry about having failed to register in time to vote. A voter in Mississippi, on the other hand, needs to register to vote with the proper authorities a month in advance of Election Day. She then needs to show a photo identification to vote–but the US does not provide government-issued IDs. This voter therefore needs to find a DMV or eligible identification-issuing office. In rural areas, these government offices are often located more than 10 miles away from most residences and are difficult to get to: nearly half a million voters do not have access to vehicles, and rural areas lack public transportation. In Mississippi, a 'perverse set of rules' requires a voter to use a birth certificate to obtain official photo ID, while it also requires photo ID to obtain a birth certificate (Gaskins and Iyer 2012: 15). A birth certificate costs US$15, not including a US$10 processing charge from the agency that mails the certificate to the potential voter. Passports and driving licences cost anywhere from US$8 to US$135 (Gaskins and Iyer 2012: 15). Voters therefore face very different costs related to voting, depending on where they reside.

Innovations in American Democracy: What Are the Problems?

L
ike many other advanced democracies around the world, the US is in a period of democratic malaise. Public confidence in all institutions, particularly in Congress, has declined precipitously, reaching a historic low of 7 per cent in 2013 (Riffkin 2014). Voters increasingly identify as 'independents' rather than as members of a political party. In the 2016 presidential primaries, voters were sympathetic to the campaigns of two outsiders, Bernie Sanders and Donald Trump, both of whom decried special interest influence. Although they had very different messages, both candidates shared a view that the interests of the so-called Washington elite were hostile to those of average citizens.

Voter dissatisfaction has paralleled a rise in political polarisation and gridlock at the national level. Since the 1970s, the Republican and Democratic parties have moved further apart ideologically than they have been at any point in the twentieth century (Voteview.com 2016). Bipartisan negotiation in Congress has therefore become more elusive, while gridlock and inaction have become commonplace. In October 2013, disagreement over funding for the Affordable Care Act, often referred to as Obamacare, led Republicans to shut down the federal government for sixteen days. Obstructionist tactics such as holding up executive appointments have also become more common. There has also been a greater degree of inter-branch conflict, with the Obama administration having implemented some of its key policies through executive agencies instead of through Congress.

As a result, more and more people perceive a representation gap: they feel as if elected officials do not work on their behalf, a trend also observed in Eastern Europe by Smilov in this Report. Instead, they think that government is run on behalf of special interests and that it is in need of sweeping reform (Pew Research Center 2015). In addition to rising cynicism among all voters, partisans also show greater levels of antipathy towards each other: Republican and Democratic supporters report not only that they distrust members of the opposite party, but also that the opposite party constitutes a 'threat to the nation's well-being' (Pew Research Center 2014). Unsurprisingly, staunch partisans are also more politically active, more likely to vote in primaries and in general elections, and more likely to discuss politics.

Further, the representation gap may be the result of actual disparities in political participation. Electoral turnout in the US is highly dependent on socioeconomic status. The cost of voting is reflected in patterns of political participation, since affluent voters are far more likely to vote than low-income voters. In data collected from the 2004, 2008, and 2012 presidential elections, approximately 80 per cent of voters making over US$100,000 per year voted, while only approximately 40 per cent of voters making less than

US$20,000 per year voted (File and Crissey 2012; Holder 2006). Affluent and educated voters have greater time and resources to devote to politics, making them much more likely to volunteer with and contribute money to campaigns, as Merkel notes more generally in his chapter in this Report. There is evidence that unequal patterns of participation translate to unequal influence in policy outcomes. Politicians are more responsive to the preferences of high-income voters, even when they represent constituencies with many low- and middle-income voters (Bartels 2008; Gilens and Page 2014; Kuo and McCarty 2015). Further, the preferences of the wealthy differ systematically from those of lower income groups, particularly on economic issues such as taxation and redistribution.

Despite growing voter dissatisfaction, there is little political will to reform democratic institutions at the national level. Reforming the campaign finance system, which now allows extremely wealthy individuals and organisations to exert enormous influence in the electoral process, is unlikely given recent Supreme Court precedent in its 2010 decision on Citizens United v. Federal Election Commission. In the national Congress, both the Republicans and Democrats can use obstruction to their strategic advantage, decreasing the likelihood that they adopt measures to incentivise compromise and negotiation. We therefore turn to two approaches at the state level to innovate electoral institutions.

Democratic Innovations: Increasing Voter Access, Decreasing Partisan Administration

In response to high levels of partisan polarisation, a number of democratic innovations seek to improve voter access to the polls and to incentivise the election of moderate, as opposed to highly ideological, candidates. These innovations target the electoral system, including the voting process, the rules governing primary elections, and the way electoral districts are drawn.

Automatic voter registration

Following the presidential election of 2012, accounts of incredibly long lines at the polls led then-President Obama to appoint a Presidential Commission on Election Administration. The bipartisan commission found that decentralised election administration led to wide disparities in Americans' voting experiences and made a series of recommendations, including online voter registration, inter-state voter registration exchanges, and expansion of opportunities to vote before Election Day (Bauer et al. 2014).

Since then, six states–Oregon, California, West Virginia, Vermont, Connecticut, and via a ballot measure in November 2016, Alaska–have adopted automatic voter registration, a common practice in many Western democracies. At least twenty other states are considering AVR measures in their legislatures, which would ensure that citizens who interact with government offices such as DMVs are automatically added to voter rolls. Voters can opt out if they so choose, but automatic registration removes the burden of registering from voters. AVR could have a transformative impact on voter registers: California estimates that it has 6.6 million eligible but unregistered voters (Brennan Center for Justice 2016). In 2016, Oregon added over 220,000 new voters to the rolls (Brater 2016).

In the states that adopted AVR, there was bipartisan support behind the measures. However, modernisation of voter registration remains politically contested. Democrats are more likely to support laws that ease burdens on voters. A state legislator in Oregon, speaking about AVR, said, 'The question should be, why would we ever have a barrier?' (Eidelson 2016). In Illinois and New Jersey, by contrast, AVR was passed by the legislature but vetoed by Republican governors. Governor Chris Christie of New Jersey mocked AVR as the 'Voter Fraud Enhancement and Permission Act' (Eidelson 2016).

Although each state creates its own rules governing voter registration, there is also political support for federal laws requiring automatic registration. President Obama and former Secretary of State Hillary Clinton have both voiced support for AVR (Obama 2016). Senator Bernie Sanders, who challenged Secretary Clinton in the race for the Democratic presidential nomination, introduced automatic registration legislation in Congress; Democratic members of the House of Representatives also introduced a bill requiring automatic registration at all DMVs. This legislation has stalled in committee, however, and is not likely to receive a floor vote under a Republican Congress.

AVR is not the only effort to ease access to the polls. Twelve states and the District of Columbia have same-day registration, which allows voters to register on Election Day immediately before they vote (NCSL 2016). Eleven states open their polls before Election Day to allow early in-person voting, while thirteen allow no-excuse absentee voting. In a few states, such as Washington and California, voting can be done entirely by mail. Voters receive their ballots a few weeks prior to the election and can drop them off in the mail or take them to a voting precinct at any time they choose.

Top-two primaries and ranked-choice voting

Another theory about political polarisation is that it is driven by political party primaries. Primary elections, in which voters select candidates who will run in the general election, are commonplace in the US. Voters select party nominees for the presidential election, for House and Senate races, and for a number of lower-level offices as well. Different states have different rules governing primary elections; in open primaries, any voter can cast a ballot, while in closed primaries, only those who have registered with a political party can vote in that party's primary.

Primary elections are low turnout events, particularly in non-presidential election years. On average, only about 17 per cent of American voters participate in presidential primaries (Patterson 2009). In Congressional primaries, turnout averages only 4-10 per cent. Those who vote in primaries tend to be older and more ideological than voters in general elections. As a result, primaries–once considered a way to democratise the party nomination process–now often produce candidates further to one side or the other on the ideological spectrum than the average voter. Primaries are also the target of large amounts of campaign funding, with ideologically extreme donors getting involved in supporting extremist candidates (Barber 2016; La Raja and Schaffner 2015). The primary process leaves many moderate voters feeling underserved by the candidates running in general elections.

One way to reduce the potential for extremist candidates to win primaries is through the adoption of top-two primaries, also known as 'non-partisan blanket' or 'jungle' primaries. In California, Washington, and Louisiana, there are no party primaries. Instead, in a top-two system, candidates of all political parties run together in a primary. The two candidates with the most votes then advance to the general election.

To illustrate how top-two primaries work, take the 2016 race for an open Senate seat in California. California is a majority Democratic state, and the Senate seat was previously held by a Democrat. The primary election for that seat included thirty-four candidates: seven Democrats, twelve Republicans, and fifteen third-party candidates. The top two vote-getters were Kamala Harris (40 per cent) and Loretta Sanchez (19 per cent), both Democrats. The next four candidates with the highest number of votes were Republicans, but each won only 3-8 per cent of the votes. The general election therefore took place between two Democratic candidates, with Kamala Harris winning 62 per cent of the votes. In many other races the two highest vote-getters were from different parties, but the theory behind the top-two system is that it reduces the importance of the party label and forces candidates to appeal to the highest number of voters so that they will get as many votes as possible. The top-two system also tries to ensure that the candidates running in the general election are less ideologically extreme by creating incentives for them to strike a moderate tone beginning in the primary.

In addition to top-two primaries, ranked-choice voting seeks to undermine the distorting effects of the American winner-take-all electoral system in which a voter's likelihood of influencing any election outcome is extremely low. Candidates stand for election in first-past-the-post races in single-member districts, and they only need to win a plurality of votes in order to win a seat. This creates incentives for candidates to mobilise their bases of supporters rather than appeal to voters across the political spectrum. Even in heterogeneous districts and states, slight partisan majorities can create winner-take-all outcomes. In a state with somewhat even numbers of Republican and Democratic voters, a turnout advantage among one party can ensure that the state legislature, the governorship, members of the House of Representatives, Senators, and the state's electoral votes for president all go to one party. As a result, many voters complain of 'wasting' their votes on Election Day, which further depresses turnout.

In a ranked-choice system, voters rank their choices among all the candidates in a race. Their most preferred candidate is ranked '1', their second preferred candidate '2', and so on. If a candidate gets a majority of first-preference votes, he or she is the winner. If, however, a candidate only gets a plurality of '1' votes, then the votes for the last-place candidate are eliminated, and the remaining votes on those ballots are redistributed as second-preference votes. Votes are then recounted and a winner declared when someone has a majority of first- and second-preference votes.

Ranked-choice voting, also known as instant run-off voting or the alternative vote, is used in many advanced democracies, including Australia for elections to the House of Representatives and Ireland for presidential elections. It has been adopted for local elections in a few American cities, including Cambridge, Massachusetts; San Francisco, California; Minneapolis, Minnesota; and Portland, Maine. While these cities have not experimented with ranked-choice voting long enough to draw an empirical contrast with first-past-the-post, reformers hope that it has a few distinct advantages. For one, candidates in a ranked-choice system, similar to a top-two primary, must appeal to moderates in order to optimise their first-preference votes. Candidates might also be less inclined to engage in negative campaigning, which might be less effective against multiple opposing candidates. Grose (2016a) found that top-two primaries in Washington and California led candidates to craft bipartisan messages and reach out to voters of opposite parties. Finally, ranked-choice systems ensure that voters can vote their 'true' preferences for third-party candidates or for minority parties (Diamond 2015).

Independent redistricting commissions

A final democratic innovation targets the system of drawing voting districts in the US. Because of the constitutional requirement of 'one man, one vote', each district should include approximately the same number of people; boundaries are redrawn every ten years after the census count of the population. The 435 seats to the House of Representatives are apportioned among the states by population; seven states have only one seat in the House, while California, the most populous state, has fifty-three.

One of the foremost reasons cited for political polarisation is gerrymandering, a term that describes the process of drawing district boundaries in order to ensure a specific electoral outcome. District boundaries are typically drawn by state legislatures, giving the majority party of the legislature significant influence in determining the demographic and partisan composition of each district. Gerrymandering can take many forms, including drawing districts of strange shapes; drawing districts to create or to undermine incumbents; and ensuring majorities of certain racial or partisan groups. Where the legislature is somewhat evenly divided between the parties, redistricting can result in stalemates over how maps should be drawn. Alternatively, the two parties may agree to bipartisan gerrymanders, ensuring that at least some districts are drawn to their electoral advantage.

While there is no central (national) oversight of the redistricting process in the US, redistricting plans are often the product of extensive litigation in the courts. Opposing parties can challenge a majority party's redistricting plan by claiming that it violates 'one man, one vote'. Stalemates over redistricting are also sent to the courts. Courts also exert tremendous influence in districting, since the courts themselves sometimes create district maps to override the boundaries drawn by politicians.

One way to obviate partisan districting is through the adoption of independent, non-partisan redistricting commissions. Six states use commissions to redistrict congressional seats, and while the commissions vary–some are composed of partisan appointees, others, like California's, are composed of citizens who do not hold political office–they nonetheless remove redistricting responsibility from partisan legislatures. An additional five states have advisory commissions to assist state legislatures with the drawing of lines.

Though there is little empirical research on the effects of redistricting commissions given that redistricting is infrequent and the commissions relatively new, research on Washington and California shows that these reforms have produced more moderate outcomes among candidates and in the legislature. In California, top-two primaries and independent redistricting were adopted in the same year. The combination of the two reforms has elected more moderate legislators to the California legislature (Grose 2016b; McGhee and Shor 2016).

Democratic Rollback

Accompanying these innovations has been a set of laws that impose additional restrictions on voters, namely in the form of voter identification requirements. Since 2010, thirty-four states have passed restrictions on voting access, including not only voter ID but also curtailment of early and absentee voting. Politicians claim that voter identification protects electoral integrity, but there is little empirical evidence that identification fraud occurs regularly at the polls. Instead, the implementation of voter ID requirements shows that democratic innovation can stem just as much from political motivations as it can from normative commitments to democracy.

It may seem incongruous that voter identification laws constitute both a democratic innovation and a rollback of democracy. After all, most advanced democracies require voters to show some proof of identification before they cast a vote. In the US, however, the history of voter identification dates to the period after the Civil War, when emancipated slaves were effectively disenfranchised through the implementation of so-called Jim Crow laws. These restrictions included poll taxes, literacy tests, and restrictive residency and registration requirements. These laws were not overturned until the civil rights movement and passage of the Voting Rights Acts in 1965.

Voter ID laws are the most recent in a series of political efforts to tackle the perceived potential of election fraud. These efforts began in earnest after 2000, when the presidential election came down to a few thousand votes in the state of Florida. That election marked the point when political leaders on the right realised that changing the rules of elections could significantly affect election outcomes. During George W. Bush's first presidential term (2001-4), the Department of Justice encouraged prosecutors to pursue lawsuits against individuals suspected of voting fraud. When lengthy investigations yielded little evidence of wrongdoing, Republicans instead turned to legislative means to reduce the potential for fraud (Lipton and Urbina 2007).

In 2005, then-President Bush appointed a bipartisan Commission on Federal Election Reform to identify ways to clean up often cumbersome voting processes. The Commission's report recommended, among other things, uniform voter identification. Although conceding that 'there is no evidence of extensive fraud in U.S. elections or of multiple voting', the Commission nonetheless recommended that states both ask voters for ID and issue identification for free to voters who otherwise would not carry it (Commission on Federal Election Reform 2005).

Since then, voter identification has become a particular political goal of Republicans at the state level (see Table 4.1). In a study of voter restrictions from 2006-11, of the forty-one voter restrictions passed, thirty-four were passed by Republican-controlled state legislatures (Bentele and O'Brien 2013). Politicians argue that these measures prevent voter fraud, although empirical and judicial scrutiny into voter ID laws finds very little evidence of fraud—and almost no evidence of the type of impersonation fraud that voter ID is designed to prevent (Ahlquist, Mayer, and Jackman 2014; Levitt 2014; Lipton and Urbina 2007; Minnite 2010). Civil rights organisations have long opposed these anti-fraud measures, arguing that they bear a distinct resemblance to the disenfranchising measures that impeded African Americans from voting for a century.

Instead, the factors related to adoption of voter ID laws seem to show that conservative legislators take issue with turnout among racial minorities.

Table 4.1 **Voter identification laws in 2016, by state**

ID Requirement	Photo ID	Non-Photo ID	
Strict	*Georgia*	*Arizona*	
	Indiana	*North Dakota*	
	Kansas	*Ohio*	
	Mississippi*		
	Tennessee		
	Virginia		
	Wisconsin		
Non-Strict	*Alabama*	*Alaska*	*Montana*
	Florida	*Arkansas*	*New Hampshire*
	Idaho	Colorado	~~*North Carolina*~~***
	Louisiana	Connecticut	Oklahoma*
	*Michigan***	Delaware	*South Carolina*
	Rhode Island	Hawaii	*Utah*
	South Dakota	Kentucky	Washington
	Texas	*Missouri*	

Source: Table adapted from the National Conference of State Legislatures, available at http://www.ncsl.org/research/elections-and-campaigns/voter-id.aspx

Notes: Republican legislatures are italicised. A strict voter ID requirement means that voters without identification must 1) vote by provisional ballot, and 2) take additional steps after Election Day in order for their votes to count – otherwise, their vote will not be counted.

* Mississippi and Oklahoma's voter ID laws passed by voter referendum; both are Republican-majority states.

** Michigan's Republican-led state legislature passed a strict voter ID law in December 2016.

*** North Carolina's law was struck down by a federal court in July 2016.

In states where minority turnout had increased since the previous presidential election, state legislatures were more likely to pass strict ID laws (Bentele and O'Brien 2013). In addition, seven of the twelve states with the highest levels of Hispanic population growth have also adopted voter identification (Weiser and Opsal 2014). Some politicians have been brazen in acknowledging the political effects of these laws; the Republican Pennsylvania House Majority Leader was quoted as saying that 'voter ID . . . is gonna allow [former Massachusetts] Governor Romney to win the state of Pennsylvania [in the presidential election]' (Blake 2012).

Research on voter identification laws shows a robust correlation between political motivations and adoption of voter ID. Bentele and O'Brien

(2013) examined legislative restrictions on voter access adopted between 2006 and 2011 and found that legislators used these laws to target minority voters and demobilise African Americans in particular. Further, Republicans are more likely to adopt voter restrictions when electoral competition is higher, indicating that they use these laws to ensure electoral majorities (Hicks et al. 2015). Indeed, the election of Republican governors and Republican legislators make the adoption of voter identification requirements much more likely (Weiser and Opsal 2014).

There have not been many election cycles with new voting restrictions in place, so the impact of voter ID is unclear. However, Hajnal, Lajevardi, and Nielson (2016) show that adoption of strict photo ID requirements reduced turnout of Hispanic, African American, and mixed-race voters in primary and general elections, while having little discernible effect on white turnout. Further, election administrators have been found to administer voter ID laws in racially biased ways, asking Hispanic and African American voters for identification at higher rates than white voters even when asking for identification is non-discretionary (Cobb, Greiner, and Quinn 2010). While there is some evidence that voter ID laws do not deter voters from wanting to vote (Citrin, Green, and Morris 2014), these laws nonetheless make it less likely that all potential voters will actually be able to cast a vote on Election Day.

While voter identification constitutes a serious burden for many voters, the focus on voter ID laws obscures other ways that Republican legislatures are limiting access to the polls. These laws include curtailing early voting, limiting registration deadlines, and limiting access to voting for those with felony criminal convictions. In Ohio, the legislature eliminated a period called 'Golden Week', which allowed early voting and same-day registration. This week had been popular with African American voters, who typically experience longer Election Day wait times and polling problems than white voters in Ohio (Berman 2016; DNC Voting Rights Institute 2005). In explaining why Ohio wanted to do away with early and weekend voting, the chairman of the Republican Party in Columbus said, 'I really actually feel we shouldn't contort the voting process to accommodate the urban–read African-American–voter-turnout machine' (Rowland 2012).

Whether these new restrictions will withstand judicial scrutiny remains to be seen. In a US Court of Appeals ruling, a panel of three justices struck down North Carolina's voter ID law. The court noted that the North Carolina state legislature provided no evidence of voter fraud, ruling instead that the laws were enacted 'in the immediate aftermath of unprecedented African American voter participation in a state with a troubled racial history'. The court further cited the 'discriminatory intent' behind the law, which constituted 'one of the largest restrictions of the franchise in modern North Carolina history' (US Court of Appeals for the Fourth Circuit 2016).

Conclusion

Democracy is a struggle for an ideal, punctuated by periods of progress and periods of rollback. In democratic societies, citizens are rarely satisfied with all of their democratic institutions: they may feel that there are inequities in representation or deficits in accountability, transparency, and access. Democratic institutions thus need flexibility in order to adapt to the changing needs of voters in increasingly complex societies.

In the US, however, voting rights continue to be the locus of innovations that serve both to enhance and to decrease democratic access. While there are occasional cries for reforming national institutions such as the campaign finance system, the current polarised climate makes the likelihood of significant reforms at the federal level unlikely. Instead, decentralised and partisan election administration provides politicians with discretion in determining how Americans vote.

There are some efforts at the state level, particularly among western states, to modernise electoral processes and make voting as easy as possible. But these efforts are countered by the adoption of onerous requirements that make voting more difficult. The likelihood that a state pursues a particular type of innovation is dependent on politics. Democratic legislatures, like California and Washington, have been more likely to ease voter access, while Republican legislatures have been more likely to block these initiatives and implement restrictions on voting access.

The most likely way states will ease access to the polls is through pressure to do so, either because of congressional policy or because of public opposition. Republican politicians justify voter ID laws through claims of voter fraud, facing little public opposition. Although the media reports on the impacts of voter ID laws, the fact is that most voters carry some form of identification. Those who are likely to be disenfranchised are often those who are politically marginalised in the first place. Furthermore, Democratic politicians have been tepid in their support for democratic reforms and unsuccessful at mobilising the public to oppose voter ID (Bernstein 2016).

Another possibility is that state-level experimentation with innovations in election procedure might streamline the voting process enough, encouraging other states to adopt similar measures. Policy diffusion is therefore a way that states might be more likely to adopt AVR and ranked-choice voting: in the 2016 election, Maine passed a ballot initiative to switch to ranked-choice voting throughout the state.

In November 2016, the Republican candidate, Donald Trump, won the presidential election over Hillary Clinton, the Democratic nominee. She won the popular vote by more than a million votes, but Trump won the Electoral College. There is a palpable sense of frustration among Democratic voters that American electoral institutions benefit the right. Democratic voters are more likely to live in dense, urban areas, while Republican voters are spread out in suburban and rural areas. The Electoral College was created as a compromise to amplify the votes of smaller states. However, the 2016 election marks the second election in less than two decades in which the candidate with more popular votes lost the presidency.

The gulf between so-called red states (majority Republican) and blue states (majority Democratic) has never seemed wider, at least in recent history. This chapter has argued that Democrats and Republicans approach institutional reforms very differently at the state level. They isolate different problems that require redress: Democrats want to ease voter burdens and make voting easier, while Republicans want to 'clean up' the electoral process through restrictions on voting. While Republicans actively oppose the kinds of reforms that western states have adopted, Democrats have not mobilised effectively to stop the wave of voter restrictions that swept the states after 2010.

Scholars are only beginning to weigh the effects of democratic innovations on the 2016 election. Were voters in western, Democratic states actually more likely to vote once they were automatically registered? Did voter ID laws suppress turnout, particularly among minorities, in states throughout the south and midwest? The hope is that political parties work hard to understand the empirical consequences of these reforms, and that they see voting rights as fundamental to democratic legitimacy and republican government. If it is the case that easing voter access increases turnout or that voter ID suppresses it, it is incumbent on politicians to support laws promoting access and oppose those that restrict it. The fact that voters in 2016 voted under such divergent conditions points to the paradox of reform in the US. In the meantime, democratic innovation in the US proceeds at an unsteady pace, with an uncertain future.

Endnotes

1   By the 1840s, most states had done away with property qualifications to vote. The Fifteenth Amendment, passed in 1870, states that 'The right of citizens of the United States to vote shall not be denied or abridged by the United States or by any State on account of race, color, or previous condition of servitude.' Women were granted the right to vote in 1920 with the passage of the Nineteenth Amendment. Native Americans were granted the right to vote in 1924 with the passage of the Indian Citizenship Act. The voting age was lowered as a result of conscription during the Vietnam War: the draft applied to men aged 18 and older, but voting was limited to citizens over the age of 21. As a result of political pressure, the voting age was lowered to 18 so that people serving in the military could also cast votes that might determine their fates. The 24th Amendment, ratified in 1964, abolished the poll tax. Poll taxes, a fee citizens had to pay in order to vote, were levied in some states to keep minority and poor voters from voting.

2   States and localities have discretion to deny suffrage to non-residents of the district (including, for example, university students and enlisted soldiers) or to voters with felony criminal convictions.

V. Democratic Innovations
Lessons From Beyond the West

THAMY POGREBINSCHI

I nnovation has become a buzzword. In academic research, politics, and media, one hears increasingly about political, social, technological, and democratic innovations. A relevant issue for public policy scholars and decision-makers since at least the 1980s, innovations have been implemented while seeking continuous improvement in policy-making and public service delivery. These 'social innovations', 'political innovations', or 'innovations in public services' have primarily involved the public and private sectors in the implementation of changes that could bring more efficiency and effectiveness to public policies, public administration, and public services.

As innovations evolve, the role that citizen participation plays in them evolves, too. Innovations were soon acknowledged as relevant not only for public management but also for democracy. Since the 1990s, citizens' demands for more participation have been increasing as consistently as their signs of political disillusionment (Cain, Dalton, and Scarrow 2003). Representative democracy has found itself challenged by low electoral turnout, decreasing party membership rates, and low levels of public trust in its main institutions, including parties, parliaments, and governments (Dalton 2004; Norris 2002).

> *Citizens' demands for more participation have been increasing as consistently as their signs of political disillusionment.*

Reforms in representative institutions have not been enough to prevent democracy from being diagnosed with a crisis (Kaase and Newton 1995; Merkel 2015a; see also chapters by Anheier and Offe in this Report) nor to avoid the discontent that has led citizens to increasingly take to the streets to protest and demonstrate. In order to improve democracy, institutional change can no longer be dissociated from citizen participation. Those willing to innovate, not only reform, have sought deeper change: involving citizens and civil society in political processes and allowing them to play a role in policy-making.

Democratic innovations conceived as new institutional designs that seek to improve governance through citizen participation have been spreading in almost every corner of the world. Experimentation with new forms of participation in politics brings together governments and civil society organisations as well as private stakeholders and international development agencies. Although efforts have been mostly driven by the belief that more participation may be an effective remedy for at least some of democracy's malaises (Geissel and Newton 2012), one can identify different patterns in how innovations evolve in the West and how they evolve beyond it.

This chapter focuses on democratic innovations in non-western countries, in particular Latin America, where the specialised literature has located not only the highest volume of institutional experimentation but also the most successful cases of democratic innovation (Cameron, Hershberg, and Sharpe 2012; Selee and Peruzzotti 2009). After briefly highlighting some features of democratic innovations in western countries, certain conditions that explain why and how Latin America became fertile ground for these new participatory institutions will be underlined. Three institutional design features of democratic innovations in Latin America (formalisation, decisiveness, and co-governance) will then be used to explain how innovations have evolved and endured in the region regardless of their aggregate impact. Based on original data from the LATINNO data set[1] for sixteen countries in Latin America, this chapter argues that Latin American innovations are highly institutionalised, unlike those in the West. Recommendations are then offered to institutional designers and policy-makers in the West to institutionalise democratic innovations by increasing their levels of formalisation, decisiveness, and co-governance.

Democratic Innovations in the West

In the older, established democracies, concern with legitimacy has been an important driver of innovation as an attempt to maintain or restore citizens' trust in and satisfaction with the political regime. Citizens have been called to participate in online and offline forums, assemblies, and conventions that have been charged with drafting new constitutions (the Constitutional Council in Iceland in 2011 and the Constitutional Convention in Ireland in 2012), electoral reforms (Citizens' Assemblies on Electoral Reform in Canada in 2004 and 2006 and in the Netherlands in 2006), and legislation in strategic areas like science and technology (consensus conferences in Denmark) and environment (*Maastoliikennelaki* in Finland). Domestic financial and political crises have also triggered new institutional designs that allow citizens to gather together and set agendas for political reform (the G1000 in Belgium in 2011, We the Citizens in Ireland in 2011, and the National Forum in Iceland in 2010).

These experiments with democratic innovations in western countries illustrate two tendencies: the need to improve forms of decision-making and the belief that deliberation can fulfil this need, offering more democratic and legitimate outcomes than aggregative methods like voting. These tendencies come together in the main institutional design for citizen participation, which has been developed and widely implemented throughout Europe and North America: mini-publics, which include various formats such as citizens' juries, citizens' assemblies, citizens' panels, consensus conferences, planning cells, and deliberative polls. All these formats share certain elements such as the random or stratified selection of participants who gather to deliberate on certain issues, often facilitated by moderators and instructed by experts (Fung 2003; Smith 2009).

Mini-publics, however, are typically small-scale and local-level non-institutionalised bodies that lack formalisation and decisiveness, meaning they are not backed up by the legal order and cannot take decisions. Given that these democratic innovations often result from civil society initiatives alone, the government is often not involved. This means that in many cases no actual co-governance takes place, and mini-publics end up having a merely (often non-requested) advisory role, with outcomes that are no more than recommendations known only to a small number of people beyond the practitioners involved in the process and scholars interested in the topic. Making the outcomes of mini-publics reach the mass public or influence macro-politics are among the main challenges that such democratic innovations face, both in theory and in practice (Goodin 2006; Niemeyer 2014).

A significant volume of democratic innovation research and practice in the West relies on or is inspired by a pioneer and widely acknowledged Latin American experiment: participatory budgeting (PB), a process in which citizens participate in the formulation of municipal budgets, as referred to also in this Report in the chapters by Merkel and by Della Porta and Felicetti. A great deal of research on institutional reform and design for citizen participation, as well as many studies on mini-publics and deliberation, has used PB as the main, if not single, empirical basis. Moreover, PB is perhaps the most widely implemented and replicated innovation throughout the West. It has spread well beyond Latin America to over 1,000 cities across the world, and by 2009 over 200 cities in Europe had implemented some variation of PB, involving around 8 million citizens in total (Sintomer et al. 2010).

Latin America's PB has been internationally acknowledged for generating a more equitable redistribution of public goods, improving well-being, reducing clientelism, and increasing levels of participation among disadvantaged groups, especially less-educated and lower-income citizens (Abers 2003; Avritzer 2009; Baiocchi 2003b; Santos 2007; Touchton and Wampler 2014; Wampler 2007). However, in its adaptation to new conditions, what has been implemented under the PB label in the West has not reflected earlier Latin American experience (Sintomer et al. 2009). There is adequate evidence that PB can be transferred effectively but also that the willingness of political authorities and pressure from civil society to embed more participatory and redistributive practices vary considerably (Bellamy et al. 2016).

PB's relatively unsuccessful experience in the West may by comparison impart useful lessons on the replication of democratic innovations and their adaptation to new contexts. But more impelling, it offers a background against which one can ask why these new participatory institutions evolve, spread, and endure in Latin America–many times with positive outcomes– while in the West their replication is as problematic as their implementation, and positive outcomes are rarely observed.

One should also keep in mind that PB is only one among more than 2,000 democratic innovations (meaning different institutional designs, and not applications or replications of one or more experiments) created in Latin America since 1990, according to the LATINNO data set. In contrast, 487 of the 631 cases in the Participedia project (which, unlike LATINNO, counts single implementations of innovations as separate cases) are located in OECD countries. Furthermore, 137 entries in the Participedia dataset reflect cases of PB, ninety-nine of which are based in OECD countries (forty-nine in the UK, nine each in the US and Italy, six each in Australia, Canada, and Germany, and so on).[2]

Is Latin America a Laboratory of Political Innovation, and if so, Why?

A few years ago, Fung suggested that 'many of us may soon turn our eyes to Latin America to understand their accomplishments in democratic governance' (2011: 857). Asking whether the latter is an 'exceptionalism or a model for the rest of us', he concluded that as for 'the vast range of ambitious and successful democratic reforms . . . there are simply no analogs of similar scale and depth in North America, Europe, Asia or Africa' (2011: 867 f.). Six factors explain why so many democratic innovations have been created and have spread across Latin America (Pogrebinschi forthcoming). These factors, which cross over social, political, and cultural dimensions, are: democratisation, constitutionalisation, decentralisation, development, the left turn, and ethnic and cultural diversity.

During the process of democratisation, Latin America has undergone a strong surge of associativism. Numerous neighbourhood committees, civic associations, social movements, and non-governmental organisations (NGOs) organised to claim access to rights and public goods (Avritzer 2002: 7). Such a quantitative and qualitative increase in associative life gave rise to a new type of politics organised around demands for rights and accountability (Peruzzotti and Smulovitz 2006: 12). This strong collective action has galvanised popular participation, leading to the emergence of new spaces for citizen engagement. The progressive institutionalisation of these societal practices has produced many new formats designed to allow non-electoral citizen participation on public issues.

As a result of their political transitions, most Latin American countries underwent a process of constitutional reform, and some of them enacted new constitutions. Social and political actors urged that the new legal order ensure comprehensive rights and designed institutions to make them effective. In several countries, social claims for more participation became a legal mandate. Deliberation has been inscribed as both a principle and an institutional design feature of several legal orders. Countries as varied as Brazil, Bolivia, Colombia, Chile, El Salvador, Ecuador, and Paraguay have enacted legislation promoting citizen participation and institutionalising deliberative practices and bodies. The result is a high number of democratic innovations implemented by the state and often taking place with and/or within state institutions.

After their transitions, nearly all Latin American countries implemented decentralisation reforms. In most countries, decentralisation has opened the doors for citizen participation at the local level and has prompted the design of democratic innovations. As the responsibility for major public services has been transferred to local governments, novel ways of holding officials accountable have been designed. Local participatory institutions have become responsible for managing social policies and monitoring the delivery of public goods. A variety of policy management bodies have been created at the local level: health councils in Brazil, neighbourhood boards in Bolivia, and community action boards in Colombia are just a few of the many new arenas of participation. Not only has the decision-making power of local governments been augmented, but also the state capacity to implement decisions and ensure concrete results expanded considerably after the decentralisation reforms.

Together with decentralisation comes development assistance. International development organisations have been major players in disseminating democratic innovations in Latin America. Many of the local participatory bodies institutionalised by national governments were promoted by international organisations, especially during the 1990s. Virtually all main development organisations have supported participatory projects in Latin America by offering governments funds under the condition that they adopt, advance, and institutionalise democratic innovations. In their efforts to fight poverty and inequality, these organisations assume that participation and deliberation can make governments more accountable and policies more effective. Such strategies involve mechanisms like PB, citizen report cards, community scorecards, social audits, public hearings, and citizens' juries.

A very different player, but equally as important as international development organisations, are political parties, in particular those situated at the left side of the political spectrum. The so-called left turn, which led left-leaning parties from 1998 onward to take over two-thirds of national governments in Latin America, has brought citizen participation to the national level, incorporating it in the decision-making process by creating democratic innovations and revitalising existing ones. Participatory practices have been actually embraced by political parties at both ends of the ideological spectrum as means to restore trust and reinstate links with voters. Nonetheless, left-leaning parties have had a larger commitment to broad citizen participation. These parties have institutionalised participation as a method of government, as in the new constitutions of Bolivia, Ecuador, and Venezuela. Some of the new Latin American left parties were born out of social movements and trade unions and have brought to government their ties with grassroots organisations thus contributing to the design of more innovative channels of communication between the state and civil society.

The last factor is the ethnic and cultural diversity that is characteristic of Latin America. Indigenous peoples in Ecuador and Bolivia have a long tradition of holding deliberative assemblies, where common issues are discussed and decided, often by consensus. This communitarian conception of democracy shared by peasants and indigenous communities has been somewhat integrated into political institutions in the Andean countries. In other countries, new participatory spaces addressing other ethnic and cultural minorities have been also created. The most frequent forms are policy councils, which provide a space for traditionally under-represented groups like women, children, youth, the elderly, and members of the LGBTQ community to voice their needs and preferences. Democratic innovations that seek to include minority groups exist in countries like Brazil, Ecuador, and Mexico, usually at national level but sometimes also at regional or local levels.

While these factors offer strong enough evidence to indicate how the conditions relevant for the creation and spread of democratic innovations are different in Latin America than in the West, they are not enough to explain why these institutions endure and in many cases, as in PB, achieve positive outcomes. The next section argues that at least three institutional design features may explain this.

What Is Distinctive About Democratic Innovations in Latin America?

While in the West, particularly in Europe, the specialised literature (Geissel and Joas 2013; Smith 2009) tends to present democratic innovations as new institutional designs that oscillate between the old instruments of direct democracy (referendums, plebiscites, and citizens' initiatives) and new arenas for facilitated deliberation (citizens' juries, consensus conferences, and citizens' assemblies), in Latin America they have multifarious forms and often combine deliberation, direct voting, e-participation, and citizen representation.

Using data from the LATINNO data set on twelve of the Latin American countries it covers, the most common institutional designs have been identified (Pogrebinschi 2016), among which are: deliberative councils, participatory budgets, conflict resolution mechanisms, popular consultation, crowdsourcing legislation, collaborative policy-making, interactive policy platforms, oversight bodies, and participatory implementation processes. In addition, the more traditional instruments of direct democracy (referendums, plebiscites, citizens' initiatives) are also present in Latin America, although to a much smaller extent than those that involve, for example, deliberation, e-participation, or new forms of citizen representation.

Despite the greater variety of forms and formats when contrasted to democratic innovations that evolved in Europe and North America, some aspects of Latin American new institutional designs for citizen participation can be easily distinguished, especially when viewed in the aggregate and in a cross-country perspective. Drawing on 1,889 cases from sixteen countries in the LATINNO data set (Argentina, Bolivia, Brazil, Chile, Colombia, Costa Rica, Dominican Republic, Ecuador, El Salvador, Guatemala, Honduras, Mexico, Paraguay, Peru, Uruguay, and Venezuela), three design features will be examined: formalisation, decisiveness, and co-governance. Despite their quite experimental character and the relative youth of the democracies in which they have evolved, innovations in Latin America tend to be significantly institutionalised, which may explain their endurance as well as some of their positive evaluations and successful outcomes.

Formalisation

As mentioned previously, many countries in Latin America underwent constitutional changes alongside democratisation processes. These changes occurred at two moments: one in the 1980s and 1990s, when the 'third wave' of democratisation is said to have hit Latin America, and one in the 2000s in the context of the left turn referred to earlier. Most Latin American countries undertook decentralisation reforms in parallel, and with those reforms legal frameworks have been built to ensure subnational autonomy and to devolve power to the local level. Together, these two factors have brought about a whole new set of governance institutions, having inscribed in constitutions and laws innovative ways through which citizens could have a role in policy-making.

In the first moment of constitutional change, in order to break with their authoritarian pasts, countries like Brazil enacted constitutions that were protective of participation rights and created participatory institutions that could assure universal access to social rights in the context of new, decentralised administrations. In the second constitutional moment, left-leaning parties in countries like Venezuela, Bolivia, and Ecuador opted to re-found their political systems, enacting constitutions that brought participation to the same level as representation and that defined a new architecture of institutions designed to include citizens in the political process. Furthermore, some countries, whose own political contexts led to the enactment of constitutions that have similarly instated strong institutional innovation, belong to neither of these two moments. Colombia's Constitution of 1991, for example, responded to the worsening of the country's political crisis and the escalation of conflict and violence in the 1980s with no less than sixty-five of its 380 articles creating new, participatory institutions (Giraldo 2011).

Beyond these new constitutions, several Latin American countries have enacted legislation promoting citizen participation and building new bodies and instances of co-governance. In many cases these institutions or institutional changes have been created by or along with decentralisation laws and have been intended to adapt the public administration to a new configuration. In other cases, governments have made such innovations mandatory in an attempt to apply participatory principles and values (sometimes present in the constitution, but not always) or to fulfil accountability requirements of international agencies that have funded projects in the country. Colombia's Law 134 (1994), Bolivia's Popular Participation Law (1994), Peru's Framework Law on Participatory Budgeting (2003), El Salvador's municipal legislation reform (2005), and Paraguay's Municipal Organic Law (2010) are examples of legislation that has devised democratic innovations by creating new bodies and mechanisms or by making their creation mandatory.

Institutional innovation in Latin America also came as a result of the strong role of the state, in particular the executive branch, in experimenting with new modes of governance and political inclusion–particularly in the context of the left turn, but not only there. Presidentialism is a rule in virtually all Latin American countries, and strong executives in unstable or not yet fully consolidated political systems not only need to conduct frequent institutional reforms but also require new participatory bodies and venues to make them popularly acceptable and legitimate. A significant number of democratic innovations have thus been created by governmental programmes and policies, regardless of their many motivations.

The context described above explains the highly formalised environment in which democratic innovations are seeded and grow in Latin America. According to the LATINNO data set and as displayed in Figure 5.1, of 1,827 democratic innovations in the sixteen countries under examination, almost half are embedded in a constitution or in legislation. Almost one-third of all cases have been initiated by governmental programmes and policies, i.e. normative acts of the public administration. Innovations that have no formalisation at all, meaning inscribed in neither legal nor administrative norms, amount to only 26 per cent of all cases.

It is reasonable to assume that the more formalised an innovation is, the higher the chances are that it is effectively implemented and will generate outcomes. This is not always true. Colombia and Mexico are examples of countries where there is extensive formalisation, i.e. a high volume of innovations inscribed in legal norms, but where many innovations never came to effect, endured only briefly, or are simply ineffective in terms of either enhancing participation or producing outcomes relevant for democracy.

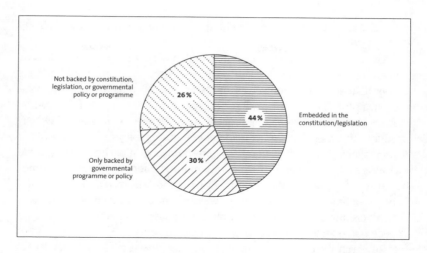

Figure 5.1 **Formalisation of democratic innovations in 16 Latin American countries**

However, the degree of formalisation is nevertheless a meaningful indicator of how institutionalised democratic innovations are, especially if one considers democratic innovations as actual institutional changes and not simply isolated or spontaneous events.

Decisiveness

A key issue is the effectiveness of democratic innovations. Relatively few studies track the impact of experiments, and even fewer provide explanations for their successes or failures. The specialised scholarship has also focused little on the effectiveness of innovations, having instead prioritised the scrutiny of the process itself, i.e. whether democratic innovations produce internal outcomes related to participation and deliberation, regardless of their external impact.

Studies of innovations in the West have mostly focused on how they affect matters like citizens' empowerment (Fung 2004) or the development of personal skills and civic competences (Grönlund, Setälä, and Herne 2010; Talpin 2007). These epistemic and ethical outputs internal to innovations say nothing, however, about their real outcomes and improvements to political systems. The few studies that do address political outputs of democratic innovations are usually circumscribed to local policy impact, thus not allowing inferences to effectiveness on the macro democracy level. For the most part these studies have sought to assess effectiveness by measuring whether innovations have solved specific local problems such as water pollution

(Geissel 2009; Geissel and Kern 2000) or the delivery of community policing (Fung 2006).

The problem with the effectiveness of democratic innovations is directly related to their capacity to take decisions. If the new institutional designs do not take decisions themselves, or if they do not transform, i.e. innovate, the way political decisions were previously taken, for example by including citizens in the decision-making process, then chances are low that they may produce outcomes that impact on democracy and policy-making. One of the main reasons why deliberation has been claimed as superior to aggregative methods such as voting is that it allows not only more legitimate outcomes but also better informed decisions (Fishkin and Luskin 2005). However, if democratic innovations are not designed or entitled to take decisions or if their decisions are not binding at all, then a lack of effectiveness is to be expected and an impact on democracy hard to verify.

Research on democratic innovations in the West has produced very little evidence regarding the decisional power of new institutional designs. The widely implemented deliberative polls, for example, have produced extensive evidence that deliberation can indeed transform preferences and lead to better-informed decisions (Fishkin 2009). However, deliberative polls have been mostly used so far as almost scientific experiments: their decisions are usually not integrated into political processes, and they are not considered consultative bodies expected to influence policy-makers in actual decision-making processes.

The same happens to mini-publics. Research shows that even the more exemplary cases of citizens' assemblies are deemed successful because of their ability to show how participation and deliberation can be improved, not because of the actual decisions they have reached or how they have transformed political decision-making. The British Columbia Citizens' Assembly for Electoral Reform, for example, after a thorough process of deliberation and participation, came up with a decision that depended on a referendum to be considered valid. As the referendum did not confirm the Assembly's decision, it had no impact at all on policy-making, despite the knowledge and many other democratic goods the process can be said to have generated (Warren and Pearse 2008). The lack of competence of democratic innovations to take meaningful decisions, i.e. decisions that impact on the political system, may well be one of the reasons that explain the scepticism of some western scholars towards these types of innovations (see Merkel in this Report).

Decisiveness, the decisional competence of democratic innovations, thus plays a crucial role in their effectiveness and is a key indicator of the extent to which innovations are institutionalised and therefore apt to evolve and endure. One can reasonably assume that innovations that yield no decisions have less chances of impact on policy-making and of making a difference on democracy than those that yield decisions. Likewise, one can expect that innovations that generate binding decisions tend to be more effective than those that enact non-binding decisions.

One aspect that should be taken into consideration is whether decisional capacity is an aspect of institutional design that is essential to the configuration and aim of the democratic innovation. Many innovations are not aimed at taking decisions, meaning their aims and eventual outputs and outcomes do not require decisions. One example is oversight bodies, innovations that seek to monitor institutional performance and ensure transparency. The success and impact of these cases, as well as other innovations that aim at enhancing accountability, do not rely on decision-making, as this element does not fit the very institutional design at stake.

Figure 5.2 considers only democratic innovations for which a decision applies to their institutional designs and shows that, in Latin America, 66 per cent of 1,709 democratic innovations spread across sixteen countries do generate some sort of decision, 46 per cent non-binding and 20 per cent binding. The latter are decisions that must be implemented by the government, either because the government has officially committed to do so or because legal norms mandate that governments proceed this way. Just one-third of all cases (34 per cent) produce no decision at all, meaning that only a minority of these innovations come to the end of their processes without producing an output apt to translate participation (and deliberation) into policy outcomes that matter for representative democracy. Considering that each case in the LATINNO data set implies a different institutional design—one specific democratic innovation with a correspondingly specific institutional configuration, not multiple implementations of the same institutional

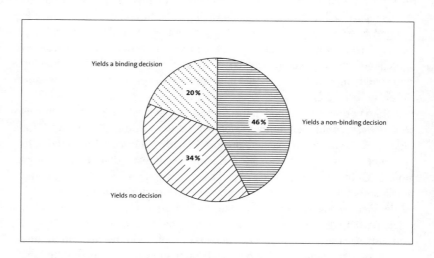

Figure 5.2 **Decisiveness of democratic innovations in 16 Latin American countries**

design—one can easily conclude that the overall volume of innovations that take decisions in Latin America indicates how well these new forms of participatory decision-making are institutionalised in the region.

Co-governance

While democratic theory focuses on how institutional innovations aspire to citizen empowerment, more equal distribution of political power, and fairer distribution of resources, many democratic innovations actually imply decentralisation of decision-making processes, devolution of power and resources, more efficient provision of public services and goods, greater transparency and accountability, exchange of knowledge and information, inter-institutional dialogue, and formation of collaborative partnerships (Fischer 2012: 458). These many goals point to a variety of new institutional designs, and in the West most of them have resulted from successive reforms of public administration initiated in the 1980s with New Public Management (Hood 1991) and later evolving into different forms of state-society cooperation, such as those embraced by the concepts of collaborative governance (Ansell and Gash 2007) and interactive governance (Torfing, Peters, and Sørensen 2012).

In collaborative governance policy-making and broader political outputs are definitional components of what could otherwise be described as democratic innovation: 'a governing arrangement where one or more public agencies directly engage non-state stakeholders in a collective decision-making process that is formal, consensus-oriented, and deliberative and that aims to make or implement public policy or manage public programs or assets' (Ansell and Gash 2007: 544). Similarly, interactive governance is defined as 'the complex process through which a plurality of social and political actors with diverging interests interact in order to formulate, promote, and achieve common objectives by means of mobilizing, exchanging and deploying a range of ideas, rules, and resources' (Torfing, Peters, and Sørensen 2012: 2 f.).

Both notions, developed in the context of public administration reforms in the West, could well apply to democratic innovations that evolved outside OECD countries, in particular those in Latin America. Although due to different factors and developed in dissimilar contexts, democratic innovations in Latin America can be defined as processes that engage political and social actors in the public policy process and aim at enhancing the quality of democracy. Slightly different than collaborative and interactive governance, participatory governance as practiced by democratic innovations in Latin America seeks to correct the defects of representative institutions and to enhance the quality of democracy through citizen participation. Indeed, in Latin America a broader idea of co-governance is better suited to the participatory kind of governance that democratic innovations put forward.

POGREBINSCHI

Democratic innovations may bring political and social actors together in the agenda-setting, policy formulation, policy implementation, and/or policy evaluation stages of the policy cycle. While many innovations involve a combination of two of these stages, only a few affect all of them simultaneously. When the core aim of an innovation is achieved by an act (not necessarily a decision) that involves political and social actors together, then co-governance takes place.

The notion of co-governance thus includes innovations that, for example, focus on the implementation stage of the policy cycle by allowing citizens to use digital technologies like OpenStreetMap to collaborate with the government in the implementation of urban or social policies. Examples of this kind of co-governance abound in Latin America, a recent one being the AsuMAP, with which the government of Asunción, Paraguay involved citizens in the definition and implementation of urban policies, more specifically an urban development project to revitalise the city's historical centre.

Several of the factors surrounding the evolution of democratic innovations in Latin America, as mentioned previously in this chapter, have contributed to placing the state, meaning governments at local, regional, and national levels, at the centre of recent institutional innovation. The LATINNO data set shows that more than half of all democratic innovations implemented in sixteen Latin American countries have been initiated and organised by the government alone. Governments have also partnered with civil society organisations, international organisations, and private stakeholders on a number of occasions, but altogether these partnerships amount to little more than 10 per cent of all cases.

However, that governments initiate, organise, or finance democratic innovations does not always imply that they are involved in them, i.e. that government officials necessarily take part in the process together with citizens or groups. In many cases, the government develops the initiative, but citizens participate on their own, and outcomes may be taken over by the government or not. In other cases, government officials steer the initiative and its organisation, in addition to taking part in activities together with citizens. There are also cases where civil society organisations undertake the initiation and organisation of the innovation, but political actors are involved, and the activities undertaken matter for the policy cycle. What matters for co-governance is not who has initiated, organised, or financed the innovation but the fact that political and social actors, governments, and citizens are all involved in a process that (may) affect one of the stages of the policy cycle.

Figure 5.3 shows that co-governance is indeed very common in Latin America. A total of 68 per cent of 1,859 democratic innovations in the region entail some sort of co-governance. This means that 1,271 new institutional designs are effective in including citizens or groups of citizens in the policy process. The high level of co-governance comprised by democratic innovations in Latin America indicates a substantial institutional change in the policy

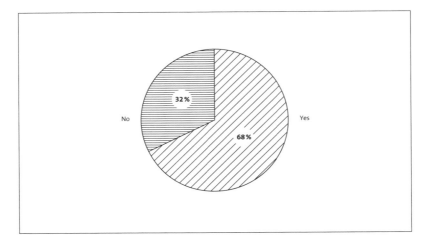

Figure 5.3 **Co-governance as feature of democratic innovations in 16 Latin American countries**

process as governments innovate by designing or taking part in designs that include non-political actors in the process by which policies are set, formulated, implemented, or evaluated. This is but one more indication of the extent to which democratic innovations are highly institutionalised in Latin America.

What Lessons Can Be Learned?

Comparativists have known for quite a while that making concepts travel is as hard as finding empirical universals (Sartori 1970). Democratic innovations are no exception to this rule, and their very nature makes conceptual stretching even more complicated. Innovations are typically problem-oriented, i.e. they arise as possible solutions to specific problems or as responses to more general malaises. This makes innovations more dependent on the contexts in which they grow. Innovations are also by nature spontaneous, in the sense that they are often unplanned or experimental and may result in ruptures, discontinuations, new modes of doing the same thing, or an attempt to do something new after concluding that the old modes do not serve anymore (Anheier and Korreck 2013). This second feature makes innovations more dependent on the moment at which they emerge.

As argued in this chapter, democratic innovations that have evolved in the West have been mostly a search for a new source of legitimacy vis-à-vis 'low-key malaises' (see Anheier in this Report) such as declining public trust in representative institutions and increasing dissatisfaction with democracy, which can be measured by decreasing party membership rates, low electoral turnout, and higher electoral volatility, among others. This explains the search for new modes of decision-making and for improvements of current methods, mostly through deliberation. Outside the West, in particular in Latin America, democratic innovations have followed another pattern, as they have been developed within political systems and legal orders that have yet to consolidate and that are at the same time dealing with high levels of social inequality and cultural diversity.

Although some measure of democratic consolidation and stability has been achieved in virtually all countries in the region, Latin America has never really adjusted to western models of democracy and perhaps will never do so, because such an adjustment would entail a different mode of democracy, one that cannot be measured with western indicators (Pogrebinschi 2013a). This explains why in Latin America some of the 'malaises' of the West, instead of being seen as signals of failure or defects, may be considered symptoms of attempts to impose a model of democracy that does not fit the context. This may also explain why in Latin America democratic innovations are so embedded in political systems, being highly formalised, comprising decision-making to a great extent, and frequently blurring the distinction between government and civil society.

The high level of institutionalisation of democratic innovations in Latin America, as gauged by these three latter features, is the most significant pattern that stands out when one contrasts the region with Europe and North America. To increase replicability of democratic innovations in other regions, identifying common institutional features of successful cases is key. The main recommendation here is, thus, that instead of searching for best practices elsewhere and trying to replicate them, policy-makers and practitioners in the West should focus on institutionalising the innovations created within their own countries. In other words, once it has been identified what works in the West, one should try to improve the chances that innovations evolve and endure by enhancing three institutional design features:

- Formalisation: democratic innovations should be, as much as possible, inscribed in constitutions and/or laws, and where this is not possible they should be backed up by normative acts of the public administration;
- Decisiveness: democratic innovations should be entitled to yield decisions, and those decisions should be binding to the greatest extent possible;
- Co-governance: democratic innovations should be linked with as many stages of the policy cycle as possible.

The greater the extent of formalisation, decisiveness, and co-governance of democratic innovations, the higher their institutionalisation, and therefore the higher the chances that they evolve and endure.

Endnotes

1   The LATINNO project collects and analyses quantitative and qualitative data on democratic innovations in twenty countries in Latin America. Its database comprises over 2,000 cases of different institutional designs for citizen participation. See www.latinno.net for information on the data and on the methodology used.

2   Data retrieved from www.participedia.net on 25 November 2016.

VI. Democratic Innovations for Re-Engaging Citizens Around the World

MATTHIAS HABER

T his chapter offers a comparative assessment of the availability and development of innovations around the world that aim to place citizens at the forefront of the democratic process by engaging them and giving them greater access to the process. The goals of these descriptive analyses are to identify where, or in which types of political regimes, citizen-focused innovations are most likely to be found and to investigate whether democracies vary in their innovative behaviour overall. Specifically, we seek to find out whether democratic innovations are more common in more advanced and consolidated democracies or whether they are more likely to be introduced in regimes that face major democratic challenges. Moreover, this chapter offers valuable insights into the various ways that governments and the general public have tried to counter the democratic malaise in their countries, as described in Anheier's introductory chapter, and allows us to better understand the challenges that countries are still facing in that regard.

Research on democratic innovations has intensified in recent years and has greatly advanced our understanding of the origin and evolution of innovative processes and their impacts on society (Warren 2012). However, in contrast to research on more established political institutions such as elections and legislatures, the field still lacks effective ways to systematically compare innovations across different political systems (Ryan and Smith 2012). We know little about the institutional designs and practices that make up the population of democratic innovations around the world. This is partly due to a relatively vague set of definitions regarding what counts as a democratic innovation and is also a result of the struggle to move beyond case study research to large-N comparative analyses. There is no central database on the variety and spread of democratic innovations, and where researchers have collected data, such data tend to be geographically and temporarily limited (Smith, Richards, and Gastil 2015; see also Pogrebinschi in this Report).

The descriptive analyses presented here constitute one of the first attempts to map the diffusion of citizen-focused democratic innovations around the world and to investigate how the prevalence of those innovations relates to the type of democratic regime. We use the categorisation

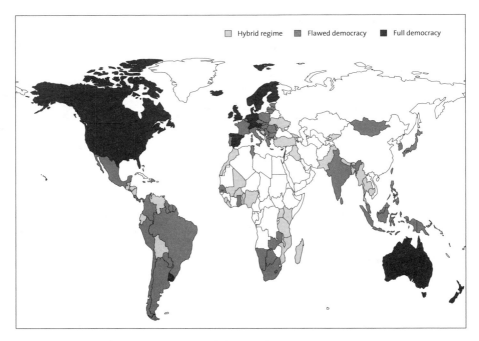

Figure 6.1 **Types of democracies around the world**
Source: Based on EIU (2016)
Note: Countries without shading are either authoritarian or are not included in the EIU Democracy Index.

scheme from the Economist Intelligence Unit's (EIU) 2015 Democracy Index and group countries into three types of political regimes that have formal institutions of democracy: full democracies, flawed democracies, and hybrid regimes (EIU 2016).[1] In full democracies, civil liberties and political freedoms are respected and reinforced by a political culture conducive to the thriving of democracy. Among the twenty full democracies in the EIU's index are most of the consolidated western democracies, along with Uruguay and Mauritius. Flawed democracies offer similar freedoms and civil liberties but have an underdeveloped political culture and problems in other areas, such as governance and political participation. The fifty-nine countries considered flawed democracies include many consolidated western democracies, such as France, Italy, Portugal, and Belgium, as well as a number of more recently democratised countries in Latin America and Central and Eastern Europe. Finally, hybrid regimes are generally characterised by weak rule of law, widespread corruption, irregularities in elections, and serious weaknesses in political culture, governance, and political participation. Figure 6.1 shows a world map indicating the 116 countries covered by the EIU Democracy Index that fall into either of the three categories.

Democratic innovations that seek to remedy the failure of the electorate to (be able to) perform its citizenship role are grouped into three categories: electoral reforms, direct democracy, and cooperative governance.[2] Using information from international data sources such the Varieties of Democracy Project, the International Institute for Democracy and Electoral Assistance, and the Open Budget Survey, comparative indicators of the use and dissemination of democratic innovations are constructed. The next sections address each of the three types of democratic innovations by systematically comparing the introduction and use of innovative procedures around the world. The concluding section summarises the results of this exercise and explores the implications of the analyses.

Electoral Innovations Fostering Higher Political Participation, Equal Access, and Fair Representation

Electoral innovations are often concerned with improving the convenience or changing the practice of voting and generally aim at increasing turnout and finding remedies to voter alienation. They include instruments such as reducing the voting age and allowing voters to cast their votes electronically or from abroad as well as innovations such as quota rules designed to enhance equality (for an extensive review of electoral innovations in the United States, see Kuo in this Report).

Lowering the legal voting age

Lowering the legal voting age to include citizens below the age of 18 is often proposed as a way to increase electoral participation and interest in politics (Wagner, Johann, and Kritzinger 2012). Introducing young people to voting can have a socialising effect through which voting and other forms of political involvement are established as life-long habits (Franklin 2004; Zeglovits and Aichholzer 2014). Moreover, there is evidence that allowing young people to vote also increases the turnout of their parents (McDevitt and Chaffee 2002). Finally, lowering the voting age is seen as a way to ensure that the interests of young people are represented in politics.

In the vast majority of countries around the world, citizens must be at least 18 years old to vote (see Figure 6.2). In some countries, including Bahrain, Cameroon, South Korea, and Singapore, the voting age is as high as 21. Still, a number of countries, the majority of which are in South America and

Southern Europe, permit citizens below the age of 18 to vote in federal elections (ACE 2016a). Among those that allow 16 year olds to vote in national elections are the European countries of Austria, Croatia (if employed), and Hungary and other countries such as Argentina, Brazil, Ecuador, and Indonesia (if married).

While the largest wave of minimum voting age reductions took place during the 1970s, a number of countries have lowered their legal voting ages more recently. In 2016 the Greek government lowered the voting age to 17 while explicitly citing the aim of encouraging youth to become interested and involved in political life (Maltezou 2016). In 2012 Argentina's legislature passed a bill to lower the voting age from 18 to 16, with some commentators arguing that the move was intended to enhance the electoral chances of then-President Cristina Fernández de Kirchner's ruling party (Popper 2012). Other countries include Austria (from 18 to 16 in 2007), Ecuador (from 18 to 16 in 2008), Japan (from 20 to 18 in 2016), and Uzbekistan (from 25 to 18 in 2012). A legal national voting age of 16 or 17 is mostly found in flawed democracies (10 countries) and hybrid regimes (3 countries), while Austria is the only full democracy that allows young people below the age of 18 to vote in national elections.

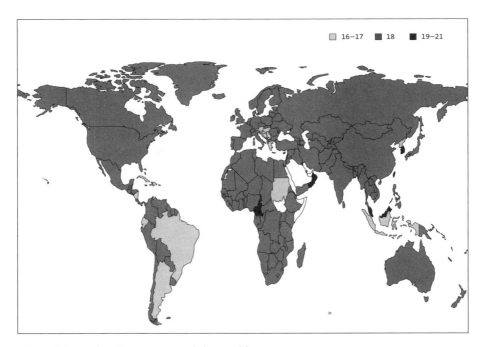

Figure 6.2 **Legal voting age around the world**
Source: ACE (2016a)
Note: Countries without shading could not be classified.

Many nations allow citizens below the age of 18 to vote in regional, municipal, or special elections. In Germany, for example, eight of the sixteen *Länder* have a minimum voting age of 16 in regional and local elections. In Scotland the voting age was reduced to 16 originally only for the Scottish independence referendum held in 2014 but then extended by 2015 legislation to all Scottish parliament and local elections.

New ways to vote in elections

Other innovative electoral tools–including e-voting, or the recording, casting, or counting of votes using digital information and communication technologies; voting from abroad; and early voting that allows citizens to vote prior to a scheduled election day–generally aim to make it easier for citizens to cast their votes and to allow those otherwise prevented from voting to maintain a political role in their home countries or localities. Electronic voting and similar innovations are often introduced to increase trust in electoral management, add credibility to election results, and increase thereby the overall efficiency of the electoral process, although there is

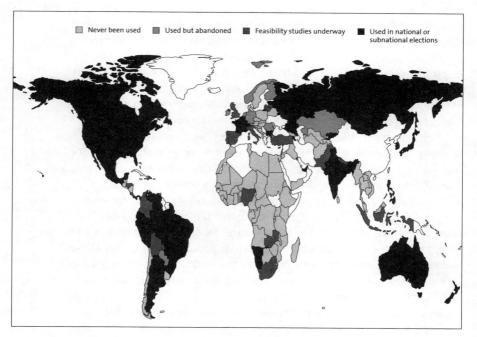

Figure 6.3 **Use of e-voting around the world**
Source: IDEA (2016c)
Note: Countries without shading could not be classified.

still little systematic, long-term research on the effects of these innovations (Newton 2012b: 149).

In contrast to the small number of countries that have lowered their legal voting ages to 16, many countries around the world have introduced some form of e-voting (see Figure 6.3). Twenty-eight countries, mainly flawed democracies in South America and South Asia, currently use e-voting in national or subnational elections. Among full democracies, five (Australia, Canada, New Zealand, Switzerland, and the US) currently have e-voting mechanisms in place at some level or another. In 2016, another twenty-one countries including eleven flawed and two full democracies carried out feasibility studies to introduce e-voting in the future. In most countries electronic voting is confined to the use of direct-recording electronic voting machines that are intended to reduce the potential for human error and improve the accuracy of the count. Of the twenty-eight countries that have introduced e-voting, only nine have also established internet voting systems that allow at least some citizens to cast their votes online. Among these are one hybrid regime (Armenia), four flawed democracies (Estonia, France, Mexico, and Panama), and four full democracies (Australia, Canada, New Zealand, and Switzerland).

As with many innovations, including electoral ones, benefits have to be weighed against risks and costs. A number of countries in Europe, including Germany, Ireland, and the Netherlands, had used or piloted e-voting procedures but eventually abandoned them due mainly to concerns about privacy, security, and potential fraud (ACE 2016b). In the Netherlands, for example, electronic voting machines had been used in elections for almost twenty years, but claims that vote secrecy could not be guaranteed led to suspension of their use in 2008 (Cross 2008). Alternatives are still being explored there. And in Germany, the country's constitutional court ruled in 2009 that e-voting was unconstitutional in part because it was impossible for voters to verify whether their vote had been counted accurately. Many countries express willingness to adopt some e-voting procedures and seek satisfactory, cost-effective ways to minimise risks and maintain voter confidence.

Another way to extend voter participation is by allowing those who are temporarily or permanently outside a country or locality to cast their votes. More than 70 per cent of the countries for which we have data and all but two full democracies have introduced procedures to do so. These include personal voting where voters must cast their vote in person at a specific place such as a consulate, postal voting where voters fill out a ballot and send it to their home country via post or email, and proxy vote where citizens choose a person who casts the vote in their stead at a polling place. Among the hybrid regimes, absentee voting is only allowed in about half of the countries. Many nations initiated external voting during World War II to allow absentee voting by soldiers fighting abroad. More recent introductions of external voting include Austria (1990), Botswana (1997), Italy (2001), and South Africa (1994). External voting may be restricted to certain groups, such as members of the armed forces or government employees. Some countries link the right to vote from abroad to the duration of absence. The UK, for example, does not grant voting rights to citizens who have lived outside of the country for more than fifteen years. Countries that currently do not allow voting from abroad are mainly hybrid regimes located in East and West Africa and Western and South Asia.

Increasing the political participation of women

Quota rules are another tool that directly concerns different stages of the electoral process. Gender quotas, for example, are introduced with the hope of increasing active and passive participation of females in electoral contests and women's representation in the legislature. On average, women constitute 50 per cent of a country's population but are often largely under-represented in political decision-making bodies. The global average of seats held by women in national parliaments is only 23 per cent (IDEA 2016b); among OECD countries, the number is only slightly higher at 28 per cent,

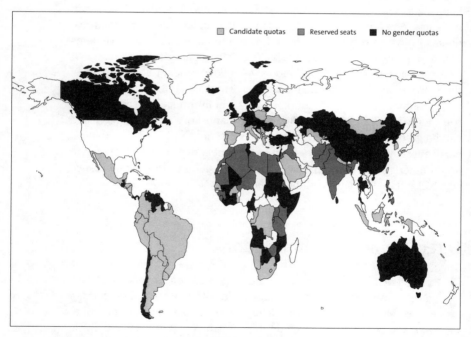

Figure 6.4 **Gender quotas around the world**
Source: IDEA (2016b)
Note: Countries without shading could not be classified.

ranging from more than 40 per cent in Finland to less than 10 per cent in Japan (OECD 2015: 88).

The three most commonly used types of gender quotas in politics are legislated candidate quotas, political party quotas (often voluntary), and reserved seats. The first two quotas set a minimum for the share of women on candidate lists, while the latter regulates the minimum number of women elected into parliament. The number of countries with such gender quotas increased slightly over the course of the 1980s and even more dramatically since 1990, largely due to the emergence of new international norms and transnational emulation of quota campaigns (Krook 2006). As of 2016, more than forty countries have legislated gender quotas for candidates running for a seat in the lower house, and twenty-nine regulate the number of elected seats reserved for women.

As seen in Figure 6.4, certain types of quotas are more prevalent in some regions, while other quota regimes are preferred elsewhere. There also appear to be links between the political and electoral system and the preferred quota type. Legislated candidate quotas are most frequent in flawed democracies, especially in Central and South America and Southern Europe, whereas reserved seats are more common in hybrid regimes in East and North Africa and South Asia. Among the full democracies, only four (Ireland, Mauritius, Spain, and Uruguay) have legislated candidate quotas, and none has reserved seat quotas for women. The prevalence of reserved seat quotas in hybrid regimes can be linked to the independence movements that took place between 1930 and 1970 in which minorities and marginalised groups often received seat quotas. After government reforms, many of these provisions were extended to women (Krook and O'Brien 2010).

Voluntary political party quotas have been introduced in several countries, including Australia, Canada, Germany, and Norway, where legislated candidate quotas or reserved seat quotas are not in place. Such political party quota systems can also be found in a number of flawed democracies in South America and Western Europe, such as Argentina, Brazil, and France, which also have legislated candidate quotas.

Direct Democratic Innovations

Direct democracy mechanisms aim to give citizens real decision-making powers in order to reengage them with politics and democracy (see Merkel in this Report). They are often seen as a useful tool to discipline the behaviour of elected representatives and to resolve political conflicts where a government is divided over an issue. Although there are various types of direct democratic instruments, the ones introduced most frequently are initiatives and referendums, described in more detail below.

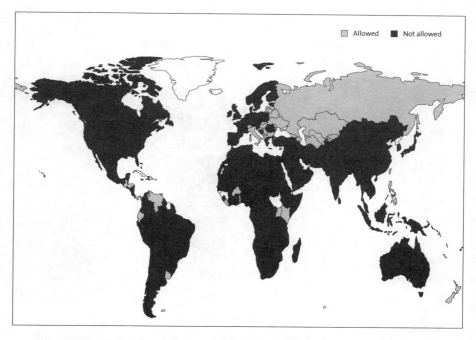

Figure 6.5 **Direct initiatives at national level around the world**
Source: Coppedge et al. (2016)
Note: Countries without shading could not be classified.

Initiatives

An initiative is a direct democracy mechanism that allows the electorate to bypass the legislature by placing proposals on the ballot. In the case of direct initiatives, these proposals go directly on the ballot, whereas indirect initiatives are submitted to the legislature for decision but not necessarily put to a vote of the electorate.

As of 2016, forty-four countries have legal provisions for direct initiatives in place at the national level (see Figure 6.5). Only 20 per cent of the full democracies allow direct initiatives, while almost 40 per cent of all flawed democracies and every second hybrid regime permits them. Although a number of countries in the Americas and in West Africa allow votes on citizen-initiated proposals, direct initiatives are most common in Central Asia and in Southern and Eastern Europe. The prevalence of direct initiatives in Eastern Europe is likely a remnant of political practices in the Soviet Union, where, until the Brezhnev era, such instruments were conceived as part of the democratisation process in post-Stalin politics (White and Hill 1996: 154). Direct initiatives are also part of the political system in Latvia, New Zealand, and Switzerland.

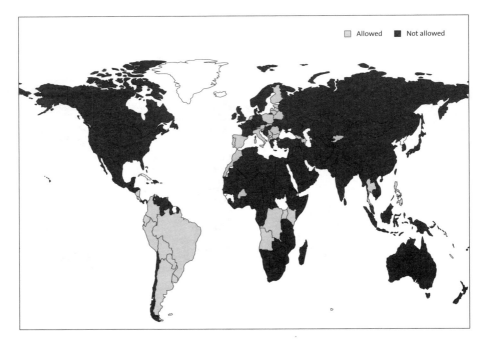

Figure 6.6 **Indirect initiatives at national level around the world**
Source: Coppedge et al. (2016)
Note: Countries without shading could not be classified.

Below the national level, even fewer countries allow direct initiatives. Only twenty-one countries around the world have introduced direct initiative measures at the regional level, and less than thirty at the local level.

As illustrated in Figure 6.6, indirect initiatives at the national level are available to citizens in forty-four countries and are most commonly found in flawed democracies in South America, where many direct democracy instruments were added since the most recent wave of democratisation, and in Eastern Europe, likely for the same reasons that direct initiatives exist. Among the group of full democracies, five, including Uruguay, allow indirect initiatives at the national level. Furthermore, indirect initiatives at the regional level are possible in four full democracies, at the local level in five. Among those that allow indirect citizen initiatives only at subnational level are Germany and the US.

Referendums

Referendums enable the electorate to vote directly on a specific, often constitutional or legislative political issue. There are two main types of referendums: legislative referendums, in which the legislature refers a proposal to the voters for approval, and popular referendums, in which the proposal is placed on the ballot through a citizen petition process. Legislative referendums can be mandatory–the law or constitution mandates that a measure be approved by the citizenry–or optional. Popular referendums are similar to the initiatives described above but allow voters to only approve or repeal legislative acts and not to propose new laws.

As shown in Figure 6.7, optional legislative referendums are available in more than 60 per cent of all flawed and hybrid regimes and almost three-quarters of all full democracies. Most countries in South America, Africa, Western and Eastern Europe, and Central Asia have in place some mechanism providing for legislative referendums. In some countries, such as Australia, Canada, Chile, Norway, and Spain, referendum results are also binding. Among the group of full democratic countries, only five, including Germany and the US, do not have provisions for legislative referendums at the national level.

The large number of countries that allow optional national-level legislative referendums stands in stark contrast to the fraction of countries that

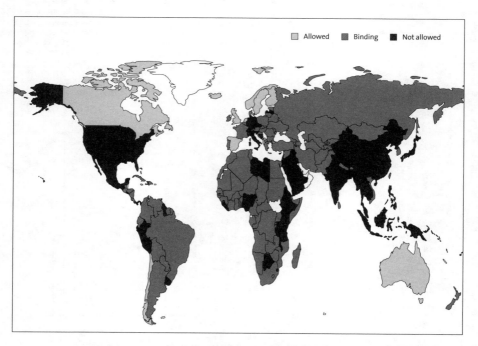

Figure 6.7 **Optional legislative referendums at the national or subnational level around the world**
Source: Coppedge et al. (2016)
Note: Countries without shading could not be classified.

have introduced popular referendums in which citizens can place a proposal to change existing legislation on a ballot. Only about 10 per cent of all
full democracies and around 20 per cent of all flawed and hybrid regimes
have instruments for popular referendums, and, except for in Albania and
Cabo Verde, they are generally binding. Countries primarily in South America, such as Bolivia, Venezuela, and Uruguay, and in Southern and Eastern
Europe, such as Italy, Slovenia, and Slovakia, allow citizens to place measures on a ballot. Binding referendums also exist in Hungary, Latvia, and
Switzerland.

The development of direct democratic innovations

Figure 6.8 shows the percentage of countries that have introduced either
legislative referendums, popular referendums, or direct initiatives and how

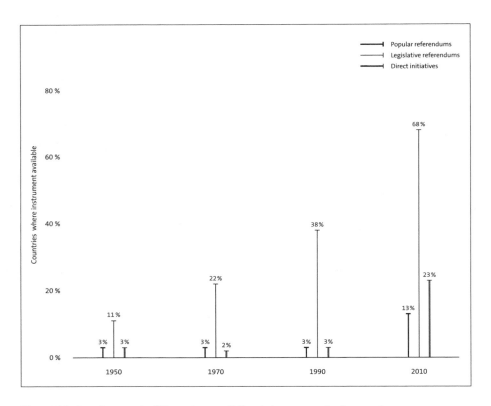

Figure 6.8 **Development of three types of direct democracy instruments
over time**
Source: Coppedge et al. (2016)

these numbers have changed since 1950. As of 2010, popular referendums had become available in only a fraction of countries, while direct initiatives and legislative referendums were much more common: citizen initiatives were available in more than 20 per cent of all countries and legislative referendums in almost 70 per cent.

Since the gradual increase in the adoption of these direct democracy mechanisms from the 1950s to the 1970s followed by the more dramatic increase in the 1980s and 1990s with the democratisation of Latin America and Eastern Europe, the number of countries allowing referendums and initiatives has not changed significantly. However, the number of times that such measures have been used has fluctuated considerably over this entire period, as illustrated in Figure 6.9. While the average between 1950 and 2014 lies near twenty votes per year, the total number of direct ballots has ranged from as low as five in 1965 to as high as forty-seven in 2003–boosted by the many national referendums regarding accession to the European Union– and fifty-one in 2009 on a broad variety of topics. Almost 75 per cent of the thirty direct democracy ballots in 2014 were cast in full democracies.

Undoubtedly some countries make use of direct democracy instruments at the national level more often than others do. As shown in Table 6.1, Switzerland leads by having held 131 direct democratic ballots of one type or another over the last fifteen years: as many direct ballots held as the rest of

Table 6.1 **Top 10 countries with the largest number of direct democracy ballots, 2000–14**

Country	Direct Votes	Type
Switzerland	131	Full democracy
Italy	22	Flawed democracy
Slovenia	18	Flawed democracy
Colombia	15	Flawed democracy
Ecuador	14	Hybrid regime
Ireland	14	Full democracy
Bolivia	10	Hybrid regime
Slovakia	9	Flawed democracy
Botswana	8	Flawed democracy
Iceland	8	Full democracy

Source: Coppedge et al. (2016)

the top ten combined and almost a third of all direct ballots held between 2000 and 2014 in any country. Other countries with a high number of direct ballots during that same period include Italy, Slovenia, and Colombia, all categorised by the EIU as flawed democracies.

Notably, only three full democracies (Switzerland, Ireland, and Iceland) are among the ten countries that use direct democratic tools most often. Indeed, as shown in Figure 6.10, no full democratic country has provisions at the national level for all four types of direct democratic instruments (indirect initiatives, direct initiatives, legislative referendums, and popular referendums) discussed here. Switzerland allows three direct instruments, with indirect initiatives only available at the subnational level. Uruguay also has provisions for three instruments, but the majority of full democracies allow no more than two. Moreover, a number of countries, such as Luxembourg,

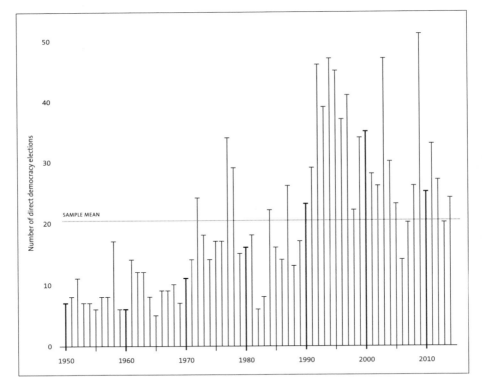

Figure 6.9 **Development of direct democracy elections (initiatives, popular referendums, and legislative referendums), 1950–2014**
Source: Coppedge et al. (2016)
Note: The dashed horizontal line indicates the average (mean) number of direct votes per year between 1950 and 2014.

Mauritius, and Norway, do not have provisions for any of the five direct democracy types (or the relevant information is not available). Germany and the US allow indirect initiatives but only at the subnational level. Across all twenty full democracies, legislative referendums are the most commonly used instrument.

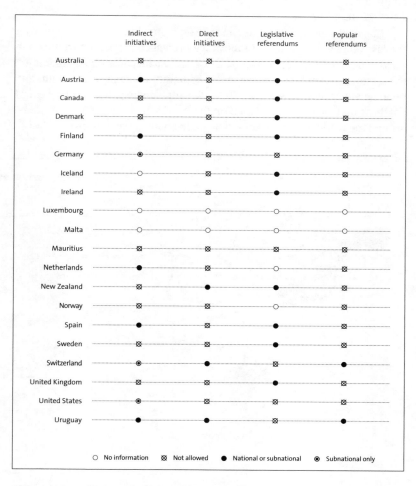

Figure 6.10 **Provisions for direct democracy instruments among full democracies**
Sources: Coppedge et al. (2016); IDEA (2016a)

Cooperative Governance

The final set of analyses focuses on the third type of democratic innovation: cooperative governance, or co-governance, which differs from direct democracy in that citizens may have direct influence on political decisions (Smith 2005: 50-60; Talpin 2012: 184; see also Pogrebinschi in this Report). Co-governance procedures are initiated mostly to improve problem-solving capacities and to develop effective and legitimate decisions. By directly participating in political decision-making, citizens gain political competency and may feel more responsible for public decisions (Michels 2011: 277-9).

Co-governance institutions can take on many different forms, and over the last years a wide range of innovative projects have been introduced in various parts of the world. Among those are participatory budgeting initiatives, citizen assemblies, village and community councils, and community policing experiments (Newton 2012a: 9). Unfortunately, there is no central database that collects information on the development of these innovations around the world, which makes it difficult to conduct comparative analyses.[3]

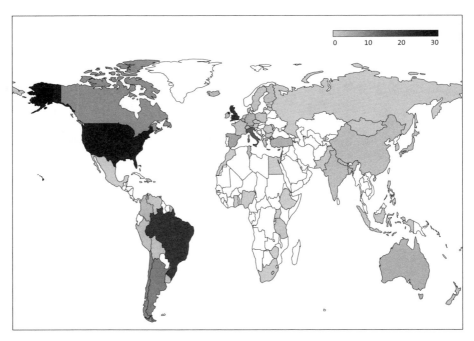

Figure 6.11 **Distribution of co-governance cases around the world**
Source: Participedia
Note: No information was available for countries without shading.

HABER

However, instead of focussing on a set of country case studies, we use data from the crowdsourcing platform Participedia, an open global knowledge platform with a focus on democratic innovations and public engagement.[4] However, although users have added roughly 650 cases of innovative projects from more than sixty countries spanning over four decades, the database does not represent the full range of democratic innovations that have been implemented around the world, nor are the cases in the database necessarily a representative sample.

Of the 183 cases in the Participedia database related to co-governance (see Figure 6.11), most are found in full democracies (89 cases) and flawed democracies (83 cases). Hybrid regimes account for less than 5 per cent of all co-governance cases. The highest number of co-governance institutions is located in the US, followed by the UK, Brazil, and Italy. More than two-thirds of all co-governance innovations happen at the local level, with only about forty cases at the regional or national levels. This is not surprising, since the local level provides citizens and political actors with more frequent opportunities for contact and cooperation. The authority of local governments over local affairs creates opportunities to experiment directly with how governance is enacted and services are administered (Freise, Paulsen, and Walter 2015).

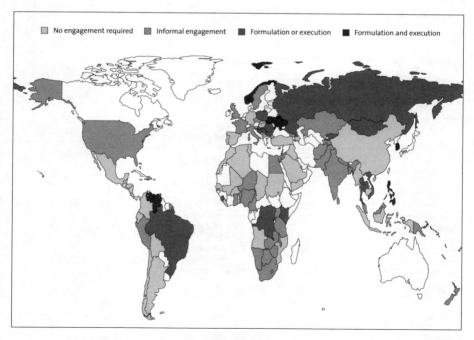

Figure 6.12 **Engagement with the public during the budget process**
Source: International Budget Partnership (2015)
Note: Countries without shading could not be classified.

Public participation in the budget process

The budget process represents a potential opportunity for citizen engagement since it affects how public resources are distributed. As shown in Figure 6.12, prepared based on a question from the Open Budget Survey asking experts whether the executive is formally required to engage with the public during the formulation and execution phases of the national or federal budget process, only in Norway, the Philippines, South Korea, Ukraine, and Venezuela is the executive obliged to engage with the public in both phases. In sixteen other countries, the executive is required to engage the public in one phase or the other. However, in the majority of countries the executive is not mandated to engage with the public directly or engages only informally. Among full democracies, only two (South Korea and Norway) have formal requirements that enable the public to engage with the executive during budget processes.

The Open Budget Survey also publishes an index of public participation in budget processes that is a composite of questions that evaluate whether governments give the general public and civil society access to budget information and opportunities to engage with the budget process at the national level. The index score ranges from a minimum score of 0 to a maximum of 100. As shown in Table 6.2, South Korea followed by Norway, Brazil, and the US are ranked the highest in terms of providing opportunities for the public

Table 6.2 **Top 10 countries ranked by the Index of Public Participation in Budgetary Processes**

Country	Score	Type
Korea	83	Flawed democracy
Norway	75	Full democracy
Brazil	71	Flawed democracy
United States	69	Full democracy
Philippines	67	Flawed democracy
New Zealand	65	Full democracy
South Africa	65	Flawed democracy
United Kingdom	58	Full democracy
Slovenia	56	Flawed democracy
Kyrgyzstan	52	Hybrid regime

Source: International Budget Partnership (2015)
Note: Based on a minimum score of 0 and a maximum of 100.

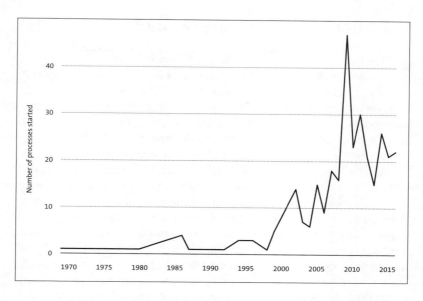

Figure 6.13 **Development of participatory budgeting cases over time**
Source: Participedia

to participate in the national budgeting process. Nine of the ten countries are full or flawed democracies; only one, Kyrgyzstan, is a hybrid regime.

Participatory budgeting

Participatory budgeting (PB) is a more direct mechanism for engaging the public in the budget process. Participedia describes PB as a decision-making process through which citizens deliberate and negotiate the distribution of public resources (for more on PB, see chapters by Pogrebinschi and by Della Porta and Felicetti in this Report). Although the PB process in Porto Alegre, Brazil, which began in the late 1980s, is perhaps the most commonly cited example in the literature, cases of PB recorded in the Participedia database date back to as early as 1969, for example a municipal participatory budgeting initiative in Argentina. Rising slowly through the mid-1990s, the number of new cases increased sharply after PB was recognised at the 1996 United Nations Habitat Conference as a best practice and taken up and spread by international networks (Ganuza and Baiocchi 2012). Based on the user-contributed entries in the Participedia database presented in Figure 6.13, 2009 is the year in which the largest number of PB processes (nearly 50) is reported to have started. Brazil is the country with the highest number of participatory budgeting institutions, followed by the UK and the US.

Conclusion and Summary of Findings

Countries around the world have implemented new institutions and rules specifically designed to increase the input of citizens into the political system and to improve the quality and quantity of participation. Yet the diffusion of these citizen-focused innovations appears to have occurred largely independently of countries' levels of democratic development. Innovations of different kinds can be found in countries all over the world, whether they have full or flawed democracies or are hybrid regimes.

As illustrated in Figure 6.14, there is no clear statistical association between types of democratic regime and types of democratic innovation. Full democracies are slightly more likely to allow online voting, while flawed democracies are more likely to provide e-voting in general. There is also a moderate positive relationship between flawed democracies and female candidate quotas as well as a moderate negative relation between flawed democracies and reserved seat quotas. Hybrid regime types are less likely to allow external voting, that is, voting by citizens not residing in the country. Furthermore, none of the direct democratic instruments show a strong association to any regime type.

If the existence of citizen-focused democratic innovations is not related to the level of democratisation, are there other factors that might explain the distribution of innovations around the world? Citizen-focused innovations are often an attempt to remedy the general public's lack of political interest

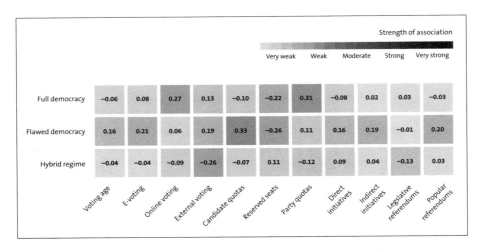

Figure 6.14 **Correlation between regime types and democratic innovations**
Sources: ACE (2016a); Coppedge et al. (2016); IDEA (2016a, 2016b, 2016c)

and trust in government. Therefore, one might assume that the presence of democratic innovations is linked to some of the democratic deficits countries are facing. Figure 6.15 shows the statistical relationship between the same twelve innovations and three distinct democratic challenges: electoral turnout for national parliamentary elections, confidence in national parliaments, and confidence in the fairness of federal elections. Contrary to the assumption, there is in fact no close association between these three challenges and the presence of an innovation. The extent of electoral turnout is not related to any type of innovation, meaning that, generally speaking, neither voting age nor the availability of online voting nor another innovation necessarily affects whether voters actually go to the polls. Countries in which citizens have low confidence in parliament are slightly more likely to have female candidate quotas and provisions for direct initiatives. Finally, lower confidence in the electoral system correlates moderately with the absence of party gender quotas.

The presence of democratic innovations is not necessarily determined by quality or longevity of democracy or by degree of democratic malaise. Instead the availability of innovations seems largely driven by countries' regional political and cultural histories. As the maps presented in this chapter suggest, there are a number of geographical hotspots where democratic innovations are more commonly found than in other regions. A particularly fertile ground for innovations is Latin America (see Pogrebinschi's chapter for a more detailed explanation). In addition to the regional clustering of innova-

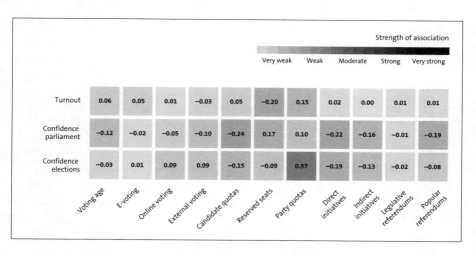

Figure 6.15 **Correlation between democratic challenges and democratic innovations**
Sources: ACE (2016a); Coppedge et al. (2016); Gallup (2016b); IDEA (2016a, 2016b, 2016c)

tions there is evidence that innovations are more prevalent in some countries than in others. Out of the twelve innovations mentioned in Figure 6.14, Ecuador has implemented nine, followed by Bolivia and Nicaragua with eight each. Outside Latin America, the Philippines, Slovakia, and Slovenia show the most democratic innovativeness with provisions for seven of the twelve innovations. An investigation into the patterns of transnational emulation of innovations is beyond the scope of this chapter but would be an obvious next step to better understanding the diffusion of democratic innovations.

Endnotes

1   Although the classification of countries into the three types of democratic regimes is largely determined by the quality of formal institutions, the thresholds between types are somewhat arbitrary and are based on numerical scores. The cut-off points on the ten-point scale are 8.01 for full democracies, 6.01 for flawed democracies, and 4.01 for hybrid regimes. Countries with scores below 4.01 are classified as authoritarian and are not covered in this analysis.

2   Another commonly used category, consultative-discursive procedures, is excluded due to lack of comparative data. Some researchers, such as Newton (2012a) identify electronic democracy as a fifth category, but since it cuts across the other categories, it is already sufficiently captured.

3   An exception is the LATINNO project, which collects and analyses quantitative and qualitative data on democratic innovations in 20 countries in Latin America. Its database comprises over 2,000 cases of different institutional designs for citizen participation. See www.latinno.net for information on the data and on the methodology used.

4   www.participedia.net

VII. Governing Exigencies
On Liberal Democracy and National Security

Ewa Atanassow *and* Ira Katznelson

How should liberal democracies navigate current exigencies of security? Do constitutional regimes face particular emergency dilemmas? Have such conundrums become especially urgent?

Violent challenges to security and public safety are characteristic problems for sovereign states that claim indivisible control over a particular territory and its population. Security dilemmas take especially intense form for regimes whose norms and forms of government include the rule of law, government by consent, individual rights, and political representation—conceptions that have been at the heart of political liberalism at least since it was powerfully and originally elaborated by such thinkers as Locke and Montesquieu.

In our time of passionate illiberalism, religious fanaticism, irregular armed force, permeable borders, and new technologies, security-related exigencies have taken new, quite urgent form. There is something ironic about this circumstance. From one vantage, constitutional democracies have never been more secure. They face almost no threat to their borders; large-scale warfare is dormant; there are very few examples of violent internal insurrection. At the same time, since the end of World War II, liberal democracies have been confronted with pervasive insecurity, compounded in recent decades by the threat of terrorism, and anxieties about appropriate responses. As this chapter aims to show, this insecurity has led to unprecedented delegation to and strengthening of executive power. This situation raises profound questions about the conditions required to enlarge the zone of security without the undue sacrifice of liberal values and institutions whose hallmarks include constraints on the decisions and acts taken by political authorities in order to safeguard the liberties of citizens.

> *In our time, security-related exigencies have taken new, quite urgent form.*

In these circumstances it is particularly important to reflect on repertoires of thought, organisation, and policy that are available within the framework of liberal norms. One might say that unless liberal democracies can find means to face present threats to security they will not have met the most elementary responsibilities of public authority. Yet absent coherent liberal doctrine and practice for emergency powers based on legitimate standards for defining exigency, exercising exceptions, learning from experience, and limiting the scope and consequences of special powers, the means chosen to do battle with insecurity pose profound and grave dangers to liberty. Statutory authority does not itself guarantee liberal results.

This chapter considers how liberal democratic regimes can effectively tackle security challenges without compromising constitutional and ethical principles. By probing the tradition of liberal thought and practice, it seeks to identify a repertoire of ideas and institutions for governing exigency within present conditions. These conditions, we suggest, are characterised by interminable threat and declining restraint on executive discretion. What policy innovations might be consistent with central liberal values? Can constitutional democracies address problems of emergency while holding onto the rule of law even if some aspects of emergency cannot be addressed through law? How can that zone be kept as narrow as possible?

Although manifestly of broader significance, this chapter focuses primarily on the United States as well as on Great Britain as the longest standing and continuous examples of constitutional regimes struggling to come to terms with these questions. Both countries have possessed disproportionate global power. Both have faced security issues with magnified intensity and scope. Not surprisingly, each has generated much experimentation in thought and institutional arrangements pertaining to the governance of exigency. These experiences and the lessons they present have wide applicability.

Liberal Resources

Any survey of liberal capacities for dealing with emergency must come to terms with the penetrating critique of Carl Schmitt (2006 [1922], 2007 [1926], 2014 [1921]). From the vantage of post-World War I Germany, this philosopher of jurisprudence came to be persuaded that liberal states were unable to grapple with conundrums of security without stepping wholly outside their self-conscious remit. Institutionally and ideologically, Schmitt considered liberal parliamentary order as ill-equipped to deal with the fundamentals of security and sovereignty. His scepticism about the capacities of liberal polities went hand in hand with the view that exigencies demand action outside the rule of law. Schmitt's plan for an exceptional sovereign–a 'sovereign dictator' embodying the nation's will–offered a decidedly non-liberal solution to the challenges of emergency. As it turned out, the Nazi regime to which Schmitt gave allegiance would offer a radical instance of his proposed solution. More recently, his fierce critique of liberalism has been taken up most notably by Agamben (2005), who, like

ATANASSOW *and* KATZNELSON

Schmitt, treats the liberal tradition as both inattentive to and simply incapable of dealing with or resisting the growing dominance of states of exception.

It is just this emphasis on exception that an important group of inter-war and post-war twentieth century American thinkers rejected as they forged a liberal alternative to the Schmittian perspective. This body of work continued a long lineage of liberal thought about emergency that Schmitt had missed. From its founding moments, liberalism confronted central puzzles associated with how a decent political order should act with respect to national exigencies. Far from ignored, the problematic of emergency, safety, and regime preservation under conditions of danger has been deeply embedded in the liberal tradition from its initial formation.

Indeed, liberal solutions to the question of emergency, including their internal strains, had been already articulated by John Locke and Alexander Hamilton. Both statesmen were deeply concerned with these issues. Both were aware of ancient Rome's institution of temporary dictatorship under emergency conditions, which had offered a republican model for addressing the problems of security and survival of a constitutional order. As analysed by Machiavelli, this model was confined to dealing with a concrete situation under the supervision of constitutional authorities, and it assumed both strict time limits and disinterested virtue: the dictator's commitment to speedily restoring the legal order.

Locke's *Second Treatise on Government*, a foundational statement of liberal constitutionalism and a blueprint for the American founding, comprehensively argues that the rule of law is the *sine qua non* of a well-framed government. Locke identified the legislature and its mechanisms of political representation as a good polity's locus of legitimacy and effective action, while reserving ultimate sovereignty to the people. Accompanying his analysis is a crucial chapter on prerogative recognising the inherent limitations of any legal framework and of the law-making body whose central role is to uphold it. Hence, Locke argued, there exists an abiding need for discretionary, but not unconstrained, executive power to address emergency situations.

> ... the good of the society requires that several things should be left to the discretion of him who has the executive power. For the legislators not being able to foresee, and provide by laws, for all that may be useful to the community, the executor of the laws having the power in his hands, has by the common law of nature a right to make use of it for the good of the society, in many cases, where the municipal law has given no direction, till the legislative can conveniently be assembled to provide for it. Many things there are, which the law can by no means provide for; and those must necessarily be left to the discretion of him that has the executive power in his hands, to be ordered by him as the public good and advantage shall require ...
>
> This power to act according to discretion, for the public good, without the prescription of the law, and sometimes even against it, is that which is called prerogative.
>
> John Locke, Second Treatise, Sec. 159–160

For Hamilton, the idea of exigencies was not an abstraction. In his view, the young US faced challenges to its safety from Native Americans, internal insurrections, and global geopolitics. Like Locke, Hamilton did not merely raise a stubborn dilemma; he also identified institutional means within the ambit of federal authority and state capacity to address it. Tensions between liberty and security led him to advocate (following the British liberal tradition) constitutional provisions ensuring that the legislature would have the central say regarding questions of defence. Recognising that such questions cannot be delimited in advance, he effectively announced the need for prerogative power and underscored the sporadic necessity for the central government to be unconstrained by 'constitutional shackles'. At the same time, in the Federalist Papers Hamilton, writing as Publius, stressed the importance of Congress and pointed to legislative consent as precondition for reconciling state power with legitimacy and governing efficacy with freedom (see Federalist 21-26 in Hamilton, Jay, and Madison 2001 [1788]). It was Congress, he insisted, that 'is the essential, and, after all, the only efficacious security for the rights and privileges of the people, which is attainable in civil society' (Hamilton 2001b [1788]).

In this respect, Hamilton echoed Locke's thinking about emergencies that rested on identifying circumstances impossible to address by law-makers and law. These situations include decisions that would need to be more resolute and speedy than the legislative process could produce, as well as those 'many things . . . that the law can by no means provide for' (Locke 1988 [1680-1690]). In such moments, there was a pressing need for executive prerogative power. Yet Locke was quick to insist that these exceptions must by no means be arbitrary. Prerogative power should be limited in time and stay in play only until the legislature can resume its functions. Moreover, executive power to act outside ordinary procedures can only be validated as it is constrained by principles that proclaim the public good and the preservation of society as the supreme law (Locke 1988 [1680-1690]: 158-9).

> The authorities essential to the common defense are these: to raise armies; to build and equip fleets; to prescribe rules for the government of both; to direct their operations; to provide for their support. These powers ought to exist without limitation, because it is impossible to foresee or define the extent and variety of national exigencies, or the correspondent extent and variety of the means which may be necessary to satisfy them. The circumstances that endanger the safety of nations are infinite, and for this reason no constitutional shackles can wisely be imposed on the power to which the care of it is committed. This power ought to be coextensive with all the possible combinations of such circumstances; and ought to be under the direction of the same councils which are appointed to preside over the common defense.
>
> Federalist #23
> (Alexander Hamilton)

These two foundational texts remind readers that the puzzle of realistic liberalism, or how to be a secure state in the world of states without compromising civil liberties, was already understood in the seventeenth and eight-

ATANASSOW *and* KATZNELSON

eenth centuries to be fundamentally important for the existence, and for the qualities of existence, of representative republics. They also leave a series of profound questions and tensions--about the meaning of emergency, the duration of exception, the status of law, and the boundary of constitutionalism--with which any subsequent thought about emergency has to grapple.

These questions underpinned both Schmitt's critique of liberalism and the responses of his American critics. The leading thinkers within this estimable group included German émigré Carl Friedrich (1941), his Harvard doctoral student Frederick Watkins (1939; 1940), and Cornell University's Clinton Rossiter (1948). Individually and as a coherent group of liberal thinkers, they sought above all to place responses to emergency within the ambit of the restraining qualities of law. Resurrecting the Roman model, they explored the character of temporary abrogation, whose central aim would be the protection of the liberal order itself.

Reeling from the collapse of the Weimar Republic and other representative governments between the two world wars, they understood that liberal democracies urgently require formulas for crisis governments to concentrate uncommon executive state capacity. But unlike Schmitt, they refused extra-legality as an acceptable orientation or pattern of policy that could turn temporary measures into the norm. They also spurned his embrace of unconstrained sovereignty in the form of a dictator, legitimated by an abstract idea of 'the people' understood as a cohesive force.

Like Hamilton, the quest by Friedrich, Watkins, and Rossiter to ensure safety in ways that would be as consistent as possible with the mores, conventions, institutions, and patterns of liberal governance focused on legislatures and law-making about delegation. Drawing on the experience of the democracies that had fought World War I and on empirical wartime examples of effective government whose powers had been based on temporary delegations by legislatures, these thinkers insisted that there must be no departure from the zone of law. Furthermore, delegations had to be specific, targeted, and limited in time. Only when such authority existed could exigencies be governed within a liberal frame.

So arguing, they revisited and deepened a genuinely liberal approach to emergency. Their alternative to Schmitt's conception of a sovereign dictator sought to enclose the state and its sovereignty within constitutionalism and law--hallmarks of a liberal polity--and thus to transform sovereignty from sheer power to legitimate authority. Without such a move, they believed, it would not be possible under conditions of duress to safeguard the standing and rights of citizens, the core intention of the liberal understanding of the rule of law. The exception must not connote an empty space from which law is absent.

In this vision, sovereignty and law do not vie but, imbricated, become mutually constitutive. By offering normatively appealing guidelines, these non-Schmittian principles remain compelling. However the structural, institutional, and ethical conditions within which these mid-century thinkers wrote no longer exist. Their work was premised on a crisp partition between ordinary and exceptional times, a boundary that has become increasingly porous. Moreover, responses to the circumstances of Cold War and terrorism have produced cumulative and layered legislative delegations and enhanced prerogative power, thus calling into question the scope and character of liberty.

Fresh Challenges

As liberal states grapple with uncertainty and insecurity, at issue is how policies to govern exigencies will be sponsored, organised, and deployed, and with what consequences for core liberal aspirations and values. While tensions between liberty and security are integral to liberal governance, what is new is how such trials of liberty and security have become increasingly widespread, acute, and durable, as the *longue durée* of the Cold War gave way to a potentially even more extended era of global terrorism based on religious fervour.

There are no democracies without some constitutionally warranted approach to dealing with exigent situations. These may take the form of legislative procedures that delegate discretionary authority to the executive for specific periods, or state of siege or state of exception constitutional provisions specific to the purpose, such as Article 115 a of the German Basic Law or Article 16 of the Fifth Republic French Constitution. The two most consistently liberal polities–the British and the American–differ in this respect. Great Britain, which lacks a written constitution, proceeds only by way of explicit parliamentary delegation; yet in contrast to the American system of separation of powers, the prime minister and cabinet effectively control the legislature through the instrument of party discipline. Alone among liberal democracies, Britain formally declared a state of emergency after the attacks of 11 September 2001, also known as 9/11, by way of a parliamentary resolution.

The US, on the other hand, falls between the two poles of constitutional and legislative models. The Constitution contains no specific emergency provisions, except the Article I permission to suspend *habeas corpus* under conditions of duress, though there is no clarity about which institutional actors possess this capacity. Article II, concerned with the presidency, contains implied prerogative powers, especially within the scope of the president's status as commander-in-chief. This includes the ability under conditions of either internal insurrection or external military threat to command state militias and to designate them as under the service of the federal government.

Across the range of liberal democracies, delegation and implicit prerogative have been more prevalent than the formal invocation of emergency power. The dominant current model is a legislative one, as Ferejohn and Pas-

ATANASSOW *and* KATZNELSON

quino (2004) have convincingly argued. It is via ordinary law-making that the existence of special circumstances (the need for speed thus for suspension of normal procedures in the face of existential threat) are recognised and powers are explicitly delegated to executive actors to act expeditiously and effectively. The danger is that 'liberties won slowly over long periods of time may be subject to rapid erosion in emergencies and these new restrictions, if they are embedded in law, may not be rapidly restored if they are restored at all' (Ferejohn and Pasquino 2004: 219). The exceptional becomes normal, the extraordinary routine. The new standard then can become a fresh point of departure.

In the long history of consideration of emergency circumstances by liberal thinkers and policy-makers, a particular temporal premise has predominated. Such circumstances have been designated as having a beginning and an end. Ever since the Roman Republic, which between 501 and 202 BC witnessed the appointment of seventy-six constitutional dictators granted exceptional powers for a limited time, emergency institutions and actions have been conceived as time-bound. In *The Spirit of the Laws*, Montesquieu discussed how the parliament in Britain had authorised detention without trial in circumstances where conspiracy thought to be a threat to the state had been discerned. Those so held, he observed, 'would lose their liberty for a while only so as to preserve it forever' (Montesquieu 1989 [1748]: 159). This practice was summarised in the eighteenth century by Blackstone, the noted British liberal theorist, as a circumstance in which parliament, exclusively, 'whenever it sees proper, can authorize the crown, by suspending the *habeas corpus* act for a short and limited time, to imprison suspected persons without giving any reason for so doing' (Blackstone 1979 [1768]: 132). As Manin has underscored, these liberals helped launch a tradition of 'argument that conformed to a key liberal principle . . . that liberty may be restricted only for the sake of liberty, not just for the sake of just any kind of common good' (Manin 2008: 143).

> *What is new is how trials of liberty and security have become increasingly widespread, acute, and durable.*

In the early twentieth century, Dicey, the leading British constitutional scholar of the time, likewise underscored how such practices usually were limited to no more than one year and only applied to persons for whom it was reasonable to suspect treason, and only for that reason. Moreover, once the moment had passed, officials who had conducted the period of exception could be held accountable on how they had acted and whether they had done so within the deliberately capacious, but not unlimited, constraints of the constitutional rule of law. Crucially, Dicey also distinguished between two kinds of emergency actions: moments of insurrection or invasion where the rule of exception was legitimately consistent with liberal values, and martial law (Dicey 1982 [1915]: 145 f., 182 f.). This same reasoning informed Article I Section 9 of the US Constitution stipulating that '[t]he privilege of the Writ of

Habeas Corpus shall not be suspended unless when in Cases of Rebellion or Invasion the public Safety may require it'.

Such limitations to the time and scope of emergency powers assumed conditions in which a combination of specification in advance, policy regulation, and post-hoc appraisal could raise the probability that governing exigencies could be made compatible with core liberal values, especially the rule of law. Underneath such actions lay the supposition that emergencies are limited in time and content. This postulate underpinned a remarkable 1918 US Government document, prepared by the order of the Attorney General and running more than 1,000 pages, that chronicled 'emergency legislation passed prior to December 1917' (Clark 1918). Excluding matters of military organisation and finance, it focused on statutes, presidential orders, and proclamations that authorised 'the taking and control of private property' during the Revolutionary War, the wars of 1812 and 1847, the Civil War, and World War I. On this account, emergency acts are associated with moments that possess a clear boundary between war and peace.

It is just this core assumption that has been brought under question and, arguably, made permanently obsolete, by three developments over the course of the past century: the intensity of violence, the vulnerability of civilians, and the growing opacity of the start and end of emergencies.

The geographic range and especially the carnage of the World War I was unprecedented, if primarily confined to the battlefield. The initial six months of the war witnessed 747,000 Germans and 854,000 French dead or wounded. In 1916, casualties at Verdun reached 800,000 and 1.1 million at the Somme. Over the course of the war, fully 5 million non-combatants were killed. As the war ended, national and global designs for the new normal took shape.

Even as the totalitarian challenge in the 1920s initially seemed limited by geography and time, the radicalisation of the Bolshevik regime under Stalin and the birth of Hitler's Third Reich gave rise to a repertoire of new security threats to American and other democracies that put pressure on previous emergency formulations in liberal political systems. World War II's amplification of the means of violence, culminating in atomic weaponry and the vulnerability of civilians well beyond the Holocaust (more deaths were suffered by non-combatants than combatants in a war marked by the unprecedented use of strategic and carpet bombing) further put pressure on traditional assumptions and liberal instruments.

These fresh circumstances and the fears they generated created conditions within which there was a significant expansion to the security-related actions of government. Thus, in the US, the Federal Bureau of Investigation and the Office of Naval Intelligence commenced the surveillance of American citizens with suspected and Nazi influences in 1936. Although the country was not at war, President Franklin Roosevelt declared a limited state of emergency in 1939 and an unlimited state of emergency in 1941, well before

ATANASSOW *and* KATZNELSON

Pearl Harbor, a move without constitutional or legislative warrant. Granting the president almost unrestrained powers over the economy and civil society, these capacities were codified during the war by congressional War Powers legislation. And, of course, more than 100,000 persons of Japanese background, most of them citizens, were interned by executive order.

Following the war, the existence of atomic weaponry, still with an American monopoly, induced Congress in 1946 to delegate permanent and unprecedented peacetime capacity to the president with regard not only to such bombs but also concerning the atomic industry. By 1947, the Atomic Energy Act was complemented by a fundamental National Security Act that fashioned the still-existing main instruments of a national security state, including the Pentagon and its military organisation, the National Security Council, and the Central Intelligence Agency, alongside federal government regulations subjecting government employees for the first time to systematic loyalty reviews. Writing in 1950, Rossiter noted the country's 'extraordinary expansion in the authority of the national executive, in both relative and absolute terms' in the face of what seemed like an emergency without end (Rossiter 1950: 417).

The Cold War circumstance of a quasi-war without temporal boundaries led quite swiftly to new circumstances. With the formal end of World War II, President Harry S. Truman terminated the 1939 and 1941 national emergency declarations of his predecessor. But he specifically exempted his own December 1950 declaration of emergency during the Korean War, which remained in effect into the Vietnam War years and which was followed by national emergency declarations by President Richard Nixon in 1970 and 1971.

The war in Vietnam led to congressional hearings and attempts to recoup legislative capacity regarding emergencies. This pushback culminated in the passage of the National Emergencies Act, signed into law by President Gerald Ford in 1976, which put previous declarations of emergency into dormancy within two years. It also offered means for Congress to negate future executive declarations through a legislative veto (ruled invalid by the Supreme Court in 1983) and specified that presidents must in the future clarify the exigencies at hand should they take such action, which would have to be time-bound.

Clearly there was a significant effort to restore the core features of the liberal tradition—but with limited effect, as it turned out. Though this high point of congressional assertion following the debacle in Vietnam provided for each chamber to meet within six months of a declared emergency to decide whether it should continue, in practice deferral to the president has proved the rule. Moreover, no fewer than twenty-three targeted executive declarations of emergency were promulgated in the next quarter-century, up until the terror attacks of 9/11.

Concurrently, Congress passed significant emergency legislation. The International Emergency Powers Act of 1977 authorised the president to regulate international and domestic finance during periods of national emergency in consultation with Congress. The Foreign Intelligence Surveillance Act of 1978 (FISA) created a special federal court, the Foreign Intelligence Surveillance Court (FISC), which holds non-public *ex parte* sessions to oversee search warrants. This key law sought to secure a role for not only judicial but also congressional oversight over intelligence surveillance activities in a manner consistent with the need for secrecy. Further, in 1994, the Communications Assistance for Law Enforcement Act enhanced the ability of police to conduct electronic surveillance by requiring telecommunications companies to design their systems to make surveillance possible.

The events of 9/11, of course, quickened the pace as Congress swiftly delegated enormous capacity to the executive branch to fight terror in the Patriot Act (2001), Homeland Security Act (2002), Intelligence Reform and Prevention of Security Act (2004), Protect America Act (2007), FISA Amendments Act (2008), Patriot Sunsets Extension Act (2011), FISA Amendments Act Reauthorization Act (2012), and USA Freedom Act (2015). The latter represented an attempt to set limits on bulk telephone data collection and on FISA court classification of decisions, but it left intact the national state's capacious and capable post-9/11 instruments that put under pressure traditional liberal rights, limitations, and procedures.

This legislative course went hand in hand with truly unprecedented executive actions authorising the lethal targeting and indefinite detention of terrorism suspects. The basic structure was created by the administration of President George W. Bush between November 2001 and February 2002 in a presidential military order that established military commissions for the trial of non-citizens in the war on terror, a Department of Justice memorandum denying Guantanamo detainees *habeas* rights, and a presidential memorandum on the international legal status of terror detainees announcing the non-applicability of the provisions of the Third Geneva Convention. In 2010, the Department of Justice produced a memorandum justifying the killing of a US citizen, Anwar al-Awlaki, in Yemen without trial, and President Barack Obama issued an executive order in 2011 that, while authorising the periodic review of persons held at Guantanamo, recognised as legitimate their indefinite detention.

These policies have cumulatively narrowed legislative power, widened executive prerogatives, and shrunk the secure range of rights possessed by citizens and foreign prisoners. One does not have to embrace Schmitt's historical and conceptual account or Agamben's reconsideration to note how conditions of 'exception' have become wider in scope, more heterogeneous in character, and ever more routinely characteristic and seemingly durable features of liberal democracies. The liberal centrepieces of law as legislated, implemented, and enforced and of rights that are intended to offer protection against encroachments on basic freedoms have been transformed by responses to the permanence of exigency.

Policy Orientations and Options

With this shift in the landscape, it has become ever more urgent to consider how to strengthen the liberal repertoire that can be deployed to govern exigencies. While the puzzles posed by previous generations of liberal thinkers remain the puzzles of the current era, and while the articulations and proposals of those thinkers have much to offer, today's challenges are not simply resolvable by pointing to past solutions. Fresh circumstances have placed great pressure both on constitutional constraints and on the distinction between the temporary and the permanent. The manner in which governments respond to present conditions will be shaped in part by expectations and values and by dispositions about the order of political priorities.

A central challenge is that of discerning norms to guide choices about discretion and constraint together with devising institutional arrangements that reinforce liberal imperatives to compensate, at least in part, for the erosion of once clearer boundaries and guidelines. How can security and liberty, including mechanisms of accountability, be served simultaneously? Is it possible to mitigate the prospects that managing security, even without overt intent, can not only undermine fundamental liberal norms but also inhibit means of learning and correction? Based on the liberal resources discussed above, five broadly portable guidelines are suggested.

First, the character of emergency must always be mediated by law. In this respect, Schmitt's distinction between types of dictatorship is both chastening and fundamental. He recognised that any exceptional policy behaviour that reacts to threatening situations—even actions that, in Hamilton's language, appear to be free from constitutional shackles—constitutes a profound exception to the normal course of liberal law. Schmitt contrasted situations in which actions are undertaken to protect a constitution under threat ('commissary dictatorship' in his terminology) from those that stand wholly outside an existing legal order and seek not to protect but to negate it permanently in order to bring about a new non-liberal order (a 'sovereign dictatorship'). On this approach, power dislodges law. It was just this move that the American liberals who wrote about emergencies in the 1930s and 1940s stoutly refused—as do we.

Second, wherever possible, the elaboration of a distinction between temporary action and permanent policy should be advanced. Notwithstanding many persisting qualities of security situations, political actors can continue to recognise this traditional division through a wide range of means, not least the requirement that key legislative acts and delegations of power to the executive should be fixed in time, subject to formal renewal. Advocating just such a constitutional requirement regarding the armed forces, Hamilton insisted on 'an important qualification even of legislative discretion', taking note of 'that clause which forbids the appropriation of money for the support of an army for any longer period than two years'. He commended this provision as 'a great and real security against military establishments without evident necessity', and for generating a public debate on a recurring basis on the character of existing exigencies (Hamilton 2001a [1788]).

Third, prudent definitions of necessity should govern policy decisions taken to anticipate and respond to security exigencies. The quest for such a standard characterised by prudence and discretion has a long-standing lineage within liberal thought. For Locke, the prerogative of the executive is conditioned on the criterion of clearly serving the public good. For Hamilton, governmental action regarding threats must seek to combine energetic action with respect for individual rights and a sensibility that is prepared to restrain executive and legislative authority. For the nineteenth century German émigré Frances Lieber, a scholar who advised President Abraham Lincoln during the Civil War concerning the proper conduct of Union troops, the state's actions under emergency conditions should be appraised by way of a reasonable person standard. Official acts, he wrote, 'should be adjudged to be necessary in the judgment of a moderate and reasonable man . . . reason and common sense must approve the particular act'. Further, he argued, 'if these conditions are not fulfilled, the act becomes unlawful, with all the consequences attending to illegality' (cited in Witt 2015: 26).

> *Policies of exception must not portend invisibility or isolation from democratic institutional practices.*

Fourth, at no point should political leaders be exempt from oversight that must be continuous. Policies of exception must not portend invisibility or isolation from democratic institutional practices. To the contrary, within requirements of probity, each of the institutions of government–the judiciary, the legislature, and within the executive itself–must have opportunities for information sharing, judgments, and supervision in real time.

Fifth, and no less important, the conjunction of liberalism and exigency requires possibilities for retrospective judgment, the capacity to appraise after the fact. We know that challenges concerning security are permanent features of governance. A process of calm learning and evaluation, tied to sanctions when liberal norms have been grossly violated, is particularly attractive for political regimes committed to democratic deliberation within the zone of collective choice.

In considering how to realise these standards, a starting point might well be the strengthening of existing safeguards. In the US, the FISC, as an example, is presently characterised by limited staffing and the absence of enforcement capabilities when putatively binding orders are violated by security agencies, now documented as a frequent pattern (Benkler 2014: 21). Likewise, existing congressional oversight mechanisms are hindered by an inability to check the veracity of information provided by national security

ATANASSOW *and* KATZNELSON

agencies, in part the result of a lack of adequate research capacity. Further, the rules of the game so strictly prohibit disclosure that members of the legislature not serving on specialised intelligence committees–let alone, citizens more broadly–are precluded from gaining a sense of what is happening, even when there is reason to suspect significant violations of rights at home and of international law abroad. Although in a liberal polity the burden of argument must rest first with government, the weakness of existing mechanisms has made the risky and illegal choice to leak information about such matters as the acquisition and analysis of bulk telephone data and the targeting of computers the dominant means to check practices that most pressure the liberties of citizens.

There are models–some dating from the nineteenth century–that might offer more robust and satisfactory options. As an example, the wartime decision by President Lincoln to issue an Emancipation Proclamation on 1 January 1863, warranted only by his powers as commander-in-chief during a period of unprecedented domestic insurrection, was soon legitimated by the most difficult constitutional means, the passage of a constitutional amendment, the Thirteenth, which eliminated chattel slavery. Unlike the suspension of *habeas corpus* that was rooted in the Constitution, Lincoln's wartime executive act concerning slavery would have been Schmittian if it were not promptly accompanied by a constitutional process and the understanding that the exercise of war powers, themselves justifiable from within the founding document, were not ultimately outside the rule of law. In the pre-Civil War American republic, slavery was at least as prominently as matters of war and peace the basis of considering exigencies. Protecting slavery joined with security matters in 1814 during the Battle of New Orleans against British forces, when General Andrew Jackson declared martial law. But unlike General Jackson, President Lincoln was deeply anxious about the implications for the liberal tradition by the exercise of emergency powers and thus limited his abolition order to particular military conditions.

This restriction was advanced by Lieber, who in his code of conduct for Union forces during the fratricidal conflict had advocated limiting martial law exclusively to enemy territory. In the decades after the war, he also considered the experiences of abrogating *habeas corpus* and abolishing slavery and their lessons about the exercise of emergency power in a liberal democracy. Lieber stressed that exceptional executive actions on behalf of security must be limited not only by the character of the exigency but by some hardwired rules, including an absolute prohibition of torture, without which, he believed, it would be impossible to maintain a political community defined by liberal values embedded in law (Witt 2015).

To the end of protecting the constitutional polity, Lieber combined the idea of a reasonable person standard with institutions of retrospective judgment, whose central purpose is less to punish than to understand for the future. Exercises of judgment during an emergency, he convincingly argued, must be accompanied by ex post exercises of judgment about conduct that had prevailed during the emergency.

Building on this orientation, an ambit of governance beckons. By the standards elaborated here, no constitutional democracy has yet displayed sufficient institutional imagination. Delegation without requirements for renewal, without prudential tests, without timely oversight, and without retrospective appraisals remains the norm. The lack of constraint by law is too often so wide as to sanction a permissive lawlessness. Nevertheless there is no lack of promising models. In the US, an independent judiciary has long constrained executive and legislative action in many policy areas in the name of constitutional requirements. Although there is a significant tradition of abnegation in areas of national security, that constraint is not hardwired. Likewise, the US Congress more than any other national legislature possesses an extensive committee structure with a wide array of powers of investigation and oversight. Unfortunately, in the recent past, the relevant congressional committees have been constrained in their oversight role not only by requirements of secrecy but by limited and sometimes misleading information provided by the country's intelligence agencies. Still, the institutional core is in place to meet the standards elaborated here. At issue is a matter of will.

The US, however, lacks significant instruments for appraisals after the fact. Two existing institutions of British governance offer compelling possibilities that demand broader consideration within other constitutional democracies.

Great Britain has a tradition of public inquiries that has been deployed to assess how governments have conducted themselves in matters of national security. In 2000, the Regulation of Investigatory Powers Act established an Investigatory Powers Tribunal, an independent court to handle complaints both under that act and under the Human Rights Act of 1998, consistent with the European Convention on Human Rights, concerning allegations that the country's security and intelligence agencies may have practised unlawful intrusion and surveillance. The Tribunal assesses whether the acts of these agencies have a lawful parliamentary warrant, whether, if lawful, they are governed by proper regulation, and, in such cases, whether implementation of these regulations has been properly followed. A 'no' to any of these matters can lead both to a public rebuke of the government and to an order that compensation be paid (Investigatory Powers Tribunal 2016: 3-13).

The most recent example is the Iraq Inquiry led by Sir John Chilcot, which was charged to consider Britain's policies regarding Iraq (2001–2009) and whose findings were published in July 2016 after an investigation lasting some seven years. It found that British participation had not been warranted by the situation at the time, that the consequences of the invasion had been dangerously underestimated, and that the government had failed to achieve its announced goals as an occupying power. Among the lessons drawn by the Inquiry, it above all emphasised that 'all aspects of any intervention need to be calculated, debated and challenged with the utmost rigour' (The Iraq Inquiry 2016: 12).

Conclusion

This chapter has analysed a particular form of democratic subversion: the danger posed by the exigencies of protecting the external borders and securing the institutional integrity of liberal democratic regimes. As states in a world of unequal states oriented by incommensurable values, liberal democracies face the pressures of security and self-preservation. They have both the right to self-protection and the duty to defend their citizenry against those who contest their legitimacy and seek to subvert their core institutions. Yet, along with external threats, democratic subversion may also result from the very measures taken to ensure self-preservation. Insofar as liberal democracies are grounded in and defined by constitutional and moral principles, exceptions from these principles threaten to undermine the viability and legitimacy of the liberal democratic order. As Rogers and Willoughby put things in 1921, governing exceptional circumstances is 'a dangerous matter', as it 'means a reversion, to an extent at least, to autocratic government. Not only is the door thus opened to oppression of the individual', they added, 'but the possibility is ever present that those in authority, once vested with autocratic powers, will not be willing to surrender them when the occasion for their use is past' (Willoughby and Rogers 1921: 23).

> *A liberal approach to governing emergency must be grounded in normative goals beyond state security.*

Hence a liberal approach to governing emergency must be grounded in normative goals beyond state security. In light of these goals, liberal states identify their main adversaries to be regimes and actors who subvert not just the state itself but its central values of rights, consent, law, and political representation.

Calling attention to the dangers inherent in any departure from the constitutional and moral norms and to historical trends that have made such departures ever more significant and in a sense normal, this chapter emphasises the need to subsume such exceptions, to the greatest extent possible, within the constitutional framework. Looking back at a long Anglo-American tradition of liberal thinking about states of exception, this chapter has articulated normative guidelines and pointed to enhanced legislative oversight and other institutional arrangements as means to govern exceptions in a liberal frame. We recommend both strengthening existing mechanisms of supervision and control, and the creation of new means that build on appealing examples drawn from two centuries of American as well as current British practice.

In conclusion, it is important to underscore that for a liberal state the end of governing exigency cannot be a fail-proof environment from which risk and uncertainty are forever banished. Nor can the tensions between security and liberty be permanently resolved. Rather, the question posed and addressed here is how liberal societies can achieve and maintain a resilient framework within which the inherent conundrums of liberty and security are negotiated and mitigated, even as they cannot be erased.

VIII. The Limits of Democratic Innovations in Established Democracies

Wolfgang Merkel

Western representative governments are under pressure. Satisfaction with and esteem for political parties and governments are near historic lows in many countries. Growing segments of society have become estranged from the representatives and institutions that govern them. New right-wing populist political entrepreneurs have moved into this representational void and have successfully mobilised voters with the slogan 'we below' against 'them at the top,' referring to the traditional political elites in Washington, London, and Berlin, among others. A new divide appears to be emerging: the cleavage between well-educated, cosmopolitan elites and higher classes on the one hand and communitarian-populist lower classes on the other. Yet what both sides have in common is a growing demand for more direct forms of democratic participation and decision-making. Old forms of direct involvement such as referendums and new forms such as deliberative democracy have been revived or newly invented as proposed cures for the malaises of representative democracy (Alonso, Keane, and Merkel 2011).

Forms of direct involvement have been revived or newly invented as cures for the malaises of representative democracy.

Can forms of direct democracy indeed serve as a cure for the current malaises of representative democracy? Can direct democracy make the established democracies of the OECD world more responsive, accountable, and legitimate? Wherein lie the strengths and weaknesses of direct democracy? Three forms of direct democracy will be discussed in this chapter:

- **Referendums**: Referendums are certainly not a new form of participation and legislation. In Switzerland, they have been part of the institutional repertoire since the mid-nineteenth century. However, they are gaining popularity in established democracies as a tool for letting the voices of the people be heard.
- **Deliberative democracy**: Although the idea of deliberative democracy can be traced back to ancient Greece, it is only during the last three decades that it has been implemented in the form of concrete institutions

such as participatory budgeting (PB), deliberative polls, and so-called mini-publics.

- **Digital democracy**: The global spread of internet-enabled devices now allows for new forms of political communication, participation, and decision-making. The hope is that the ease and accessibility of digital tools will lower the threshold for engaging in politics for many citizens.

In discussing each of these innovations, this chapter will focus on two questions. First, to what extent might these forms of direct democracy remedy or compensate for the recognisable malaises of participation, representation, and governance? Second, to what extent are direct democratic elements compatible with the institutions and procedures of representative democracy?

Referendums

Referendums are often seen as an alternative to representative democracy: they are said to appeal directly to the people without the mediation of political parties and thus enable the people to decide for themselves. We know from empirical research, however, that political parties play a key role in referendums (Kriesi 2005). This does not mean that majority parties will carry the outcome of a referendum; while certainly the case on average, there have also been spectacular exceptions such as the ban on minaret construction in Switzerland in 2009 and the reform of the school system in Hamburg, Germany in 2010, which was blocked via referendum against the will of all parties in the city council. In general, parties often dominate referendum campaigns because they are already involved in political dialogue with citizens over issues of finance, organisational resources, and programmatic direction and are thus able to communicate their objectives more effectively than citizens' initiatives. The institution of the referendum also reinforces citizens' identification with the democratic system as a whole, including with parties. In the case of Switzerland, referendums strengthen the existing party democracy by opening up new legitimacy resources for the democratic system and a new form of public space for political parties. However, the representative components of Swiss democracy resemble almost entirely an ideal type of 'consensus democracy' (Lijphart 1999), with extensive direct democratic components serving as a majoritarian corrective. The Swiss system is a unique symbiotic combination of representative and consensus democracy.

Crucially, referendums fail to bring the masses to the ballot box and to mobilise those that previously dropped out of political participation. In fact, the contrary is often the case: referendums tend to yield lower rates of participation and higher levels of social selectivity than general parliamentary elections (Merkel and Ritzi 2017). Referendums on the European Union (EU), which tend to be rare, are one exception. For example, the Brexit referendum was quite democratic since the turnout was considerably higher than in previous general elections. Referendums, if used often, may face problems of participation and legitimacy. (This is mitigated by the fact that the volume of referendum decisions remains well below the legislative output of parliaments and councils, even in Switzerland.) Despite these flaws, elements of direct democracy strengthen the overall democratic system and its representative organisations by strengthening citizens' identification with their body politic. Nonetheless, they do not contribute toward solving the problem of inequality in political representation. Referendums are above all an instrument of educated, politically interested, middle class, disproportionately male voters. For these reasons, and given the occasional anti-minority bias in referendums–as was the case against Muslims and immigrants in Switzerland or homosexuals in California–it is necessary to look beyond the theoretical promises of direct democracy and examine which policy areas at what levels of decision-making are suitable for the democratisation of representative democracy. Questions of environmental policy or infrastructure projects at the local level may be more suitable for referendums than distributive or minority-related matters. It is not uncommon to find discrepancies between direct democratic expectations in theory and problematic side effects in practice, at least in Europe and North America.

Participation

Proponents of referendums emphasise these additional opportunities for political participation as a major advantage over purely representative democracies, in which citizens are only periodically called to the ballot box. In reality, the extent of participation in referendums is key to determining their legitimacy. If 25 per cent of eligible voters vote in a referendum against a law that had been passed by 75 per cent of legislators, the case for the superior legitimacy of referendums loses much of its force. In this vein, the high '50 per cent plus 1' quorum for abrogative (repeal) referendums, such as in Italy, is exemplary from a democratic-theoretical perspective and provides for greater legitimacy than the relatively low quorums in place in Switzerland, California, or the German states.

Referendums can hardly attenuate, let alone solve, the problems of declining participation and rising social selection in established democracies. As noted above, rates of participation in referendums at local, regional, and national levels remain below those in general elections (Merkel and Ritzi 2017). Given that referendum voters are most often well-educated and wealthy men, the politically active demos is thus more than halved and becomes even more imbalanced in composition than in general elections.

While referendums do constitute greater opportunities for participation, they also reproduce the over-representation of those already disproportionately represented in the traditional institutions of democracy. Moreover, the problem of legitimacy remains unsolved: as a rule, disadvantaged minority groups do not end up deciding on legislation for the demos as a whole. The direct democratic therapy of referendums appears to only aggravate the representative democratic disease of social selectivity by expanding opportunities for over-represented groups to participate and thus inadvertently advancing the oligarchisation of our democracy.

Representation

Social imbalances in representation that are recognisable in parliamentary decision-making processes and their outcomes (Lehmann and Regel 2015) are not corrected by the outcomes of referendums. As noted above, the interests and preferences of the most privileged appear to prevail even more markedly in referendums than in parliamentary-representative decision-making processes. This holds for fiscal policies as well as recognition of minorities. Moreover, political parties and interest groups are generally more prominent actors in referendums than citizens' initiatives; in fact, the latter have most often taken on a prominent role when referendum proposals discriminate against certain minorities. This has especially been the case in Switzerland when initiatives have been backed by the right-wing populist Swiss People's Party (SVP). The capturing of referendums by such a political party threatens to become a blueprint for elsewhere in Europe.

Governance and policies

Referendums can serve to overcome reform barriers in periods of policy-making stagnation (e.g. Italy in the 1970s). More often than not, however, referendums serve as institutional stabilisers of the status quo; they have been powerless when it comes to regaining the ground that politics has lost to the markets over the last three decades. Referendums have been more effectual when it comes to deciding the extent to which nation-states should give up sovereignty to the EU. This was the case with Norway's and Switzerland's negative votes on EU membership, the 'no' votes on the EU Constitutional Treaty in France and the Netherlands in 2005, and Brexit in 2016. These examples made it clear to the obviously not-so-representative institutions and political elites that passive consensus on wider and deeper European integration had come to an end. While referendums on the EU yield on average much higher rates of participation than classical policy referendums, it is conceivable that referendums ought to be required whenever sovereignty rights are to be transferred via international treaties. The examples of Switzerland, Norway, and the United Kingdom (UK) show that in such cases, the public at large might establish itself as an effective veto player against further sovereignty transfers. If one subscribes to the notion of national democratic constitutionalism, a veto position might be considered a form of (national) democracy protection. If one prioritises cosmopolitan values and post-national open societies, however, (national) democracy might be seen to produce integration costs.

There is a commonly overlooked dilemma inherent to referendums: the role and size of the quorum necessary for validity. If the quorum is set too high, few referendums will stand a chance of reaching it; the significance of referendums for actual policy-making would remain even less than it is today. Even in Switzerland, 93 per cent of parliamentary decisions enter into force without referendums (Vatter 2014: 374). The relevance of referendums for policy-making is thus in inverse proportion to the passion with which they are advocated or rejected. If, on the other hand, the quorum is set too low, there is the possibility of falling into a legitimacy trap. More referendum outcomes would become law, but potentially with the approval of less than 25 per cent of the population eligible to vote. There is hardly any democratic-theoretical legitimisation for the abrogation of legislation previously passed by a large majority in parliament via a referendum with such low turnout (as was the case in the failed reform of the school system in Hamburg). A low quorum favours the rule of well-to-do, well-organised minorities. It is therefore a democratic-theoretical imperative to set quorums at appropriately high levels. The pragmatic objection that referendums would only rarely pass is irrelevant from the perspective of legitimacy.

Deliberative Democracy

Approaches to deliberative politics are, in a sense, the opposite of referendums. It is not the people at large who are called upon to decide but rather small groups. Decisions are to be taken on the basis of the better argument, unencumbered by power and interest-driven manipulations, optimally leading to a broad consensus and a reasoned politics. This does not rule out majoritarian decision-making at the end of deliberation, as is often argued by proponents of the 'systemic turn' in deliberative democracy (Dryzek 2012; Mansbridge 2015). The systemic turn describes the strong tendency within deliberative democratic theory to prioritise the development of mini-publics that can discuss and decide on local issues at the expense of theoretically more demanding aspects of reasoned politics. However, if taken seriously, deliberation involves highly demanding procedures that call for symmetrical access to social discourses. In the purist Habermasian conception (Habermas 1992) and despite intentions to the contrary, deliberative politics remains an elite enterprise that at best works within more egalitarian, middle-class communities. What might work in middle-upper-class Princeton is more likely to fail in the predominantly lower-class Bronx, and deliberation is hardly suitable for deciding on questions such as war and peace, redistribution and social justice, and taxes.

In practice as well as in more practice-oriented theoretical variations, the concept of reason-driven deliberation may be watered down and adapted to actual political possibilities. This applies, for example, to the national public policy conferences in Brazil (Pogrebinschi 2013b), which despite considerable participation from civil society are fundamentally state-managed from the local to the national levels and thus hardly meet the conditions for a domination-free discourse. Though the policy conferences represent a pragmatic attempt to integrate state and civil society into policy-making processes in the fields of health, infrastructure, and social policies, they are more reminiscent of corporatist mass events under state auspices than of randomly selected citizens' assemblies with deliberative rules of discourse. Nonetheless, these conferences can be seen as a recognisable upgrading of the political role of civil society in Brazil.

At the same time, the theoretical advantage of bringing forth a more reasoned and common-good-oriented politics through deliberative procedures remains limited in practice. The British Columbia Citizens' Assembly (Canada) that took on the issue of electoral reform in 2004 is one of the most often cited, but nevertheless very rare exceptions. In Europe, deliberative assemblies play a limited role at the local level. The participatory budgeting (PB) schemes introduced in some municipalities around the globe are neither financially very relevant nor in high demand from citizens. The prototypical PB scheme, as in Porto Alegre, Brazil, still seems to be an exception in terms of finance and citizens' participation (see Pogrebinschi in this Report for information on PB in Latin America).

Apart from expert commissions, local advisory councils with hearing rights, intra-party consultations, deliberative polls, and parliamentary committees, deliberative politics has only marginal significance for national politics in Europe. An across-the-board spread of deliberative citizens' assemblies is hardly conceivable given the organisational complexity involved. Nonetheless, there are indications that the deliberative paradigm as a regulative idea can influence conflict resolution at the level of elites when public attention can be generated. When antagonistic interests enter into conflict, however–as is often the case with distributive politics in pluralist capitalist societies–it is more than probable that the idea of deliberation recedes into the background and that interests and power resources come to dominate conflict resolution. This is not a priori negative but rather a constitutive element of all pluralist democracies. When ethical or moral questions are up for discussion, deliberative elements take on greater significance in processes of political consultation and decision-making, especially when the outcomes of these processes have not been dog-matically predetermined by fixed worldviews. Though there remains a signifi-cant discrepancy between the immense body of theoretical work on delibera-tive democracy and its low real-world significance in advanced democracies, there seems to be a growing awareness of the deliberative method in different political arenas, including international organisations, transnational non-gov-ernmental organisations (NGOs), and parliamentary and civil society debates.

Democratic theories should be subject to a double test: one of internal theoretical consistency and another of practicability and by extension polit-ical relevance. Failing the first test would mean that it would not be mean-ingful to speak of a theory at all; failing the second test would mean that a theory runs the risk of being no more than an elaborate game of intellec-tual fancy. Indeed, deliberative elements of democratic theory only become relevant politically once thinned out normatively (see for example Dryzek 2012; Gutmann and Thompson 1996; Mansbridge 2015; Pogrebinschi 2013b; Warren 2009). While this normative thinning out allows for greater practica-bility, it also leads to a loss of theoretical consistency and normative dignity.

Participation

Classical organisations for political participation, such as political par-ties and large associations, lost much of their traction by the turn of the twenty-first century. For members of the middle and upper class, civil soci-ety forums and conferences may supplement traditional forms of political organisation. For all others, this cannot be expected. The random selection of discourse participants would do little to improve representativeness for two reasons. First, potential participants would need to register their will-ingness to participate, and second, the discourse participants would need comparable cognitive and argumentative resources at their disposal. Yet, in terms of the latter, less-educated individuals tend to have fewer capabili-ties and less training to argue in public, and it is precisely their exclusion that constitutes one of the malaises of contemporary democracies. The argument that facilitators could compensate for this social selectivity is not entirely convincing (for a different view see Offe 2011: 30). At worst, modera-tors might take on such prominent roles that their own selection, training, and supervision would raise a classic problem of democratic theory: who guards the guardians, and who moderates the moderators?

Deliberative discourses promote participation above all for the middle class and hardly for those already absent from the traditional organisations and institutions of representative democracy. The more these discourses shed their deliberative character, as in the case of national public policy con-ferences in Brazil, the more they also open themselves up to wider swathes of society and can thus be seen as instruments for expanding participation.

Representation

In most conceptions of deliberative democracy, deliberative forums are not envisaged as representative organs. Indeed, the random selection of participants is meant to replace the representation of socioeconomic class, values, and interests. Moreover, the process of transforming individual preferences into fair and reasoned preferences oriented toward the common good is meant to overcome precisely the particularity of the interests involved. If this were to succeed, a flaw of liberal pluralist democracies might be remedied or at least attenuated: namely, the asymmetrical influence of economic power on collectively binding political decisions. Yet it appears unlikely that these interests can be eliminated from real-world deliberative discourse in capitalist societies. Nonetheless, it might be possible to strengthen a public sphere that forces the questioning of particular interests and their mediation vis-à-vis the common good. Whether this can be done better through deliberative processes than through parliamentary debates and government decisions remains a matter for discussion. At the very least, however, deliberative discourses may intensify the moral pressure to justify one's own position. The upside is that additional possibilities for representation may arise for the politically active in the form of citizens' assemblies or councils, PB processes, and policy conferences. This would be an especially welcome development if social selectivity can be minimised and any potential legitimacy deficit avoided. In addition, democratic deliberation can contribute toward representing social discourses that otherwise stand little chance in the interest- and power-laden spheres of representative democracy. One example would be the transnational discourses of NGOs on topics such as human rights, migration, sustainability, and global justice.

Policies and governance

The Brazilian public policy conferences have shown that civil society participation in policy formulation can change political decision-making processes. Pogrebinschi and colleagues (Pogrebinschi 2013b; Pogrebinschi and Samuels 2014) have emphasised the positive influence of these conferences on central policy areas in which the life chances of large portions of society may be considerably disadvantaged: healthcare, social policy, and education. This has been possible in the context of Brazil, which has one of the highest levels of inequality in the world.

There is as yet no empirical evidence that such distributive measures have found acceptance in the established democracies of the OECD world. Policy areas that contribute to inequality–namely, financial market deregulation and tax system reform–would hardly be appropriate for deliberative discourses given their complexity and interest-laden nature. Why should wealthy capital holders allow their preference for low taxes to be swayed by the better argument of the less well-off? Moreover, there is a never-ending (philosophical) debate on the distributive question of who is entitled to get what between the poles of meritocracy and individual need. This leaves us with other policy areas, such as issues of tolerance and gender equality, where democratic deliberation may have a better chance to shape real political discourses and decisions.

Direct democracy in the form of referendums carries the risk that the 'worse I' (Offe 2011) comes out in the privacy of the voting booth; exclusion rather than inclusion is an additional, frequently incurred risk of referendums. Deliberative discourses, on the other hand, are meant to enable the development of the 'better I' and the more reasoned 'we' under the light of the public sphere. A concept for establishing such discourses on a relevant scale and without discrimination of lower social strata has yet to be presented in the context of the established capitalist democracies of the OECD world. This does not discount the idea of deliberative discourse as such, but it does indicate that the normative project of deliberative-democratic theory has yet to overcome its cumbersome relationship to real-world politics in antagonistic capitalist societies.

Digital Democracy

Cyberspace appears to constitute a new opportunity structure for democracy, promising to lower the transaction costs of political information, communication, and action and to open up a new dimension of political participation. We are still at the beginning of the political possibilities of digital democracy. It is only a matter of time until the majority gains access to internet; the question is whether and to what extent the internet will be used for political purposes. Empirical studies have shown that roughly half of internet users do not use it as a source of political information (Vowe 2014: 34). Of the other half, only a small proportion does so regularly and an even smaller proportion actively.

At least two dimensions of political use of the internet should be distinguished. One dimension relates to the use of digital communication and participation platforms by the traditional organisations and institutions of representative democracy: political parties, elected officials, and governments. In most countries, these institutions use the internet to communicate with interested citizens (see Box 3 for more on participation and digital democracy). In political parties in particular, stronger forms of member participation in internal decision-making processes will develop–a process that numerous parties have already begun–with greater transparency as another foreseeable gain for democracy. Parties that have yet to leverage

Box 3 **Political participation in a digital world**

The political aspects of digitalisation and digital communication are often associated with speaking, contributing, or posting. Active communication roles are the focus. Indeed, digitalisation has changed the way democracy takes place. In the Indian general election of 2014, the largest ever in terms of registered voters, Prime Minister Narendra Modi and his supporters dominated social media channels to effectively challenge powerful media institutions with counter-narratives. In the US, former President Barack Obama made it possible for individuals to contribute to his campaigns by making small donations online, a form of participation that reached out to those who would not necessarily go to the post office to mail a US$5 check. And in Germany, party-internal communication via digital mediums has enabled those at headquarters to work closely together with party members and field offices distributed around the country. Digitalisation has enabled publics to demand immediate reactions and statements from politicians, effectively accelerating the communication of politics.

As much as speaking is emphasised, it may be the listening that is really the big change brought about by digitalisation. That is largely what all the excitement about big data is about: it is a new way of listening. Internet polling, monitoring Tweets, and using digital trace data are all forms of listening. The major difference between big data and traditional methods is in the quantity. Focus groups (another type of listening) allow political campaigners to understand which messages work with their groups, and which do not. Big data analysis allows them to listen in a different way, by paying attention not to individuals but to larger trends.

One result of this is targeting. Targeted advertisements promise a better return on investment, including the energy put into making and spreading them. Micro-targeting allows political groups to choose who receives which messages and to compose their messages accordingly. If an organisation knows roughly how much money someone earns, it can ask that person to donate more or less than others, for example. However, and this is more important for politics than for businesses, which also use these methods: targeting practices also involve choices about whom an organisation does not want to speak to. This poses normative problems for political actors, since as representatives of entire populations they should arguably not be selective about their audience and target groups.

Targeting, however, is not just used to mobilise individuals to participate in politics by voting or donating. It can be and indeed often is used for organising as well: empowering individuals to act on behalf of organisations that they are not necessarily a part of. The Modi campaign targeted people who accessed the internet via mobile phones in areas with low internet penetration, encouraging them to share information with or hold events for people who could not access the internet, thereby bridging a particular digital divide. The Obama campaign persuaded young digital natives in the Jewish community in New York, for example, to travel to Florida and convince their grandparents to vote for Obama, bridging a different kind of digital divide.

While digitalisation has changed the way democracy takes place, it has not necessarily made things more or less democratic. With digital inclusion come digital divides. And with digital divides will come new ways of trying to bridge them, and many will attempt to do this digitally as well.

Andrea Römmele

---

digital platforms will in the future be able to withstand rising demand for digital participation only at the expense of further losses in members and votes. Online participation becomes especially effective politically when it succeeds in linking up with the offline world.

The truly innovative side of digital democracy only becomes evident beyond the horizon of conventional organisations. Internet debate forums, online petitions, digital letter-writing campaigns, and online-offline mobilisation are on the rise. The internet is increasingly being used for active politics, with a digital civil society emerging. Especially for NGOs with watchdog functions, Web 2.0 offers possibilities for intensifying the monitoring of political institutions. Keane is correct in tracing the contours of an emerging 'monitory democracy' (Keane 2011). Though the internet has strengthened political civil society and will continue to do so, there are no indications that this is leading to a return to politics of or by the people. Even the various forms of e-democracy exhibit–as do most non-conventional forms of politics or reform proposals–an in-built social selection filter.

Moreover, there are a number of risks. The digital world holds the danger of information overload and volatility as well as the illusion, possibly even arbitrariness, of participation. Signing an online petition with the click of a mouse costs nothing–not even the discursive scrutiny of pros and cons. This kind of activism may generate the illusion of effectual political intervention; 100,000 online signatures do not have the same effect as signatures collected through face-to-face interaction on the streets. Neither the seriousness nor the discursive effect on society is the same across the two cases.

If one considers the internet solely as a reservoir for protest, the constructive side of the critique misses out. If the 'worse I' (Offe 2011) votes in referendums, there are countless indications that the anonymity of the internet brings out even worse I's. The hate speeches and denunciations carried out through digital smear campaigns may violate civil rights and have the potential to destroy livelihoods, while the violators, hidden under the cloak of anonymity, do not have to fear the consequences. This may be nothing more than the infantile disorders of digital democracy. As yet, however, few indications point to a lasting turn toward an open and fair online discourse. It can be argued that open discourses fundamentally cannot flourish in a sphere of anonymity. The readiness to engage via social networks and media must be coupled with a sense of responsibility and commitment; only then can the democratising potential of the internet be realised. Apart from this unresolved problem, digital democracy offers considerable opportunities for greater participation and control of authority. There are no systemic incompatibilities with representative democracy. Yet as is the case with so many innovations, true opportunities cannot be had without risks.

What remains of the hopes and fears of a departure into the world of digital democracy? Do technologies of digital participation lead to greater, more socially balanced, and more effectual political participation? Although it is still too soon to make a systematic and empirically robust judgment, experiences, pilot studies, and observations allow for reasoned conclusions.

Participation

The new electronic media have not led to a rise in voter turnout, as shown for example in pilot projects in the UK (Hall 2012). It is evident that young people in particular make use of the option to cast votes electronically–but only if they are already politically interested: 'Technology can increase the convenience of voting; but inconvenience is not the major reason why people (including the young) do not vote' (Smith 2005: 21).

Transaction costs for voters have historically been greater for information acquisition than for the act of voting itself. Here, the internet provides an unparalleled diversity of offerings. Even if mainstream media cannot be short-circuited from below through the internet's pluralism in information acquisition and opinion formation, this pluralisation of information sources can, at least under some circumstances, promote democracy. This diversity, however, comes with risks. On social networks especially, the boundaries between information and opinion formation become blurred far more easily than in major newspapers and public radio and television broadcasts. Quality control takes on less of a role, if any, when it comes to non-mainstream information providers; the dangers of manipulation and disinformation are certainly greater. It has become more difficult to identify credible sources of information on the internet. Moreover, the question in established democracies today is whether there is not so much a problem of diversity as a problem of selection. In any case, a greater supply of information does not automatically lead to greater political awareness or competence.

Social networks like Twitter and Facebook offer new possibilities for unconventional forms of participation. Online mobilisations for offline demonstrations against the Transatlantic Trade and Investment Partnership (TTIP) and the Comprehensive Economic and Trade Agreement (CETA) were successful in Germany and other European countries. These new opportunities hold not only for street demonstrations, but also for online petitions. Whereas the Occupy movement was able to effect surprisingly little mobilisation on the streets outside the US, it has continued to gain significance through the articulation of protest and the raising of issues on the internet. There is considerable potential here for the future, though this potential will take on greater political significance in less democratic contexts. The internet and new media have so far proven much more effective in the mobilisation of protest against something than in the collective construction of something. Parallels to referendums are striking in this respect.

Representation

Although the boundaries between participation and representation become blurred far more easily in the digital world, here too forms of representation can be observed. Online campaigns run representatively by NGOs for swift and direct intervention in political decisions have taken on an increasingly important role (see for example Hall's chapter on online advocacy related to refugees in this Report). The main instrument in these campaigns is the electronic petition. Many NGOs themselves originated from online campaigns and constitute hybrids between participatory grassroots movements and political lobby groups. One of the first petition mobilisation organisations was MoveOn, founded in 1998 in the US. Today, organisations such as Avaaz operate successfully at the transnational level or, like Campact in Germany, at the national level. These groups intervene in political decision-making processes through campaigns and protest mobilisations.

Without a doubt, the internet has widened the palette of political participation. However, this holds true only for those already interested in politics, relatively well-educated, and probably also young. Digital socialisation will remain effectual even as digital natives come of age. There are no indications that the effects of education and political interest will not continue to be the major drivers of individual political participation.

This becomes especially evident in light of exponentially growing watchdog initiatives such as Transparency International, Human Rights Watch, and election-monitoring organisations. Keane (2010: 585, 2011: 223 f.) sees in these civil society initiatives elements of a new, post-traditional form of 'monitory democracy'. The control of elected representatives in state institutions through unelected but morally legitimised and de facto accepted representatives improves the functioning of representative democracy. To this end, the internet offers an easily accessible arena for information and participation and thus enables more transparency than was the case in the post-war decades of traditional politics. The question of the legitimacy hierarchy between socially respected but unelected civil society representatives and elected but often little-respected representatives of political parties cannot be addressed at length here (see Alonso, Keane, and Merkel 2011). Generally speaking, the arguments here assume that in case of collision between different forms of representation, those that are grounded in free and fair general elections should take normative precedence.

Moreover, digital platforms have considerable potential for more substantial forms of communication, participation, and decision-making in political parties. These platforms, if used in a disciplined and controlled manner and in a spirit of solidarity, can enable the membership base to take on a greater say in internal affairs and thus help to fight back Michels's (1911) 'iron law of oligarchy' a little over a century after its initial formulation. However, extensive party-internal communication through online forums, social networks, or specific software such as LiquidFeedback can sow the seeds of self-destruction as the recent fate of the Pirate Party in Germany demonstrates. Parties can also make use of new digital possibilities to intensify their communication with voters and citizens beyond tight time and space restrictions. Digital forms of participation and representation might work their unique effects not by circumventing or supplanting traditional political organisations but by supporting and controlling them in their representative functions vis-à-vis citizens. At the same time, this positive technological modernisation cannot by itself compensate for the loss of trust that parties and parliaments in most countries have incurred over the past three decades.

The internet and its political platforms also promote a digital habitus of unboundedness, arbitrariness, and short-term thinking (Han 2012), which sustains the illusions of some that it is possible to do politics with an easy click of the mouse. Guggenberger (2012: 12) writes that, on the contrary, 'political participation requires a foundation of perseverance, experience, and predictability, without which it runs idle'. Yet it is precisely the erratic, volatile, and non-binding character of digital communication that renders the formation of such continual relations of trust difficult. Effectual political participation without civic responsibility does not work. Politics is and remains 'a strong and slow boring of hard boards with both passion and perspective' (Weber 1919: 66).

Digital communication is bringing about a structural transformation of the public sphere. The general public now has the opportunity to become an actor in its own right. It remains to be seen how large the sections of this public are, which groups take part in it, and what democratic political quality this participation takes on. As noted above, however, once again it is above all those with education, spare time, and other resources at their disposal who engage via digital communication. Thus far, the internet has not changed social patterns of political participation and representation.

The democratic effect of digital politics will also depend on how internet communities and the entire digital civil society deal with the silent majority that has yet to be incorporated in decision-making processes. Ensuring this incorporation, albeit in a not entirely sufficient manner, is one of the strengths of representative democracy that neither direct democratic referendums nor deliberative citizens' assemblies nor digital-participatory procedures can come close to replicating. The 'sluice-gate model' proposed by Peters (1993) and Habermas (1992) for the relationship between civil society and parliament must also apply to the internet: decisions that are to take on authoritative applicability must, beyond being subject to direct votes on carefully worded questions, pass through the 'sluices of democratic and constitutional procedures situated at the entrance to the parliamentary complex'. Digital communication thus does not replace representative institutions but can render them more transparent and responsive in the future (monitory democracy). This, in short, is the upside. Yet responsiveness does not imply responsibility. A forward-looking democracy requires both a binding of the representatives to the represented as well as a certain distance of the governing from the governed in the interest of acting responsibly with a long-term view. Responsibility, however, has not been one of the strengths of digital democracy. Responsibility by way of the current and future common good of society arises rather in the pluralism of large collective organisations and the compromise-oriented deliberation of parliamentary discourses than in the atomistic participation landscape of the internet.

Conclusion

This is not a pessimistic outlook, but one that attempts a realistic reflection on democratic innovations in addition to a positive normative examination. Key institutional bastions of representative democracy and nation-state sovereignty cannot be relinquished carelessly. Optimistic promises about the future based on normative considerations do not by themselves fulfil the strict criteria of democratic legitimacy checks. The foundations of representative democracy face great challenges but nothing like wholesale disintegration (Merkel 2015a). These challenges cannot be met primarily with more referendums, more deliberation, or more digital democracy alone. The thrust of this chapter's argument is the following. One of the diseases of representative democracy is the lack of participation and representation by a third or even half of society: those segments that have dropped out of even the simplest forms of participation such as voting. All democratic innovations, with the exception of referendums, are cognitively and temporally much more demanding than voting. They privilege well-educated people who are already interested in politics and whose interests are already well represented in politics. Giving them more opportunities while others abstain from deliberation and digital forms of participation threatens to aggravate, as opposed to cure, the malaises of representative democracy.

Based on this analysis, the following policy recommendations can be drawn:

- Democratic innovations should be carefully screened for which and how many citizens actually participate in them. If only a small and socially biased selection of citizens participate, these actors should retain the opportunity to monitor those who govern and to criticise them in public discourse, but they should not be entitled to decide. Authoritatively binding decisions (except referendums) need the approval of parliaments to be democratic.
- Civil society-based watchdogs should be supported by law and impartial public financing.
- Referendums need high quorums of participation in order to claim democratic legitimacy. Specific issues such as minority rights, fiscal matters, or immigration should not be decided through referendums. Referendums at the local level strengthen grassroots democracy and the identification of citizens with 'their' democracy more than those at the national level.
- Direct democratic innovations can complement the institutions of representative democracy such as elections, parties, and parliaments, but they should not replace them. Since most of these democratic innovations are of minor empirical relevance, key reforms of democracy have to be implemented with regard to elections, parties, parliaments, and governments.
- In general, elections and electoral campaigns should be publicly financed in order to avoid the asymmetrical influence of business interests and rich donors.
- In order to avoid a further decline in voter turnout, compulsory elections such as those in Australia, New Zealand, Belgium, or Luxembourg could be introduced. The right to vote should be reconceived as a proud republican duty of citizens. Taxes or conscription are an incomparably higher and legitimate demand from the democratic state than compulsory voting in national elections, which takes in well-organised democracies no more than 30 minutes every few years. However, every citizen should also have the opportunity to cast a vote for 'none of the above' at the ballot box.
- The power of parliaments should be strengthened once more, not least their control of the executive in national and supranational policy-making and of markets.

IX. Democratic Innovations and Social Movements

DONATELLA DELLA PORTA *and* ANDREA FELICETTI

T he study of social movements represents an opportunity to understand the democratic malaise in contemporary society and its sources and to identify some possible ways to redress it. The democratic malaise is often expressed or countered through social movements, which in doing so may assume very different, or even opposite, connotations: on one hand, a well-documented galaxy of proactive movements denouncing and countering injustice and lack of democracy (Della Porta and Diani 2006); on the other, a rising tide of populist movements that openly contest progressive as well as egalitarian and substantial notions of democracy (Kriesi and Pappas 2015). Both types of movements shape democratic life in profoundly different ways, and in some cases movements represent sources of democratic innovation. This chapter examines democratic innovations associated with movements such as the Global Justice Movement (GJM), the World Social Forum (WSF), and the anti-austerity movement in order to argue that the nature of social movements deeply affects their ability to contribute to democratic innovation.

> *The nature of social movements deeply affects their ability to contribute to democratic innovation.*

A cursory introduction to some of these movements' essential features is in order before discussing the specifics of democratic innovation. The GJM is defined as 'networks of individuals or groups that mobilize internationally for global justice' (Della Porta and Rucht 2013: 7). While groups within the GJM[1] have different thematic focuses, ideological leanings, and strategies, they all see in democracy a desirable political order to be pursued both at the societal level and within their own processes. Rather than a network, the WSF is 'a set of initiatives of transnational exchange among social movements, NGOs, and their practices and knowledges of local, national or global social struggles' carried out against neoliberal globalisation and against exclusion, discrimination, and cultural imposition (Santos 2006: 6 f.). The movement has its symbolic home in the Brazilian city of Porto Alegre, which not only played a vital role in the beginning of the movement but has also provided fertile testing ground for innovations envisioned by the movement. Finally, the anti-austerity movement comprises the more recent wave of protests in 'opposition to austerity measures in the global North', denouncing also the 'crisis of political responsibility in the so-called advanced democracies' and the consequent 'deterioration of democratic institutions' (Della Porta 2015: 3). The anti-austerity movement can be connected to a wide range of mobilisations that, after having first erupted in Iceland in 2008, have spanned across a large number of countries, including Greece, Ireland, Portugal, Spain, and the United States. In general, these movements share similarities but also exhibit differences that have evolved over time, though all of them can be seen as fundamentally progressive movements calling for more democracy.

Social movements like these not only transform democratic states through struggles for policy changes but also express fundamental critiques of conventional politics, thus addressing meta-political issues and experimenting with participatory and deliberative ideas. Today, movements are increasingly understood as a central component of democratic systems: critical actors who may promote inclusion and foster epistemic qualities of social and political systems (Parkinson and Mansbridge 2012). (See Box 4 highlighting the contribution of civil society organisations to democratic innovation.)

Of course, this capacity may be curtailed to the extent that a movement embraces populist and exclusionary positions. In fact, social movements are not always champions of progressive values, and far-right social movements do indeed exist (Caiani, Della Porta, and Wagemann 2012). As an example, the German-born movement Pegida (Patriotic Europeans Against the Islamisation of the West) essentially combines 'fear of "Islamisation" with general criticism of Germany's political class and the mainstream media' (Dostal 2015: 523). Since the start of regular protests in Dresden in October 2014, Pegida has inspired a host of mobilisations across Europe. As such, it illustrates a movement that is critical of progressive values and inclined to challenge egalitarian and inclusive ideals associated with substantive notions of democracy. While Pegida is critical of party democracy, no substantial form of democratic innovation has been observed emerging from the movement. Nonetheless, referring to this type of movement provides a sobering reminder that the ability of movements to innovate democracy is not universal. Rather, the capacity to produce democratic innovations seems intimately tied to the activities of movements that are committed to promoting substantial space for democratic interaction internally as well as at the societal level.

As illustrated in the following, social movements promote innovation on two different fronts. First, they enhance political participation by promoting internal practices of democracy. Second, they can play a key role in introducing democratic innovations into existing institutions. Yet, as shown later in this chapter, social movements also face challenges in doing so.

Box 4 Innovation and relevance: Emerging trends in organised civil society

A vibrant and free civil society is an essential element of any democratic polity. Civil society organisations (CSOs) can be a source of renewal, even innovation, not only where democracy is at risk, but also where it is well established. CSO initiatives at the national and supranational level range from ensuring fair elections to holding policy-makers accountable, and, at least as important, to maintaining civic space.

CSOs have developed platforms that allow, among other things, monitoring of elections to track fraud and sometimes related violence. For example, Ushahidi, meaning 'testimony' in Swahili, is both a crowdsourcing information platform originally developed to track post-election violence in Kenya and an organisation that has promoted the platform's adaptation for monitoring elections, managing crises, and enhancing people's voice in policy decisions.

Efforts by CSOs to demand transparency and accountability frequently take novel turns. In Romania, for example, Funky Citizens developed the country's first fact-checking platform, alongside other 'civic tech' applications for monitoring public budgets, corruption, and the judiciary. In Russia, activists—mainly from the Anti-Corruption Foundation—used open property registries in other countries to track down Russian politicians that own foreign real estate but did not report it on their mandatory income declaration. Access Info Europe has taken accountability issues to the European Union level by demanding transparency and access to information including drafts of proposed legislation, meeting minutes, and financial reports such as travel and expense reports. The International Consortium of Investigative Journalists focuses on cross-border crime, corruption, and accountability of power and recently made the headlines by publishing the Panama Papers.

Notably, such democratic innovations seem to be emerging from newer CSOs rather than the more established ones. Indeed, recent memorable mobilisation campaigns happened either under the lead of a small cause-based organisation (like #Kony2012, #icebucketchallenge, or #bringbackourgirls) or without any centralised lead (protests against weakening of anti-corruption laws in Romania, #refugeeswelcome, #occupy, or #womensmarch). More established CSOs have played only a minor if any role in such events, sometimes because they are simply too slow, sometimes because they choose to remain on the sidelines in order to avoid alienating mainstream members or jeopardising good relations with decision-makers. The hard work of reaching out, raising awareness, and building relationships to effect long-term change—the strategy typically pursued by more traditional CSOs—is not capturing the interest of those today who want their voices heard immediately and directly. The role of CSOs as an efficient 'dialogue pipeline' between people and decision-makers is in need of revision—a process that should include all stakeholders.

At a time when their long-term efforts have finally won them a seat at the table with economic and political decision-makers—on both the national and international levels—more established CSOs are not only experiencing a seeming innovation slump; in many countries, they are also the primary victims of a recent spate of laws and regulations said to address cyber security and the fight against terrorism, or limit foreign funding and external political intervention. Those regulations effectively shrink the civic space and thereby damage trust in civil society and political actors.

Olga Kononykhina

Democratic Innovation Within Social Movements: From the Forum to the Camps

A primary contribution of social movements to democratic innovation is found within movements themselves, which are not only interested in internal democracy but also capable of learning how to promote it. An analysis of emerging trends within social movements that mobilised in the recent wave of protest against the 2008-9 financial crisis and for democratisation illustrates this important form of democratic innovation. These progressive social movements have emerged as self-reflexive actors that experiment with new ideas of democracy, which then form the basis of proposed changes to democratic governance.

Citizens and activists involved in the Arab Spring protests at Tahrir Square in Cairo, the *Indignados* movement at Puerta del Sol in Madrid, the anti-austerity protests at Syntagma Square in Athens, or the Occupy Wall Street encampment at Zuccotti Park in New York have not just criticised existing representative democracy as deeply corrupted but have also experimented with different models of democracy. The *acampada*–a term first used in Spain to describe the full-time occupation of an open public space over an extended period of time in order to perform political activism–is a repertoire of protest and an organisational form at the same time. It represents a major democratic experiment, adapted from one context to the next. If social forums were the democratic invention of the GJM of the 1990s and 2000s, the *acampadas* of the 2010s have been an attempt to update those forums as well as overcome their perceived failures. Conceptions of participation from below, cherished by progressive social movements, have been combined with special attention to the creation of egalitarian and inclusive public spheres (Della Porta 2015; Della Porta and Mattoni 2014). The same cannot be said for movements like Pegida, in which case a much touted characteristic of their repertoire consists in their ability to organise orderly

DELLA PORTA *and* FELICETTI

and non-violent demonstrations, hardly a front-line innovation in democratic politics.

Both the newer *acampadas* and the older social forums promote forms of internal democracy that combine participation and deliberation, with some differences (see Table 9.1). While social forums mix working group and assembly formats to develop agreements among delegates from civil society groups, the *acampadas* have thus far refused to accept the involvement of representative associations and have privileged instead the participation of individuals–citizens and members of the community–in building consensus. From a relational point of view, whereas the social forum process is oriented to networking, *acampadas* follow a more aggregative logic based on individual mobilisation (Juris 2012). From a cognitive point of view, while forums aim at building political alternatives, *acampadas* embody more prefigurative politics by experimenting with practices that enact imagined desirable political courses for the future. These differences are in part the product of learning processes after a perceived decline in the innovative capacity of the social forum process. However, they also reflect adaptation to the legitimacy crisis of late neoliberalism and its social and political consequences as well as to national opportunities and constraints.

Transparency, equality, and inclusivity are values cherished by these two types of movements, though with some important differences. Social forums are an innovative experiment promoted by the GJM. Distinct from a counter-summit, which is mainly oriented towards public protest, the social forum is a space of debate among activists. Its format epitomises the cognitive processes

Table 9.1 **Dimensions of democracy: from the forum to the camps**

	Social forums	*Acampadas*
Transparency	Open meeting places	In open public spaces
Equality	In associational democracy	In communitarian/ direct democracy
Inclusiveness	Movements of movements	The people
Consensus	Within spokes councils and social movement organisations	In assemblies, open to all
Argumentation	Rational/political	Prefigurative/emotional
Orientation	Cognitive work towards the public good	Construction of the commons
Preference transformation	Within the GJM	Within the 99 per cent

that developed within protest events as arenas for encounters. The charter of the WSF defines it as an 'open meeting place' for all civil society groups, with the exception of those advocating racist ideas, those using terrorist means, and political parties. Hundreds of workshops and dozens of conferences (with invited experts) are organised during a very short span of time and emphasise the production and exchange of knowledge. In fact, the WSF has been defined as an ideas fair, a place to exchange information (Schönleiter 2003: 140). Different activities converge on the aim of providing a meeting space for a loosely coupled, huge number of groups in order to lay the groundwork for broader mutual understanding. The open debates are designed to increase awareness of others' concerns and beliefs, as opposed to eliminating differences. Diversity and transparency are highly valued but difficult to practise. In the social forum process, assemblies are important and so are workshops, during which activists exchange information and network rather than properly decide (Della Porta 2015; Della Porta and Mattoni 2014).

The *acampadas* of recent years have been established in open air spaces in order to reinforce the public and transparent nature of their process. Meeting in public spaces also stresses the inclusiveness of the process, and the refusal to allow delegates represents a further emphasis upon equality. Not only are Tahrir Square, Puerta del Sol, Syntagma Square, and Zuccotti Park open air spaces, but they are also highly important meeting places for local residents. The *acampadas* have symbolised a reclaiming of public space by citizens in all their variety. In Egypt the heterogeneity of participants was mentioned with pride: 'people of different backgrounds, of different classes, just sitting together talking' (Gerbaudo 2012: 69). In Europe the *acampadas* sought to construct a public sphere in which problems could be discussed and solutions sought. Unlike the temporary global convergence spaces of social forums, *acampadas* are presented as 'rather occupation and subversion of prominent urban public spaces' (Halvorsen 2012: 431).

If associational and participatory conceptions have sometimes clashed on issues of representation and accountability in social forums, direct, unmediated democracy is often called for in *acampadas*. General assemblies in the *acampadas* have been described by activists as 'primarily a massive, transparent exercise in direct democracy' (Della Porta 2015). Unlike social forums, which refer to themselves as spaces for 'the movement of movements' and welcome associations of different types (Della Porta 2009c), *acampadas* are presented as spaces for the people. The main institution of *acampadas*, the general assembly, often held daily, testifies to a broadly inclusive effort. Assemblies have taken on a central role in the elaboration of strategic and tactical decisions for movements: from the creation of general programmes to the everyday management of camps. General assemblies often break down into commissions, which then reconvene with the spokespersons of various commissions appearing before the assemblies. In *acampadas* thousands of propositions on topics ranging from politics and economy to ecology and education have been put forward and in many cases approved by consensus (Della Porta and Mattoni 2014). In these movements, inclusion, absolute and of all, has been a main principle of the assemblies: 'The strength of this movement is that we are many and different . . . the spaces that make us strong, happy and active are those that everyone can perceive as her own' (for original text in Spanish, see Toma la Plaza 2011). The long-term occupations of squares thus create a new agora in publicly owned spaces, with assemblies mobilising not only activists but also local communities with handmade placards and individualised messages.

Another democratic innovation coming from the GJM and further elaborated in the *acampadas* is the consensual method. Several (but not all) organisations central to the social forum process have adopted consensual decision-making internally, but the method has been practised in different ways by different groups: in some cases pragmatically and aiming at reaching agreements, in others with the ambition of creating a community (Della Porta 2009a). In *acampadas*, collective thought is expected to emerge through inclusivity and respect for the opinions of all. Across Spain, consensual deliberative methods were proposed by young activists (Della Porta 2015; Della Porta and Mattoni 2014). While in previous movements direct democracy through consensus was experimented with in spokes councils, in *acampadas* it has been applied to the general assemblies, which may involve hundreds or thousands of people. According to Graeber (2013: 23), 'The process towards creative thinking is really the essence of the thing'. Deliberation through consensus is in fact seen as an instrument against bureaucratisation but also against the routinisation of the assembly and as a way to build community (Della Porta 2015).

Consensual decision-making in *acampadas* has integrated certain structures derived in part from the consensual processes devised by the GJM (Della Porta 2009b). Building upon those initial experiments, the *Indignados* in Spain further developed rules to better ensure equality and inclusivity. For example, regulations for assemblies have covered speaking time limits, hand gestures, rotating speakers, and the preparation of *compte rendus* (to be read at the next assembly meeting). A commission on conflicts, managed by students, used psychology and group dynamics techniques to improve participation and deliberation. Organisers also developed special techniques for assemblies; for example, participants were arranged in semicircles with corridors that allowed them to move around (Della Porta 2015; Della Porta and Mattoni 2014). Anyone could call for a working group; people then divided into small circles, coming back together after some time, with a speaker reporting on the debate in each group (Nez 2012). In Zuccotti Park in New York, instead of conducting up-or-down votes on more controversial proposals, groups worked to refine such proposals until universally accepted (Kauffmann 2011: 47).

Similar to social forums, *acampadas* are sites of contention but also of information exchange, reciprocal learning, individual socialisation, and knowledge building (Fritsch, O'Connor, and Thompson 2016). However, while engagement in consensus-oriented discussions is very important in the social forum process, emotions and prefiguration have been given a larger role in the construction of the commons in the *acampadas*. During forums as well as during their preparation–sometimes up to a year long–a crucial aim is the sharing of knowledge by activists from different countries, groups, ages, and so on. In this process, alternative visions are built about globalisation, Europeanisation, and the development of capitalism. Knowledge is exchanged mainly among activists, and in many cases exchanges have been facilitated by associations of various types.

In *acampadas*, the cognitive function is also central, but its production extends from activists to citizens. The oft-stated aim is building a community. While forums have been described as sorts of universities where abstract knowledge is embedded in specific contexts, *acampadas* have privileged the personal knowledge and experiences of individual participants. While forums privilege reason, emotions are more openly emphasised in *acampadas*, which are planned as places of talking and listening, where collective identities are constructed and sustained through the development of strong emotions. While the social forum process certainly favoured intense moments of transnational encounters, the stationary nature of *acampadas* helps build longer-lasting relations. The GJM chose summits as its targets, and 'summits are transient by their nature; they only last a week. That made us transient too. We'd appear, grab world headlines, then disappear' (van Gelder 2011: 46). In contrast, she noted, *acampadas* are in theory without a predefined end, and 'this is wise. Only when you stay put can you grow roots' (van Gelder 2011: 46). Open public spaces have in fact facilitated the creation of intense ties through encounters among diverse people who suddenly felt that they shared a common belonging. Both cognitive and affective mechanisms are embedded into networks of relations.

Spreading Ideas Into Institutions: Illustrations From Brazil and Iceland

Some of the democratic innovations mentioned above have been at the heart of institutional experiments that were inspired by principles of participation and deliberation. Besides engaging in internal practices of democratic innovation, social movements are also vehicles for transferring innovation to institutions, performing this role in a variety of ways and with different results.

This section introduces two cases of innovation in which social movements have played pivotal roles. The first one is a long-established, well-known case of successful governance innovation: Porto Alegre's participatory budgeting (PB). The second is the less well-known, shorter-lived Pots and Pans Revolution in Iceland, which triggered anti-austerity protests throughout the rest of Europe but, unlike PB, did not lead to change in governance. Nonetheless, the process, which had far-reaching effects on politics in Iceland, is particularly interesting from an innovation standpoint. In fact, the Pots and Pans Revolution gave birth to an unprecedented inclusive, direct process for reforming a core aspect of democratic governance: the country's constitution. Interestingly, the two case studies can be related to two successive waves of mobilisations. Porto Alegre is an illustration of GJM, while the mobilisations in Iceland can be related to the global movement against austerity.

Since beginning in the late 1980s, Porto Alegre's PB has provided a raw model for a long list of deliberative participatory experiments around the world, especially in Latin America and Europe, with different qualities in terms of participation, deliberation, and empowerment (Cabannes 2004; Ganuza and Baiocchi 2012; see also Pogrebinschi in this Report). Recognising its success, the United Nations has defined participatory budgeting as one of forty best practices at global level (Allegretti 2003: 173).

As a long-term experiment, Porto Alegre's PB has acquired an articulate and complex structure, oriented toward achieving two main objectives: social equality and citizen empowerment. Fundamental criteria in the distribution of public funds are the levels of well-being and of privatisation of public services in different neighbourhoods. The PB process is organised to overcome the limits of assemblies, in particular in terms of blocking decisions, without renouncing the advantages of direct democracy.

The PB model emphasises the participation of all citizens interested in determining decisions related to public expenditures. The process of PB in Porto Alegre involves up to 50,000 people per year and combines working groups and assemblies on various thematic policy areas and territorial sub-areas of the metropolitan city. PB managed up to 20 per cent of the city's annual budget, and about one third of requests presented by citizens were approved (Santos 1998: 493). Decisions made through the PB process are, however, implemented by the government administration. Various rules aim at increasing active and egalitarian participation and include rigorous and equal turns in speaking, election of delegates in proportion to the number of participants in public assemblies, and the fixed annual agenda of the main assemblies.

Citizens are encouraged to mobilise their neighbours 'because the more people that go to the meetings, the more likely they will be able to win the prioritizing vote that determines which neighbourhoods will benefit first' (Abers 2003: 206). Interestingly, the 'extremely competitive component' of PB 'gives it its vitality': 'if [PB] did not provide the prospective of providing returns to their specific needs or concerns, most people would not go to the meetings' (Abers 2003: 206). The local administration also offers incentives for participation in various ways. For instance, it hires activists and organisers from neighbourhood movements to help with organising the process, and city administrators have visited neighbourhoods where participation was particularly low (Abers 2003: 205). In Porto Alegre and in similar experiments in West Bengal and Kerala in India, this has brought about high rates of involvement by poorer, less educated citizens and by women (Baiocchi 2003a: 53).

Besides participation, deliberation also plays a role in the process. According to Baiocchi (2001), PB in Porto Alegre includes rules aimed at improving communication. Information about rules and procedures, specific budgeting skills, and mediation techniques to improve discussion quality as well as orient it to the achievement of collective goals are all taught during the process. Moreover, there is a didactic component embedded in meetings devoted to learning procedures as well as specific competencies related to budgeting and skills in debating and mobilising resources for collective goals.

A strong emphasis on the direct participation of regular citizens, resonating with the experiments in the *acampadas*, characterises the second case under examination, which stems from the turbulent events in Iceland following its 2008 banking system collapse and subsequent economic and financial downturn. By the second half of 2008, political protests had erupted against a government perceived as corrupt and incapable. Equipped with kitchenware and shouting chants, people took to protest in front of the Icelandic parliament, giving birth to the so-called Pots and Pans Revolution. The mobilisation that continued until January 2009 was an early manifestation of the global uprising against the neoliberal order (Júlíússon and Helgason 2013: 189). Meanwhile, in late January 2009 a left-wing coalition supporting constitutional change replaced the centre-right Independence Party and the Social Democratic Alliance's grand coalition government.

The ensuing constitutional reform process was highly participatory (crowdsourced). It started with a National Assembly in Reykjavik in November 2009. The deliberative and participatory one-day event was organised by the Anthill, a movement of grassroots organisations. The assembly hosted 1,500 people, among them ordinary citizens, politicians, and economic leaders, discussing the country's main values and the future of Iceland in the aftermath of the crisis. The event was a clear manifestation of the movement's demand for more grassroots politics to redress the fate of a country severely damaged by elite-driven policy choices. More generally, the Pots and Pans movement laid their claim to reshaping the very governance of the country (Blokker 2012; Burgess and Keating 2013: 424). The discussions of the National Assembly were made public in order to elicit public sphere debate and eventually laid the groundwork for constitutional reform.

Following this deliberative moment, in June 2010 the Icelandic parliament initiated a constitutional revision process. A constitutional committee then arranged a National Forum, conducted in November 2010 with 950 randomly selected citizens. Its goal was to develop general guidelines for the work of a to-be-elected Constitutional Assembly. After the election process of the Constitutional Assembly had been invalidated by the Icelandic Supreme Court, the government decided to appoint as members of a Constitutional Council those who had been elected through the contested vote (Landemore 2015: 169). The reform proposal developed by the Constitutional Council was then subjected to a consultative national referendum, the first in the history of the country. Even though turnout was not particularly high (slightly below 50 per cent), voters approved the proposal. However, the government eventually dismissed the proposal and its plans for constitutional reform due in part to the relatively low electoral turnout and opposition to a proposal drafted by a politically-appointed Constitutional Council, rather than a directly elected Constitutional Assembly. Moreover, were the government to have accepted the Council's proposal, the document would by law be subjected to another national referendum. An additional challenge was posed by the fact that a final decision on the proposal would have to be made by the parliament that would be in place only after upcoming elections (Blokker 2012; Landemore 2015).

As argued by Landemore (2015: 167), the failure to translate the proposal into a law should not lead one to overlook the fact that 'for the first time in human history, a country's foundational text (or at least a draft proposal for it) was written with the more or less direct participation of its people'. In fact, the most important aspect of the Icelandic constitutional reform lay in the way in which the process was carried out (Kriesi 2014a: 316). The proposal of constitutional change was drafted in an iterative process between the public at large and the Constitutional Council. The various drafts of the document were subjected to constant comments and feedback via social media (Bani 2012). The final document was eventually accepted with full consensus of all twenty-five members of the Council. The process was far from perfect but nonetheless it achieved inclusiveness to the extent that it promoted '(i) direct popular participation at various stages of the process, (ii) elements of descriptive representativeness where direct participation wasn't possible, and (iii) transparency' (Landemore 2015: 168). These aspects combined ensured not only formal procedural legitimacy but also 'some degree of epistemic reliability' (Landemore 2015: 168).

Social Movements and Democratic Innovation: Roles and Challenges

The cases of PB in Porto Alegre and the Pots and Pans Revolution in Iceland shed light on the roles that social movements play in incorporating democratic innovations in formal political processes and on the challenges they meet in their attempts to do so.

For one, the two case studies suggest that social movements have an important role in setting the democratic innovation agenda by demanding and envisioning new modes of political participation in governance. In the case of the process leading to the creation of PB in Porto Alegre, social movements were essential during the start-up phase. To begin with, the PB system was initially set up through collaboration between local government and movements (Koonings 2004: 83), a process characterised by disagreement and critical engagement, to be sure. As Ganuza and Baiocchi (2012: 3) noted, the PB model actually implemented by the Porto Alegre government differed substantially from the one proposed by movements in at least some respects and 'de-emphasized the role of existing associations and their leaders in favor of the individual citizen' (Ganuza and Baiocchi 2012: 3). Moreover, PB was conceived as 'an integral part' of a comprehensive and working administrative project, in an effort to combine collective action logic and administrative logic (Avritzer 2006: 627).

Two important corollaries follow. First, once a democratic innovation is introduced in governance processes, social movements are no longer 'privileged interlocutors to speak on behalf of the whole' (Ganuza and Baiocchi 2012: 4). Rather, they become but one of many voices involved in the process. Second, participation in such forms of democratic innovation 'is premised on accepting certain limits of the public debate, mainly based on administrative limits and schedule', which may be uncongenial to more radical movements (Ganuza and Baiocchi 2012: 6 f.).

In the Icelandic case, social movements effectively introduced democratic reform of the constitution into the country's political agenda. Within only a few months of the first protests, movements had managed to engage both Icelandic society and its political system in debates about constitutional change (Júlíússon and Helgason 2013: 201). As argued by Landemore (2015: 185) 'the deliberative, more controversial part of the process had to an extent taken place in the two years prior to the National Forum 2010, with the Pots and Pans Revolution and months of ruminating on the collapse of the economic system'. Indeed, social movements contribute to deliberative politics not only when they themselves are deliberative but also when, through non-deliberative behaviour, they are instrumental in promoting inclusive and effective societal debate on critical issues (Dryzek 2009). In the Pots and Pans Revolution, movements were crucial actors in bringing about the demand for change. However, in setting the stage for other groups, including institutions and the public at large, to join, movements started to lose their own central role in the process.

Both cases also suggest that social movements contribute to framing discourses on governance in markedly democratic terms. In the Brazilian case, social movements intended PB to be a means to adopt 'the concept of citizenship as a banner for improving democracy and using it to empower and benefit the poor and excluded popular masses' (Koonings 2004: 82). The presence of movements or active civil society organisations is key for avoiding that during PB processes 'participants will utilize political strategies of accommodation that reproduce traditional elite-mass relationship rather than contentious politics' (Wampler 2008: 69). Finally, the collaboration between government and social movements in PB effectively allows for the institutionalisation of a 'form of participatory democracy based on the associational tradition created by community movements' and 'the constitution of a more democratic political cal culture with strong pro-poor distributive effects' (Avritzer 2006: 634).

> *Social movements contribute to framing discourses on governance in markedly democratic terms.*

The Pots and Pans Revolution successfully framed the idea that more democratic governance should be achieved through substantial democratic processes in the first place and then provided practical support. In fact, the movements involved promoted the idea that a new start for Iceland was tied to what seemed lacking in the old model: democratic participation. Thus, social movements demanded that constitutional revisions for a more democratic constitution (Gylfason 2012) be achieved through a participatory and deliberative model (Blokker 2012; Burgess and Keating 2013: 425).

In both the Icelandic and the Brazilian cases, the democratic frames promoted by social movements underpin changes in governance processes. Nonetheless, as these processes unfold, the radical frame becomes but one of many contending frames that affect institutional procedures and the behaviour of political actors. The primacy of the democratic frame is thus far from granted.

Finally, social movements stand out as key providers of practical support to the implementation of democratic innovations. In the case of PB, social movements are important participants in these processes and influential partners in their implementation (Wampler 2000: 20). Social movements are among 'the carriers of the new values and the practitioners of new strategies' (Wampler and Avritzer 2004: 297). Pre-existing networks, including social movements, provide important support for implementing innovative processes like PB (Wampler 2000: 6). In fact, movements are not only instrumental in promoting greater participation, which gives PB more legitimacy, but their presence also positively contributes to the successful implementation of these processes. The successful democratic decentralisation that occurred with PB in Porto Alegre can be explained in terms of the synergy between local parties in power that were committed to bottom-up democracy-building and a rich network of active social movements and civil society organisations that were capable of mobilising the population (Heller 2001). Over time, movements involved in Porto Alegre's PB seem to have gained valuable experience not only in mastering the novelties of the process but also in coping with administrative and liberal democratic logics that collaboration with institutions involves.

With support from the Icelandic government, social movements were central in allowing the popular constitution-making process to occur. Social movements in particular played an important role in relation to citizens' assemblies and the process leading to the crowdsourced constitutional proposal. Without protesters starting and actively contributing to the process, the innovative Icelandic approach to constitutional change may not have occurred at all (Blokker 2012; Burgess and Keating 2013; Landemore 2015). The fact that the constitutional change never made it into law should not preclude appreciating the process and the role social movements played in it. At the same time, there are potential challenges that social movement innovation needs to address. In the Icelandic case in particular, the tension between administrative and liberal democratic logics on the one hand and more radical democratic views on the other seemed to accumulate during the process and eventually jeopardised its chances of success.

Conclusion

Addressing increasing democratic malaise is a core challenge for contemporary democratic societies. The critical role that social movements play in denouncing injustice and their efforts to redress, to some extent, endemic oppression and marginalisation is well known. In particular, social movements are important actors in articulating democratic malaise. They mobilise against perceived failures in the performance of governments, for instance, by protesting against markedly anti-egalitarian economic policies. Likewise, they denounce the deterioration of democratic politics. However, social movements' contributions to these efforts vary from case to case, as right-wing movements tend not to engage in or even to oppose these endeavours, supporting exclusionary policies instead.

> *Social movements are neither panacea nor irrelevant actors in the fight against the democratic deficits of contemporary societies.*

Besides expressing democratic malaise, social movements often, although certainly not always, contribute to democratic innovation. This is quite naturally not the case with social movements whose interest in democracy, if present at all, is restricted to compliance with minimal notions of democracy, rather than furthering democratisation. Pegida represents a good case in point, as its open advocacy for restriction of minority rights on racial or religious grounds arguably undermines, rather than innovates, the democratic project. Progressive social movements that are actually interested in and capable of democratic innovation participate in this endeavour in at least two ways: by promoting democratic engagement internally

DELLA PORTA *and* FELICETTI

and by innovating institutional governance. With respect to the former, a tendency to engage with innovative democratic practices is part and parcel of the repertoire of progressive social movements. This ability is connected to movements' substantial efforts to learn from the past, adopting a process of internal democratic innovation on a trial-and-error basis.

Social movements also contribute to democratic innovation at the institutional level. In this respect, movements can influence agenda-setting, affect the framing of innovations, and support their successful implementation. However, movements also encounter specific challenges at these different stages of the innovation process. In terms of agenda-setting, when interfacing with institutions, movements generally lose the centrality as agents of innovation that they usually enjoy in the public sphere. Within institutions, social movements have to collaborate and compete with other powerful actors determining the institutional agenda. This complex relationship affects also the way in which innovations are developed, with movements struggling to promote their own innovation discourse vis-à-vis that of more traditional actors. Finally, the adoption of social movement-led innovation depends on the ability of movements to win electoral contests, which, in a representative government, is usually necessary to transform innovation proposals into binding laws (for exceptions, see Pogrebinschi in this Report). Even when a proposal for a democratic innovation attains the necessary level of support, challenges are not over. In fact, successful implementation of democratic innovations usually demands that social movements accept and are able to engage with public agencies whose actions may be rooted in an administrative logic that is distant from that of social movements.

Overall, the success of movements in promoting radical democratic values and practices in the context of liberal democratic systems is far from guaranteed. Yet, as this chapter has shown, it is possible to achieve this objective, and social movements play a greater role in democratic innovation than one may think.

The attitudes of policy-makers may be key for enhancing the ability of movements to fight against democratic malaise by innovating conceptions and practices of democracy. This implies two important endeavours on the part of policy-makers. The first is the need to recognise that superficial or standardised reactions to social movements need to be replaced by selective attitudes. Movements are neither panacea nor irrelevant actors in the fight against the democratic deficits of contemporary societies. Policy-makers should first consider the goals and practices of different movements as indicators of their worthiness as agents of democratisation and should then relate to them accordingly. Second, policy-makers need to acknowledge that in engaging with institutions, even actors genuinely interested in and potentially capable of innovating democracy face substantial challenges. Policy-makers' abilities to establish positive and supportive attitudes towards social movements do not only mean the difference between successful and unsuccessful attempts to innovate democracy. Openness on the part of policy-makers also represents a formidable way to unite actors interested in democratisation in order to counter threats that endanger the pursuit of a more substantial democracy.

Endnotes

1   Groups that are part of this global movement go by various names in different countries, such as alter-globalisation, 'no global' or new global, global justice, Globalisierungskritiker, and altermondistes (Della Porta 2007; Della Porta and Rucht 2013: 7 f.).

X. Innovations in Activism in the Digital Era
Campaigning for Refugee Rights in 2015-16

NINA HALL

New digital technologies offer citizens, interest groups, and political parties innovative ways to communicate, mobilise, and organise. The internet has heralded many innovations in collective action, from online petitions to viral memes and Twitterstorms. Digital organising and campaigning can have far-reaching effects in a world with over 10 billion devices connected to the internet and where 1 billion people own smartphones (Kissinger 2014). However, commentators are divided over the significance and impact of digital communications on democracy. It is not clear whether the internet has enabled greater and more informed political awareness and participation or whether it degrades political culture by encouraging so-called slacktivism and clicktivism. These are particularly important questions given the loss in confidence in established political parties and the growing strength of populist parties and far-right movements in many western democracies, as Anheier's introduction to this Report highlights.

> *Digital organising and campaigning can have far-reaching effects.*

Some have argued that the internet has degraded political culture by diverting attention and action towards tasks that have little sustained or long-term impact. For these critics the internet has not profoundly changed political action but rather created an illusion of effectual political interventions (see Merkel in this Report). This is problematic for democratic participation as many citizens, particularly those in younger generations, may channel political action into Facebook and Twitter rather than taking action on the streets or through other established forms of lobbying and advocacy. In this view, the internet encourages clicktivism, as opposed to contributing to transformative change or addressing democratic deficiencies (Gladwell 2010; White 2010).

In contrast, others have pointed to the speed, ease, and low cost of communication in the digital era (Shirky 2008). They have emphasised the role of the internet in the Arab Spring, the Occupy movement in the United States, and the *Indignados* protests in Spain (Gerbaudo 2012). Individuals use digital technologies to connect with others, share information, and mobilise, and in doing so they can trigger pivotal political changes (Margetts et al. 2016). Proponents of this view see digital technologies as transformative and addressing many problems in democracies, such as by enabling greater political awareness and participation in western democracies or by pushing for democratic reforms in less democratically consolidated countries. However, this perspective tends to focus on how individuals use the internet and overlooks the importance of formal organisations to sustain social movements (Bimber, Flanagin, and Stohl 2012).

In fact, there are critical shifts occurring in advocacy organisations in the internet era. We now have new, permanent advocacy groups that use the internet to mobilise and lobby for economic, political, and/or social change (Hall and Ireland 2016). This chapter examines the role and contribution of new online advocacy organisations in western democracies. It focusses on groups that identify as progressive and that aim to counter populism and foster democratic participation and political awareness. These groups use online and offline methods to mobilise large membership bases at opportune moments and to drive progressive change (Karpf 2013). However, it is worth noting that also populist movements have used digital media to organise and influence political debate. In the US, new alt-right groups used social media extremely effectively to spread misinformation in their support of President Donald Trump's 2016 election campaign. They were 'shockingly effective' at identifying memes–hashtags, images, video clips, and other media that go viral–to influence mainstream news and undermine Hillary Clinton's campaign (Marantz 2016). The advantage of online organising is that a small group of individuals– even just one person–can without any editorial interference reach thousands more people than the mainstream media can. In short, digital technologies are used by many different groups, from terrorists to populists and from progressives to conservatives, to spread their messages. The focus here is on advocacy organisations that use digital technologies to push for progressive change.

In the last twenty years we have seen the emergence of a distinctive, new, and innovative model of digital advocacy organisation. These groups campaign on a range of issues, from the environment to LGBTQ rights, and their memberships can number in the thousands if not millions. This model exists in many different countries, from the US (MoveOn), the United Kingdom (38 Degrees), and Australia (GetUp!) to Canada, South Africa, New Zealand, Poland, Sweden, Switzerland, Italy, and Romania. Unlike hashtags and digitally empowered social movements such as Black Lives Matter or Occupy Wall Street, these are permanent organisations with professional campaigning staff. Furthermore, they are not simply online petition platforms such as change.org, as their campaigns extend beyond the internet. They may also be on the streets demonstrating.

These advocacy groups all share an organisation model: they are independent, grassroots or netroots, member-driven, and member-funded organisations. They are distinguished from earlier forms of political organisation by their digital campaigning tools and by their organisational structures and strategies. Traditional advocacy organisations were based around a common identity such as women or senior citizens or around single issues, for example Greenpeace and the environment or Amnesty International and human rights. These new digital-based advocacy groups work across many issue areas simultaneously, and their mode of activism differs. Whereas traditional non-governmental organisations (NGOs) often work tirelessly on single issues, trying to reframe public debate and put their issues on the political agenda, these new groups look for key tipping points, when there is public attention around a particular issue, and then seek to galvanise public opinion to shift decision-makers. Their strength is in identifying these moments and responding rapidly with campaigns–often launched on the same day–to leverage these windows of opportunity. They are not agenda-setting organisations but rather specialise in rapid-response campaigning. This model has been reported to perform exceptionally well in terms of 'impact and force implication', as organisations with relatively few resources can engage supporter bases for sustained periods of time and have 'achieved some degree of policy and cultural change' (Mogus and Liacas 2016: 5). In addition, many of these new advocacy organisations belong to a common international network, the Online Progressive Engagement Network (OPEN), and meet on a regular basis to share tactics and strategies.

This chapter examines five advocacy campaigns in the UK, Ireland, Australia, Germany, and Austria and how they have used online and offline tactics to campaign for refugee rights. One of the few comparative studies of digital-based, multi-issue advocacy organisations, it draws on publicly available information from websites, social media, and mainstream media as well as interviews with lead campaigners in several digital advocacy organisations, staff in refugee and migrant civil society organisations, and journalists and independent experts with knowledge on migration and refugee policy in their countries.[1] This study is a unique global comparison of how digital-based activist organisations worked on refugee rights in 2015 and 2016 in an increasingly polarised political context and contributes to a growing body of literature highlighting the continued importance of organisations for collective organising and mobilising in the digital era (Han 2014; Karpf 2012, 2016)[2].

Studying refugee advocacy in 2015-16 is particularly important, as the supposed refugee crisis has challenged democratically elected political elites across the world. Although the majority of refugees live in developing countries, the crisis is often framed as a European one (McCormick 2016). The increase in refugees worldwide comes at a time of growing populism that draws on xenophobic sentiments and advances anti-immigration and anti-refugee rhetoric and policies across many western democracies. In June 2016 the UK made the radical decision by referendum to leave the European Union, a decision partly motivated by public concerns about immigration. In

November 2016 Donald Trump was elected the next US president after having campaigned for strong anti-immigration policy. Earlier the same year the Alternative für Deutschland (AfD) won a large proportion of votes–around 20 per cent–in many state elections in Germany. In Austria the far-right presidential candidate successfully challenged the results of the May 2016 election so that Austrians had to return to the polls for an unprecedented second presidential election in December 2016, which was ultimately won by the moderate candidate. In a context of highly contentious and nationalistic politics, it is important to understand how and in what ways digital-based advocacy groups have mobilised in support of refugees. This chapter asks: what did these activist organisations do to promote refugee access and rights? And were their interventions merely clicktivism, or did they in some way strengthen democracy and democratic participation?

Refugee Advocacy in 2015-16

In late August and early September 2015 there was a global tipping point on refugee issues. On 24 August German Chancellor Angela Merkel announced she would open the country's borders and disregard the EU's Dublin asylum system whereby refugees were required to register in their first country of arrival. Then on 2 September a Syrian toddler named Alan Kurdi drowned while attempting to cross from Turkey to Greece with his family. A photo of his body washed up on the shore featured on newspaper front pages and social media forums around the world. Public opinion shifted dramatically at this time: people were appalled by the loss of life, and even tabloids that had been anti-immigrant featured sympathetic coverage of the event. In fact, a number of campaigners and experts interviewed for this chapter referred to this tipping point as the 'Alan Kurdi moment'. Governments in Europe and beyond were forced to reconsider their policies and faced a hard question: how many refugees were they willing to accept? This section focuses on advocacy campaigns in five countries, especially during the September 2015 period, on the actions taken by advocacy organisations, and on outcomes.

The UK and 38 Degrees

After Merkel's decision to open Germany's borders, then-Prime Minister David Cameron was adamant that the UK would not accept any more refugees. Within twenty-four hours of the images of Alan Kurdi having surfaced, Cameron acknowledged that he was 'deeply moved' but gave no indication of any new UK policies to take in more refugees (Dathan 2015). All the major newspapers had covered the story, and the tabloid *Daily Mail* ran an unusually sympathetic story towards refugees, headlined 'The final journey of tragic little boys washed up on a Turkish beach: Mother and sons who died in sea tragedy are taken from morgue after heartbroken father says goodbye to the family he couldn't save' (Stanton et al. 2015).

The morning of 3 September 2015, immediately after the Kurdi story had broken, 38 Degrees called a special meeting and launched a rapid campaign to put pressure on Cameron to shift his position. They initiated petitions under the slogan 'Refugees Welcome' that stated: 'We don't want Britain to be the kind of country that turns its back as people drown in their desperation to flee places like Syria' (38 Degrees 2016). 38 Degrees asked people to start their own petitions to demand that local councils accept more refugees. Six hundred and thirty-three local campaigns were launched across the UK, from the Scottish highlands to Norwich and Oxford, and gathered over 137,000 signatures. These petitions also led to the formation of local refugee welcome action groups and resulted in more than 78,000 emails sent to members of Parliament and thousands of phone calls. On 7 September Cameron announced that the UK would accept 20,000 Syrian refugees over the next four to five years. This was a dramatic shift in position, and although it cannot be attributed solely to the work of 38 Degrees, they were able to launch at a rapid pace and mobilise thousands at breathtaking speed.

The work of 38 Degrees went beyond an online petition. Their members (anyone on their email list) raised more than 300,000 British pounds for refugee causes such as refugee assistance packs for new arrivals to the UK. The organisation also played a role in bringing together UK NGOs and civil society organisations to provide the practical support councils and communities needed to resettle refugees. They used crowdsourcing to create the National Refugee Welcome Board, a national, independent coordination entity, and enabled it to start operating. In addition, 38 Degrees worked with partners to send lawyers to Calais, France to file cases on behalf of refugee children in order to bring them safely to the UK. Thus the work of 38 Degrees went beyond simply initiating an online petition: they raised funds, supported the establishment of a new national entity, and worked with others in the refugee sector to directly support refugees.

Ireland and Uplift

Ireland was insulated from the large increase in refugees entering Europe, largely due to its location and its opt-out from the European resettlement plan. In late August 2015 Uplift's director, Siobhan Donoghue, began receiving messages from members stating that they wanted the government to do more and that they would be happy to offer rooms to refugees. Motivated by these members' concerns, Donoghue decided to launch an online petition in solidarity with refugees just a day before the Alan Kurdi story broke and Uplift received 38,500 signatures. After the Kurdi story, the Pledge a Bed petition was launched, and 14,000 beds were pledged–remarkable given that the total population of Ireland is just 4.5 million and that Uplift had only one permanent staff member and a volunteer working. The mainstream media covered the success of the petition, and the government had to respond to the Irish people's pledges to house refugees.

Uplift, working with other refugee advocacy groups, also organised vigils around Ireland in solidarity with refugees. As Donoghue explained in an interview with the author: 'One member encouraged me to create a physical space, as it was important to give people a space to connect with others.' They held vigils all around the country, from small towns in West Clare to Dublin, where over 1,000 people encircled the river Liffey holding hands. Other refugee organisations through the Refugee Migration Coalition also held vigils and escalated pressure on the government. Finally, on 10 September 2015, Taoiseach (Irish Prime Minister) Enda Kenny announced that he would extend protection to 4,000 refugees, up from 600, by the end of 2017 under the EU resettlement and relocation programme.

Uplift's campaign is not the only explanation for this change in decision, but it was an important part of the civil society movement. Furthermore, the government decided to enlist the public's pledges of support, many of which were made through Uplift. The Irish Red Cross was officially appointed to manage pledges on the government's behalf and has followed up with individuals to check if they are still willing to host refugees and for how long and even to check their housing conditions. This is an unusual example of the government inheriting a public online petition with at least the stated intention of delivering on its promises. However, in December 2015 a coalition of refugee and migration advocates criticised the Irish government for 'not living up to the commitments made after considerable pressure from the Irish public to respond proactively to this situation' (Refugee Migrant Coalition 2015). As of July 2016 the Irish government had taken on 273 refugees, and many Irish pledgers were still waiting to host. As one Irish Red Cross staff member explained, the government's resettlement plan had been slowed down by delays in refugee processing in Greece and Italy.

Australia and GetUp!

Although Australia is far away from Europe and has a long history of anti-refugee policies, it was also touched by the Alan Kurdi moment. Immediately after Kurdi's death, over twenty refugee advocate organisations including GetUp! established the Light the Dark campaign to 'send a message to the world that Australians Say Welcome' to refugees (GetUp! 2015). A call went out to rally around the hashtags #refugeeswelcome and #LightTheDark and to lobby the government to accept more Syrian refugees. They targeted then-Prime Minister Tony Abbott, who stated on 6 September that Australia would not increase its overall refugee quota. From Monday 7 September vigils were held in all the major cities, and over 10,000 people across Australia attended. On 9 September, Abbott declared that Australia would welcome an extra 12,000 Syrian and Iraqi refugees under pressure from politicians at the state and national levels and from the public.

This was a significant shift in the space of a week. As Daniel Webb, Director of Legal Advocacy at the Australian based Human Rights Center, explained to the author, Abbott 'was left with little choice, such was the public outcry. In just about every other moment, there's been more political capital in cruelty than compassion . . . but in that moment the political dynamic changed.' However, it is difficult to attribute the decision solely to GetUp! or the Light the Dark campaign: 'I don't think that the Abbott government listens particularly to those campaigns. . . . The government saw . . . a growing global expectation that Australia would do something given how big the need was. I don't know that he was particularly moved by Light the Dark', as Ben Doherty, an Australian journalist working for *The Guardian*, explained in an interview.

In February 2016, however, GetUp! in coalition with several refugee advocacy organisations did indeed have a significant impact on public opinion and government policy. They ran a campaign called Let them Stay to ensure that 267 asylum seekers (including thirty-three babies) could remain in Australia, where they were at the time for medical care, instead of being returned to offshore detention centres in Nauru or Manus Island. The detention centres are part of Operation Sovereign Borders, a broad strategy to stop asylum seekers from reaching mainland Australia by fiercely patrolling the northern sea border with Indonesia, forcing boats to turn back, and putting asylum seekers in offshore detention camps. Human rights experts, psychologists, and doctors have documented the horrific conditions in the detention centres where many asylum seekers have been abused or committed self-harm (Farrell, Evershed, and Davidson 2016). The campaign resulted from a court case against the Australian government that had been handled on behalf of the asylum seekers by Daniel Webb at the Human Rights Law Centre. When the case looked as if it might fail, Webb approached GetUp!, as, in his words, 'they're a formidable campaign machine'.

GetUp! and its partners—the Human Rights Law Centre, the National Council of Churches Australia, and the Darwin Asylum Seeker Support and Advocacy Network—made front-page news in the major Australian newspapers with photos of the babies who were going to be forced back into detention. They sought to win over the public by highlighting how refugees were much like locals: they featured stories of the refugees, their jobs, music tastes, and hobbies. The core campaign group worked closely with the broader refugee sector, lobbied politicians, and formed a broad-based movement of churches, medical practitioners, and teachers who called for

the government to #LetThemStay. For several weeks the campaign continued to headline news reports, with politicians and many members of civil
society coming out in support. Thousands attended protests. The campaign
culminated in a dramatic stand-off between guards and doctors at Lady
Cilento Children's Hospital in South Brisbane. The doctors refused to release
a one-year-old girl, dubbed Baby Asha, into the hands of the Australian government and were supported by protestors outside. The government was
finally forced to back down and allow all the asylum seekers to stay. This was
a remarkable turnaround, given the Australian government's intransigence
on refugee policy. However it was only a partial victory: the government
reserved the right to deport the asylum seekers with 72 hours' notice and on
26 July 2016 deported a Sudanese man to Christmas Island.

Germany and Campact

Campact in Germany was faced with a different political situation at the Alan
Kurdi moment. Merkel, driven in part by humanitarian motives, had opened
the country's borders in late August. Thousands of refugees arrived in Germany and were welcomed with open arms at the Munich main train station.
There was a strong *Willkommenskultur* in Germany, where thousands of
small civil society initiatives emerged across the country and where people
offered refugees a home, a bed, a dinner, or legal assistance. Thus advocacy
needs were very different from other countries: refugees needed assistance
in Germany, not entrance to Germany. Campact was part of a broad wave
of civil society refugee initiatives: in October 2015, they launched *Das Will-
kommensnetz*, an online platform to connect interested people with refugee-
related volunteering opportunities.

Public sentiment towards refugees shifted on New Year's Eve 2015. Several migrants were arrested in Cologne and other cities for sexually harass-
ing women in public places. Although it was not immediately clear to the
public if the migrants were newly arrived refugees, the alleged incidents
provided fuel for those arguing that Germany should not welcome so many
refugees, particularly Muslims who had different views on women's rights.
In an immediate response, Avaaz, another international digital-based advocacy group, launched an online petition and video showing refugees giving
German women roses to illustrate that not all refugees were sexual abusers
with problematic views of women. Following the Cologne attacks, political
support for the AfD grew, and the party won a significant proportion of seats
in many state parliaments during 2016. The AfD argued that 'Islam does not
belong in Germany', and a survey conducted in May 2016 suggested that this
view was supported by 60 per cent of Germans (Brady 2016).[3]

In early 2016, Campact worked with Amnesty International, Pro Asyl,
NaturFreunde, Oxfam, and other NGOs to hold a national action day against

racism. On Sunday 19 June they organised human chains in several major cities (Berlin, Munich, Leipzig, and Hamburg) and in many other smaller cities where thousands held hands to protest 'against racism, for human rights and diversity' (Nienaber 2016). Campact's refugee campaigns, like the others examined here, illustrate a combination of offline and online activism, and they have worked closely with other advocacy groups. However, Campact's policy or legislative successes are more difficult to identify: this is partly because there were no clear easy wins in Germany in contrast with the UK, Australia, or Ireland. In addition, much of Campact's campaigning energy and attention focused on stopping the EU-Canada and EU-US free trade agreements during 2015 and 2016.

Austria and #aufstehn

#aufstehn (stand up) launched an email action in late July 2015 directly targeting mayors to encourage them to welcome refugees before the German or Austrian borders had been opened to refugees and the Dublin protocol suspended. Many refugees had arrived in Austria over the summer and were facing overcrowded camps without enough food or adequate sanitation. #aufstehn launched a campaign to show the government that there was good will and sufficient space in Austria for refugees. Executive Director Maria Mayrhofer explained in an interview with the author that the government was shifting the responsibility at the time: 'The national government said that the province governments should take care of it, and the province governments said the mayors should take care of it.' #aufstehn argued that there were over 2,100 townships and municipalities in Austria and enough space to provide housing. They set up an email protest with the call *'In unserer Gemeinde ist Platz!'* (In our community there is space!) and urged for *'Zimmerstattzäune'* (rooms instead of fences). #aufstehn initially asked 2,000 people to join the campaign through social media and email, and almost 4,000 people wrote to their mayors encouraging them to welcome refugees in their town or city. #aufstehn reported that working at the local level was effective, as people had greater contact with their local mayors, and many mayors who were already considering housing more refugees were 'relieved that people were backing them', while some others 'were convinced by people writing to them', as stated by Mayrhofer. In fact, #aufstehn found that there was a strong correlation between places from where people sent letters and places where the intake of refugees was subsequently raised. Another asylum NGO, SOS Mitmensch, acknowledged that it is difficult to identify and attribute the impact of this campaign but that in the European summer of 2015 only one-third of communities in Austria had housed refugees, compared to over three-quarters in the summer of 2016.

Austria's border control and refugee policies shifted in August in response to the increasing number of refugees and to Merkel's decision to open Germany's borders. On 27 September 2015, seventy-one migrants were found dead in the back of an unventilated food truck near Vienna, and the government began inspections of vehicles attempting to cross the border with Hungary. In coordination with Germany, on 4 September the government announced that migrants would be allowed to cross the border from Hungary into Austria and onward into Germany. However, in December the Austrian government started to build a fence on the Slovenian border as part of a new border management system. On 17 January 2016 the government announced it would further extend border controls and repel even those refugees who did not intend to ask for asylum in Austria, in other words those seeking to enter Germany through Austria.

On 11 March, in response to these increasingly restrictive policies, #aufstehn launched the campaign *Anstand statt Notstand!* (Decency not emergency!).[4] The campaign showed two images comparing Austrian streets to a refugee camp and asked people to 'call on the Austrian government to, instead of creating an artificial state of emergency, finally act with decency and reason regarding the refugee issue' (#aufstehn 2016). More than 11,000 people signed this petition, and #aufstehn estimates that it reached over 230,000 people. However, they and other asylum and refugee organisations did not manage to stop the government, and on 27 April then-Chancellor Werner Faymann declared a state of emergency in Austria due to the refugee crisis. This came directly after the far-right candidate from the Freedom Party of Austria had won the first round of the presidential election. The situation continues to evolve, and #aufstehn has been involved in demonstrations, media appearances, and press conferences pressuring the government not to declare another emergency.

Innovations in Activism

How innovative were these campaigns? And what impact did they have on political awareness, participation, and refugee rights? Most of the campaigns were rapid responses that took advantage of a particular window of opportunity: the Alan Kurdi moment. Campaigns were launched within a matter of hours to encourage citizens to pledge a bed (in Ireland, UK, and Austria) and/or lobby the government to increase the refugee intake (in the UK and Australia). Organisations with extremely small numbers of staff were able to mobilise thousands of people and capture significant media and political attention. The fast pace of campaigning, combined with low transaction and organising costs, is one of the remarkable features of advocacy based on email, online petitions, and social media (Mogus and Liacas 2016). All of these campaigns were able to quickly scale up and have an impact at a moment of high public interest.

Furthermore, what is remarkable is the range of online and offline tactics these organisations used, summarised in Table 10.1. Some organisations (in the UK and Austria) used online petitions to directly target councillors and mayors. These campaigns had an impact on refugee rights because they targeted local politicians, who tend to receive less lobbying attention than members of national parliaments. In addition, activists in Austria reported that citizens are in close, direct personal contact with mayors in some towns, which complemented online petitions. Digital-based campaigning allows for the diffusion and decentralisation of campaigns at much greater ease and lower cost and is often more effective when reinforced with face-to-face action.

In fact, all of these campaigns went beyond the digital sphere. Many of the activist groups got people on the streets by holding vigils (in Australia, Germany, and Ireland). They worked with established refugee advocacy organisations and sought mainstream media coverage. Scholars who view digital activism as purely clicktivism miss how these groups combine offline and online tactics in a highly sophisticated style to increase and enrich political debate and participation.

There were also notable differences in the campaigns. Some groups (GetUp!) had more strategised, planned campaigns, while others followed the rapid mode of campaigning, reacting to a change in political opportunity structures. Some groups (38 Degrees) had more sophisticated technologies and were thus able to launch distributed petitions, while others did not have this technology. The ability to capture mainstream media attention also differed: GetUp! ran targeted advertisements and made front-page news for several days in a row in February 2016. What is significant is that these digital-based advocacy groups combined offline and online tactics, mainstream media, and social media to lobby for refugee rights and increase political awareness and participation on this issue.

In several cases, campaigns for increasing refugee numbers were at least partially victorious. Conservative governments in Australia and the UK and the Irish Labour-Fine Gael government pledged to welcome more refugees. It is difficult and beyond the scope of this chapter to attribute these initial victories to each organisation's campaigns. Firstly, there were many other advocacy groups pressuring these governments to welcome more refugees. Secondly, there was a broad shift of public opinion fuelled by the Alan Kurdi story and by global developments including Merkel's decision, which may have paved the way for other conservative leaders, especially in Australia, to make similar decisions. It is also possible that Cameron's decision in the UK swayed Abbott in Australia.

However, in many cases governments have not fulfilled their pledges (in Ireland and the UK), and/or have seen the continuation of anti-refugee policies (in Australia and Austria). Meanwhile in Germany, Merkel has stood strongly behind her decision to open the country's borders but has also pub-

Table 10.1 **Examples of tactics used by digital-based advocacy organisations**

	38 Degrees (UK)	Uplift (Ireland)	GetUp! (Australia)	Campact (Germany)	#aufstehn (Austria)
Organisation (country)					
Tactics					
Online petitions (local)	●				●
Online petitions (national)	●	●	●		
Social media campaigns	●	●	●		●
Creation of volunteering network platform				●	
Targeted mainstream media campaign			●		
Vigils and demonstrations		●	●	●	●
Material support (assistance packs for new arrivals)	●				
Crowdsourcing and institution building (National Refugee Welcome Board)	●				

licly acknowledged that this position resulted in losing votes to the AfD. This highlights the importance of campaigning over a sustained period of time for refugee rights and access. Otherwise, governments can make pledges but never deliver. In fact, one major shortcoming of multi-issue, rapid-response advocacy groups is that they often quickly shift attention to other issues and do not follow up to ensure their victories are adequately implemented. Another limitation is that these groups generally do not have expertise on the issues on which they campaign but rely on other organisations for this. Another weakness of this member-driven advocacy model is that it may be prone to populist tendencies and the tyranny of the majority. For instance, some groups were more reactive to their members' preferences and stuck with their refugee campaigns only as long as there was member interest. If members do not respond to an email or petition to 'welcome refugees', these organisations may choose to shelve their campaigns. In some cases professional campaigning staff will override group members and decide to run a campaign even in the face of membership apathy. How they decide which issues to campaign on and how they decide when to drop campaigns are crucial for assessing their ability to counter populist tendencies.

Further investigation should examine the contribution of these advocacy organisations within their national civil society and political contexts. Some groups were more embedded in the refugee and migrant advocacy movement than others. For instance, Uplift's director, Siobhan Donoghue, had previously been the director of the Migrant Rights Centre, and GetUp! worked closely with others in the refugee sector, particularly the Human Rights Law Centre and Darwin Asylum Seeker Support and Advocacy Network. There were also important differences in national political contexts that influenced what groups could campaign on and achieve. Many of the countries (except Ireland) had conservative governments that were traditionally unsympathetic to calls for increasing access for refugees or migrants. The situation was very different in Austria and in Germany, given the large number of migrants and refugees that had arrived overland in the summer of 2015 and Merkel's open-border policy in Germany, which contrasted with Austria's declaration of a state of emergency. The success of digital advocacy organisations is determined in part by how closely they work with other refugee advocacy organisations and by who holds political power.

Conclusion

The utility of new digital technologies for mobilising citizens is now well-established. However, the effect of these new tools is still being debated. A common concern is that online petitions and social media fuel clicktivism. Meanwhile, others point to the transformative power of digital technology for connecting individuals in non-hierarchical ways and with low transaction costs.

We should examine how digital technology is used by this new generation of activist organisations, born in the digital era and using online and offline technologies to campaign, that have led innovative campaigns on refugee rights and have contributed to important victories for refugee access in many cases. These victories cannot be solely attributed to any single organisation, as these organisations worked in partnership with existing civil society movements. Rather, new digital-based organisations have a particular niche: at a key tipping point, they mobilised thousands to pledge solidarity with refugees. They did this through rapid, reactive campaigning: seizing a window of opportunity after the Alan Kurdi moment and mobilising through mass emails, online petitions, and pledges to 'host a refugee' or 'offer a bed'. These were conducted alongside street action—vigils (in Australia and Ireland) and solidarity demonstrations (in Germany). In summary, scholars and practitioners interested in democratic innovations should pay greater attention not just to the new tools of organising but the new structures of organising. These groups are just the tip of an iceberg of new innovative activist organisations that use digital technologies.

More broadly, the rise of digital communication can enrich democratic participation and public debate. This is particularly true when internet technologies are used to complement conventional, offline methods of organising that bring people face-to-face. In fact, many well-established NGOs such as Greenpeace and Amnesty International are increasingly using digital platforms to campaign. Civil society organisations should look at whether and how they can employ digital tactics and/or partner with digitally savvy organisations to expand their outreach and spread their messages. However, digital technologies are also being used by populist movements, terrorists, and the alt-right to further their causes. To understand the internet's impact on democracy we must examine who is using new digital platforms, for what purposes, and how. Social media platforms, particularly Facebook and Twitter, have great power in today's democracies to create the news. Facebook determines what content is shared and viewed, yet we have surprisingly little knowledge about how these decisions are made. Chancellor Merkel recently argued that 'algorithms, when they are not transparent can lead to a distortion of our perception, they can shrink our expanse of information' (Connolly 2016). Governments should pressure social media companies and internet search engines to be transparent about the algorithms that they use and should ensure that digital platforms enrich and inform public debate and do not undermine it.

Endnotes

1   Other scholars have examined individual activist organisations within their national contexts but have not compared organisations within the OPEN network (see for instance Karpf 2016).

2   These latter scholars note the advantages of digital technologies for mobilising but also see their limitations: organisations must still 'organise' and develop their members' abilities and not just 'mobilise' them to take action (Han 2014). They offer more fruitful avenues for inquiry by examining if and how organisations use the internet to mobilise.

3   This stands in contrast with 49 per cent supporting the view that 'Islam does belong in Germany' in 2010, which had been declared by then-President Christian Wulff (Wagener 2010).

4   Note that #aufstehn also ran a number of other refugee rights campaigns, which are not detailed in this chapter due to space limitations.

XI. Democracy and Innovations
A Conceptual Toolbox

CLAUS OFFE

The analyses and cases presented and the issues raised in this Report suggest a number of analytical variables. Taking them together and adding a few additional ones, we accumulate a rich and complex tableau of design options for democratic innovations and reminders of their limitations.

Innovations by design versus novelties by evolution. Interestingly, the term 'innovation' is not used by Report authors entirely consistently. Its use oscillates between, on one hand, an empirical account of novel phenomena that seem to result from evolutionary processes taking place in a polity or region under analysis and, on the other hand, explicit proposals for institutional change that authors advocate, endorse, or reject on the basis of some more or less explicit normative argument. This raises basic questions concerning the malleability versus path dependency of democratic institutions and the role of perceived crisis as a trigger of innovative institutional design.

Counter-democracy as means to protect democracy from populist assault? In his chapter, Smilov addresses the phenomenon in which depoliticised and fiduciary institutions can and do strengthen the quality of democracy, not just in Eastern Europe. Independent courts and judicial structures such as the Romanian anti-corruption prosecutorial office mentioned in Smilov's chapter, central banks, regulators, watchdog non-governmental organisations (NGOs), the Venice Commission and other expert councils, and the European Commission as well as the Council of Europe can perform an important role as effective supervisors of democratic integrity (and are typically antagonised by populist leaders). Referendums, the (allegedly) most democratic method, permit doubt as to their authenticity as the referendum process is typically initiated by political party strategists.

Universal citizen participation versus sortition. Must the number of citizens turning out in elections be maximised, or is there a role for randomly selected bodies, such as juries or jury pools in courts of law? Smilov effectively demolishes the 'noble fiction' of the 'citizen ready to contribute time, resources, and efforts' while putting public interest ahead of self-interest. This overdrawn picture of citizenship can only breed cynicism, he argues, suggesting instead participatory mechanisms, now widely discussed and advocated (for example, by van Reybrouck 2016) and which revive ancient and Renaissance methods of statistical representation by lottery.

Fairness versus discriminatory bias in elections. The extended chain of causation that turns citizens into voters, votes into seats in legislative assemblies or/and winners of presidential elections, and winning (coalition) governments into acts and programmes that affect citizens is well known to be full of all kinds of intervening variables, distortions, and biases of both an institutional and factual nature. Most of them are subtler than simple fraud and forgery. Social class is a widely documented determinant of both voter turnout and campaign finance. Kuo's chapter focuses on the peculiar case of elections in the United States, where the access of citizens to the polls is partly restricted by statutory identification, registration, residence, and clean criminal record requirements, and where the drawing of electoral district boundaries is under the strategic control of competing political parties. These deficiencies can be–and are partly being–healed by rather obvious revisions of institutional rules.

Remedies enhancing the fairness of the electoral process are less obvious when it comes to electoral systems (majority versus proportionality), the structure and functions assigned to political parties by constitutional and statutory law, political finance, and the role of (public, private, and social) media. Proposals for innovations concerning these institutional parameters of elections are not extensively addressed in the chapters of this Report. This may be due to the fact that many of these parameters appear to be written in stone in existing democracies and thus hard to change. At least there is some plausibility supporting the hypothesis of strong path dependency: once you have a majoritarian electoral system, the shift to proportionality is almost as unlikely to occur as a shift from unitary government to federalism; innovative change in the opposite direction is much easier to envision. In these and other cases, innovation appears to be at best unidirectional.

Formation versus expression of preferences. Before citizens can cast their votes or engage in other ways of supporting or opposing political forces and their policies, they must find out what it is they want to achieve or promote by doing so. Preferences are not given but formed; once formed, they need not be stable. All people like to think that their preferences are supported by good reasons, yet forming preferences in political and economic life is made difficult by the fact that all people are virtually 'multiple selves'. People are cross-pressured by the fact that most of them are simultaneously consumers, earners, and savers and/or debtors–identities that may pull them into different directions. In addition, people have interests, values, opinions, preferences, and, at the same time, the meta-preference for having the right preferences–preferences, that is, which are sufficiently well-considered to make acting on them reasonably regret-proof. Preferences are formed and reshaped as a by-product of the lived experience of political, economic, family, and associational life. They can also be shaped through formal institutions, such as the curriculum of civics classes, and elite strategies, such as electoral campaigns.

Recent developments in democratic theory have focused on preference formation through institutionalised deliberative panels, mini-publics, and even consultative chambers in which combinations of ordinary citizens and non-partisan experts are mandated to find out and publicly provide advice on what the right policy preferences might be–without, however, having a role in actually making decisions on policies, which remains the exclusive privilege of the popular sovereign and its electoral process, as well as other forms of preference manifestation. Though this logical and institutional separation of the stages of formation and expression of preferences is not addressed in the assessment of deliberative innovations in Merkel's chapter, it does come through in Pogrebinschi's chapter on lessons taken from beyond the West.

Normal versus emergency politics. What is to be done when the normal democratic process governed by constitutional and statutory laws, institutions, and procedures is interrupted and an exceptional situation–an emergency that threatens the security of state and nation–emerges? That is the classical Schmittian question that Atanassow and Katznelson address in their chapter. It is the situation when decisions overrule rules and when security concerns come to prevail over both democracy and rule of law. Rather than offering an institutional solution to this dilemma, the authors offer a rich overview of the US experience and debates as well as some eloquent warnings to the effect that existing mechanisms of supervision must be defended and, wherever possible, strengthened. The authors suggest a somewhat paradoxical move of constitutionalising the breach of constitutional rules when necessitated by an extraordinary challenge, such as an attack by a foreign power. An example of such a move is the German 'emergency constitution' of Articles 115a to 115l of the Basic Law. Yet three issues remain unresolved. First, as Article 115a Section 2 states, an emergency sets in if 'the situation imperatively calls for immediate action' and the parliament is hindered from convening. Here, a problem is that a situation cannot call for something; it is agents evaluating and interpreting the situation who call, and their call may be contested by other agents who are silenced by the situation. Second, the Basic Law specifies the emergency as a 'state of defense', but severe security challenges can also be caused by Cold War and cyber war conditions, large-scale terrorist acts such as 9/11, or civil war conditions– and even major monetary and banking crises to which the European Central Bank has in fact responded by the mobilisation of means ('whatever it takes'), the legal status of which is at least highly doubtful. Third, as Atanassow and Katznelson remind us, emergencies do not need to conform to the model of an international war being ended by the defeat of one party and a subsequent peace treaty so that normality can resume. Instead, emergency can become, under the threat of terrorism and asymmetrical wars, a permanent condition, in the preservation of which state agencies, invoking a need to protect the security of the population, may develop an intrinsic interest. There seems to be no clear proposal available as to how democracies might deal with the thorny and apparently irresolvable problem of reconciling liberty and security, or the normal and the exceptional, without degenerating into a dual regime that consists of a legal surface covering up a legally and partly unregulated security apparatus.

Civil society-initiated versus state-sponsored innovations. Revolutions, rebellions, and individual acts of violent or non-violent civil disobedience are all instances of political innovation in spite of the fact that they are not covered by the legal order under which they occur. If successful, they will be appreciated as innovative breakthroughs in future retrospect. Protest movements, as discussed in the chapter by Della Porta and Felicetti, are an intermediate case that originates from civil society yet is legitimated by state-protected civil rights. Compared to participation in the electoral process, participation in movements and protest activities is much more demanding of the resources of individual participants. The turnout and longevity of movements can therefore signal something that cannot be communicated through elections. In the latter, quantities of (political party) preferences are registered, whereas in (sustained) participation in movements it is the intensity with which causes are pursued by participants. At the other end of the analytical scale, we find institutional innovations such as the numerous cases from Latin American that Pogrebinschi reviews in her chapter. Many of these are designed, introduced, and propagated by governing elites, at least some of which see themselves as fulfilling revolutionary missions in order to improve governance through citizen participation.

Representative democracy versus direct-democratic innovations. Referendums on substantive policy issues are often advocated because of their anti-elitist appeal: decisions should not be left to (distrusted) members of the political class but should be made according to the supposedly more genuine and unadulterated will of the people. As Merkel duly notes in his chapter, the claim to greater authenticity of plebiscitarian methods of decision-making is often dubious because it is typically political parties and representative legislative bodies that determine the parameters of referendums: the timing, the phrasing of the question to be decided on by the people, the pro and con campaigns, and the quorum of turnout as well as the requisite majority required for the result to become valid. Also, compared to elections that result in the losers being still represented as a minority in parliament, the losers of referendums are definitively deprived of their voice. On the other hand, with adequate opportunities provided for a minimally informed and reflective preference formation (as opposed to a constituency being invited to express its momentary gut feelings), a minority party's option of initiating a referendum can represent an effective threat to an elite cartel of governing parties.

Territorial versus functional representation. The institutional repertoire of liberal democracies contains two modes of representation. The citizenry living in a (sub)territory–municipality, province, nation-state, European Union (EU)–is politically represented in ways that are shaped by elections, legislative periods, competing political parties, legislative bodies, and governments. They are shaped by the political will of constituencies and the individuals within them. (In Box 5, Jean Pisani-Ferry suggests ways the EU could strengthen its legitimacy among its citizenry.) The second circuit of representation consists of interest associations that are made up of members. Membership is based not on citizenship but on some specific socio-economic function performed by members (as farmers, employers, workers, civil servants, pensioners, and members of trades and industries, among others) and the particular interests that derive from and are continuously defined on the basis of those functions. Here, the operative logic is not citizenship but membership and the paying of membership dues. The representative leadership of interest associations interacts with other such associations through bargaining; it also interacts with political parties, parliaments, and ministries by voicing demands, exerting pressure backed by positive and negative sanctions, offering information and advice, and so on.

The interaction between those two circuits of representation has been

---

Box 5 **Can open government help the EU?**

Trust in the European Union (EU) and its very legitimacy have been severely affected by the (mis)management of the economic crisis and the refugee crisis. The European executive is certainly not alone in experiencing this fate. But whereas elections may restore trust in national governments, the role of the electoral process in deciding who governs Europe is too muted to confer significant legiti-

macy to the EU Commission, whose president and members, in the eyes of citizens, remain appointed bureaucrats whose legitimacy rests on output.

This does not mean that governance processes do not matter. Precisely because its legitimacy does not result from direct election, the EU can gain more than national governments from being at the forefront of the transformation of governance. Open government—through greater transparency, access to data, and extensive citizen consultation—can in principle help foster this transformation. More and more governments are adopting this philosophy, including through membership in the Open Government Partnership network (of which the EU is not a member at the time of writing).

The EU has taken steps towards greater openness by, for example, releasing data on the beneficiaries of the Common Agricultural Policy and creating a lobbyists' register, but much remains to be done to dispel the widespread perception that the EU is too secretive toward citizens and too accessible for special interests. An important challenge is to find the right balance between open access to key documents underpinning international trade or regulatory talks and the preservation of secrecy that is indispensable to effective negotiation; recent controversies over the Transatlantic Trade Investment Partnership (TTIP) and Comprehensive Economic and Trade Agreement (CETA) suggest that there is still much room for improvement in this area.

A second, major step toward changing how the EU is perceived by citizens would be making the Council of the European Union's deliberation process more open and transparent. In all democracies, parliaments deliberate in public, yet the Council, which together with the European Parliament constitutes the EU's legislative branch, deliberates mostly behind closed doors, with preparations in working groups and discussions on non-legislative acts not necessarily open to the public. Here again, a balance must be struck, because the Council, comprised of various configurations of ministers of EU member governments, is not exactly a parliament, and it plays roles in addition to that of co-legislator.

Citizen consultation is a third area for change. True, the EU relies on expert groups and open consultations. It also consults social partners (employers' and employees' associations), though less so than in the past. Digital technologies render the involvement of citizens easier than ever before, and citizens' involvement should be developed further. Yet a major issue is whether such consultations increase the EU's legitimacy: for those who feel left out and resent the power and influence of experts, more involvement of the cognoscenti in open consultation processes is hardly a way to restore trust. The more the EU strives to involve citizens, the more it actually risks increasing its distance from ordinary citizens.

The upshot is that the EU should make progress towards openness in several directions, but that it would be an illusion to believe that openness alone would be sufficient to overcome the EU's legitimacy problem. Openness can help, but it cannot substitute for effectiveness and democratisation.

Jean Pisani-Ferry

See *The Governance Report 2015* (Oxford University Press) and its companion edited volume, *Beyond the Crisis: The Governance of Europe's Economic, Political, and Legal Transformation* (also Oxford University Press), for more perspectives on the governance challenges facing the EU.

analysed by theories of (neo)corporatism, tripartism, agency capture, associative democracy, and others. This currently–under the impact of neoliberal practices and doctrines–somewhat neglected field of democratic representation can also be seen as a promising field of innovations. For instance, statutory codetermination rights of particular interest associations in the legislative process might be further enhanced in order to compensate for inferior power resources of particular groups of citizens, or associations as agencies of functional representation could be subjected to public supervision of their sources of finance and political activities. In addition, interest associations could be granted public status according to their density, the ratio of actual to potential members. Another option is the introduction of representation vouchers (see Schmitter and Trechsel 2004) that would replace the tax deductibility of membership dues with a universal grant of a modest annual amount by which every citizen could allocate funds to associations of their choice regardless of their own membership.

The internet versus physical presence and face-to-face communication. The chapter by Hall is a vivid illustration of how the use of digital media can enhance the effectiveness of civil society advocacy organisations. Others have explored possibilities to continuously consult the people and its political preferences in a real-time format. The extent to which new technologies allow us to extend and speed up the range of communication and to save costs and time can hardly be exaggerated. As technologies, they can be put to use for all kinds of organisations and purposes, including those of enhancing democratic representation.

Yet digital communication among large groups of people differs in potentially consequential ways from direct communication, say, among a group of people physically present in a lecture hall. These differences apply not only to the enormous ease with which participants in digital communication can tune in and tune out, perhaps leaving behind an anonymous 'like'. This feature can explain the short-lived and superficial character of digital communication. The other difference between digital and face-to-face communication is that in a group that is physically assembled, people gain two kinds of knowledge: they learn what has been said, and they experience who else, that is, what other concrete persons, has been exposed to the communication. The latter can trigger dispositions for collective action, debate, and informal social control that digital communication does not.

National democracy versus supranational policy impacts. A normative intuition that informs much of contemporary thinking about the quality of democratic institutions is a postulate of congruence: all those who are significantly affected by a policy should have a voice in its making. This postulate is plainly utopian (in the worst sense of the word) in today's world, where the spatial horizon of causation is systematically much wider than the horizon of participation and representation. In order to close the gap in conventional democratic ways, one would have to permit, for instance, the citizenry of half a dozen states in the Middle East to participate in US presidential elections, as they are existentially affected by what the American president decides or fails to do. States and their national policies dump enormous negative externalities upon other states and societies for which they cannot be held democratically accountable by the latter.

Absent widely acceptable and minimally realistic blueprints for the supranational extension of so far essentially national democracy–blueprints that are not even consented to be available for the EU–there are just two weak measures to fill the vast and still widening representation gap between 'policy-takers beyond our borders' and 'us', the effective policy-makers. One is the adequate representation of the (potential) victims of negative externalities in the making of international regimes, treaties, conventions, and legal provisions. Yet the bindingness of supranational norms is still largely contingent on the readiness of states to adopt and enforce them. The other possible measure is to create a representation of the interests of the victims of negative externalities within the political systems from which they originate. Such representation might result in the transfer of compensation payments, development aid, and a large variety of diplomatic and peace-making activities. But these policy areas are far beyond the reach of largely parochial, nation-state-focused democratic innovation.

So much on some major design alternatives that innovators of democratic institutions and practices must address and cope with. In doing so, innovators must make explicit which deficiencies or symptoms of malfunctioning of contemporary democracies they seek to remedy. As demonstrated in the introduction to this Report, we can do better than summarily refer to a condition of crisis or malaise of democracy. Much of the discussion has focused on attitudes and patterns of behaviour that can be observed on the input side of the political process (referred to earlier as 'by-the-people' issues), such as declines in trust, participation, commitment, engagement, turnout, membership, and activism. At least as interesting and worthy of further conceptual elaboration and empirical research is the output performance of contemporary liberal democracies: what can they credibly and irreversibly do 'for the people'? If the capacity of democratic governance to protect, shape, and improve life chances of citizens is as deficient as much contemporary evidence suggests, the general decline of participation, trust, and commitment is entirely unsurprising.

XII. Innovations at a Glance

HELMUT K. ANHEIER, SONJA KAUFMANN, *and* REGINA A. LIST

The opening chapter of this Report briefly introduced the many deficits of modern-day democracies and quickly shifted the focus to this year's main topic: identifying innovative responses to the many and complex problems democracies face. By such innovations, we mean novel rules and approaches that seek to address the challenges confronting democratic institutions and practices. The promise of these innovations is to counteract, if not remedy, such deficits and their underlying causes. Their aim is to bring about more effective and efficacious ways to achieve better outcomes and hence greater legitimacy as well as stability of the democratic order.

However, by innovation we do not imply uniqueness of a rule or approach in the sense that parts, most, or all of it has never existed before. Governments can and do copy from one another, as do political parties and indeed most organisations and social movements. For example, while most countries allow for, and conduct, some kind of referendum, some do not. So if a country were to introduce the possibility of referendums and adjust them to prevailing circumstances in addressing a particular challenge to its democratic regime, it would be regarded as an innovation in that context and instance.

Why Democracies Innovate

Democracies are living systems and, like societies and economies, are rarely stable but subject to gradual changes and unforeseen discontinuities, even jolts. Plattner (2010) suggests that liberal democracies today owe much of their resilience to an ongoing balancing of two leading sources of internal opposition: populism, or in Offe's terms, popular sovereignty, on the one hand and radical pluralism, i.e. minority rights and preferences, on the other. These sources are inherently in tension with each other, and both are at work to different degrees across democratic societies and over time. To some extent, they can cancel each other out or neutralise potentially negative outcomes that might arise, but sometimes one becomes more dominant, triggering in turn reactions by the other.

The elements of democratic malaise highlighted throughout this Report are closely related to the imbalances that Plattner and Offe, in his contributions to this Report, identify. They may well be signs of deep-seated changes occurring in societies–changes that seek answers within, and through, democratic systems that are not yet established or ready for such tasks. In this respect, Merkel argues in his chapter that the tension-ridden nature of democracy and the many challenges today's democracies face should not be mistaken for breakdown and disintegration. A search for resilience requires recalibration. Indeed, the democratic malaise many democracies experience implies attempts at change and a search for remedies–the kinds of innovations identified and reviewed in this Report.

Innovations arise out of tensions and frictions, as the chapters have shown. They often emerge, as Smilov argues in his chapter, from certain myths, for example, the unquestioned dominance of a noble fiction of the citizen eager to contribute time, resources, and efforts for the advancement of the public interest. While this myth has an empowering effect for some groups, motivates the building of democratic institutions and processes, and adds to the resilience of democracies, it falls short of a reality characterised by deficiencies that include disinterested and self-serving individuals, semi-loyal elite, entrenched power structures, and malfunctioning, even corrupt, institutions. Thus, democratic innovations can emerge as the result of contradictions between ideals and reality.

Democracies are facing a similar contradiction in seeking to respond to the sense of pervasive insecurity felt by citizens facing societal, economic, and cultural changes, among others, and most visibly the threat of terrorism. The novel measures described in Smilov's chapter and emerging from Eastern Europe to address rising fears (real or imagined) among the populace seem to stretch the limits of liberal democracy. In seeking to resolve the tension between satisfying the need for security and upholding liberal values and institutions that Atanassow and Katznelson identify in their chapter, democracies have no choice but to develop innovative solutions.

The application of particular models in new contexts also presents opportunities for innovations. Perhaps this is one reason why Latin America and Eastern Europe appear to be innovation hubs of sorts, as indicated in the chapters by Pogrebinschi, Smilov, and Haber. Various models of democracy or elements of these taken from consolidated democracies may not fit the historical circumstances and current needs of the importing polity. In some cases, there will be adjustments at the margins, in others novel approaches will emerge altogether, and in yet others reactions will lead to rejection, even triggering some kind of rollback.

Goals and Types of Democratic Innovations

What are some of the main goals and types of democratic innovations? As Offe points out in his contribution at the beginning of this Report, there are two sets of issues innovations could address: 'by-the-people' issues and 'for-the-people' issues. Though the latter are also present, most of the innovations highlighted in this Report focus more on 'by-the-people' issues, that is, those concerned with citizen participation in the democratic political process–setting agendas, expressing preferences, making decisions, and ensuring accountability.

The democratic innovations found throughout this Report and summarised in Table 12.1 aim to achieve at least one of the following goals:

- **Increasing active involvement in the democratic project** in places where citizens are dissatisfied or disillusioned with current politicians in office or the political system in place and are disinclined to participate by voting, taking part in political parties or associations, or even presenting themselves as candidates for elected office.
- **Enhancing the voice of citizens** through formal democratic processes such as elections as well as other opportunities to make substantive contributions to decision-making and to make their opinions heard.
- **Bolstering legitimacy and trust in the democratic process** where scepticism of traditional democratic institutions and mechanisms is on the rise, accountability and authority are in question, or political leadership seems to ignore citizens.
- **Safeguarding institutions and ensuring the rule of law** in order to maintain a balance between security and liberty, majority and minority rule, and other tensions that are innate to democracies while preventing or at least limiting backsliding and hollowing out of democratic principles.

The main categories of types of intervention this Report has covered are:

- **Government-initiated direct democratic innovations** that are introduced by the government of the day, often in an attempt to gain or consolidate power but also often in response to ideas or experiments started by social movements or civil society groups.
- **Bottom-up citizen engagement approaches**, most often emerging from civil society or social movement efforts to develop new ways for citizens to make their voices heard.
- **Electoral reforms** that seek to expand or improve opportunities for citizens to vote in elections and for those votes to have impact.
- **Institutional provisions** that either strengthen the polity's capacity to monitor and manage democratic processes or create openings for new types of institutional actors.

Table 12.1 **An overview of democratic innovations**

Category	Tool/Strategy	Challenge	Basic proposition	Advantages/ Potential	Disadvantages/ Limitations
Government-initiated direct democratic innovations	Referendums	Distrust in representatives and perceived lack of legitimacy of political decision-making	Include citizens in decision-making processes on specific issue areas	+ Gives citizens the chance to voice their opinions beyond elections + Reinforces identification with democratic system	– Only affected or interested groups take part, imposing their views on all – Low turnout endangers legitimacy of vote – Does not engage those already disengaged – Only appropriate for certain issues
	Deliberative citizens' assemblies e.g. mini-publics	Many less dominant voices not heard in government decision-making	Decisions should be made based on the better argument in broad consensus and without manipulation or domination of interests	+ Allows consideration of broader range of perspectives + More appropriate for ethical or moral questions than for distribution issue	– Organisational complexity limits application – Not always tied into decision-making
	Co-governance e.g. participatory budgeting, Brazilian national public policy conferences, Icelandic constitutional reform, British Columbia Citizens' Assembly	Gaining legitimacy for policy decisions	Structured and institutionalised decision-making on policy with citizen participation	+ Improves problem-solving capacities + Increases citizens' identification with decisions	– Can be hijacked by political leaders or other dominant participants

ANHEIER, KAUFMANN, *and* LIST

Category	Tool/Strategy	Challenge	Basic proposition	Advantages/ Potential	Disadvantages/ Limitations
Bottom-up citizen engagement	Repurposing of mass protest e.g. mass protests in Eastern Europe such as on Maidan Square in Kiev, Ukraine	Corrupt practices, authoritarian tendencies, and self-entrenchment of majoritarian governments lead to erosion of democracy	Mass protests are no longer used as last resort in existential crises, but to show dissatisfaction with government, certain parties, and elites	+ Have become a quite powerful tool (revision of proposed policies or appointments after protests) + Open and inclusive structure allows everyone to participate	– Lose their role as weapon of last resort in existential crises – Become an instrument of routine opposition rather than a device for radical transformation of political system
	New ways of organising protests e.g. *acampadas* such as the Occupy movement	Protests organised hierarchically leaving little room for an individual's meaningful participation and impact	Long-term occupation of significant public spaces with direct individual involvement Assemblies, debates, and processes open to all	+ Privileges individual involvement, personal knowledge, and emotion over organised groups and expertise + Transparency and openness in non-hierarchical processes builds confidence in participation	– Difficult to move from protest to policy – Despite intentions, not necessarily long-term occupation
	New forms of advocacy organisation through online platforms e.g. GetUp! (Australia), Campact (Germany)	Fast-paced public sphere and global events challenge conventional advocacy	Ad hoc, issue-specific mobilisation via online platforms, opening a new dimension of political participation through lower transaction costs of political information, communication, and action	+ Enables independent, grassroots or netroots, member-driven and member-funded organisations with relatively few resources to mobilise significant support + Gives broader society access to information and participation	– Unlike mainstream media, no editorial control guaranteed – Does not automatically translate into action (clicktivism vs. offline activism) – Most effective when used in combination with conventional forms of advocacy – Anonymity brings out the 'worse I'

Category	Tool/Strategy	Challenge	Basic proposition	Advantages/ Potential	Disadvantages/ Limitations
Electoral reform	Automatic voter registration US-specific issue	Registering to vote creates a hurdle to participate in an election	Create automatic voter register based on other public records (e.g. driving licenses, social security rolls)	+ Removes the burden of registering from voters + Increases access to voting + Reduces administrative errors	− Potential for errors in registering ineligible voters
	Non-partisan blanket primaries (top-two primaries) and ranked choice voting US-specific issue	Low turnout in primary elections often produces candidates who are more ideologically extreme than the average voter, thereby leading to partisan polarisation	Open primaries, with a large number of candidates and the top two candidates moving forward to the general election regardless of their party affiliation	+ Creates incentive for candidates to appeal to voters across the spectrum + Votes are not 'wasted' compared to first-past-the-post system	− Primary election results may not fully reflect the party preferences of the voters
	Voter ID laws US-specific issue	Perceived or potential voter fraud	Require specific forms of ID—some easier to acquire than others—before validating a person's vote	+ Ensures validity of voting process	− Creates hurdles for certain socioeconomic and racial groups − Can restrict fair and universal access to elections
	Non-partisan commissions to draw voting district boundaries	Gerrymandering: drawing of district boundaries to favour a specific political party or candidate and to ensure specific electoral outcomes	Non-partisan redistricting commissions are tasked with drawing constituency boundaries	+ Prevents manipulation of district boundaries to deliberately advantage one party, candidate, or socio-economic group	− May not completely eliminate partisan tactics

ANHEIER, KAUFMANN, *and* LIST

Category	Tool/Strategy	Challenge	Basic proposition	Advantages/ Potential	Disadvantages/ Limitations
	Lowering voting age	Young people are tuned out of politics	Lowering voting age on national or subnational level	+ Gives voice to young people who may be affected in the long run by outcomes and policies + Encourages youth to engage in politics and to become habitual voters	– Young voters might still lack motivation to participate or they might seek alternative forms of participation
	Quotas e.g. for gender, language, minority groups, regional representation	Certain groups in society are under-represented #in legislative bodies	Increase participation of disadvantaged groups by guaranteeing their representation	+ Increases actual representation of under-represented groups + Encourages members of those groups to run for office	– Free choice of voters is restricted – Votes are 'wasted' on candidates that cannot take a seat because of the quota
	New/other forms of voting e.g. online, absentee, and early voting	Voters who are unable to vote in person on election day de facto surrender their voting right	Allow citizens who are not able to cast their vote in person on election day to participate in elections by other means, such as mail-in ballot, online voting, voting from abroad, or voting prior to election day	+ Allows people to exercise their right to vote + Increases voter turnout	– Certain forms are vulnerable to manipulation and fraud (especially online voting)

Category	Tool/Strategy	Challenge	Basic proposition	Advantages/ Potential	Disadvantages/ Limitations
Institutional provisions	Safeguard institutions for governing emergencies e.g. Investigatory Powers Tribunal (UK), FISC (US)	In times of emergency, governments may expand their power in far-reaching terms, endangering civil rights and liberties	Install institutions, laws, and procedures to review or limit power extension Assess rightfulness of government action after the fact	+ Ensures accountability of leaders during and after the fact + Offers clear guidance in balancing liberty and security needs + Limits delegation to duration of emergency + Prevents rollback of gains achieved prior to emergency	− Need for confidentiality might hinder oversight, at least during an emergency
	Party-media hybrid e.g. Berlusconi in Italy, Ataka and National Front for the Salvation of Bulgaria (both originating in a regional TV network)	Distrust in elected representatives and the state	Politicians/media personalities make use of their media exposure as political capital Political parties emerge out of media programmes	+ Creates greater possibilities for broad communication between politicians and the populace	− Campaign financing is strictly regulated, while media financing is not − Uncritical and unfiltered dissemination of political messages − Fears stoked through tendentious and partisan reporting
	Unelected, independent expert bodies e.g. central banks, watchdog NGOs, anti-corruption agencies	Need for independent supervision of government, especially where traditional institutions are distrusted	Provide other channels of oversight and representation beyond elections and parliament Often recommended or mandated by law or by external institutions such as the EU or donors	+ Distances important functions from partisan influence + Draws in apolitical expertise + Provides opportunities for making political leaders accountable	− Positions in supposedly independent supervisory agencies may be filled with loyalists

ANHEIER, KAUFMANN, *and* LIST

As shown in Table 12.1, each of these main categories covers a range of innovative tools or strategies that either respond to specific challenges and deficits or address more general issues of the democratic system in place. These measures typically rest on a basic proposition or set of assumptions on how to respond to the issue at hand. Yet, innovations not only offer potential remedies and bring about advantages; in some cases, they also face limitations and can lead to future deficiencies. Of course, innovative measures not covered here certainly exist, as do other analytical approaches and useful categorisations (Geissel and Newton 2012; Smith 2009). The purpose of the table is to convey the rich set of options democracies have to respond to challenges, but it is not meant to offer a comprehensive overview of the entire spectrum.

Democracy Challenged – Democracy Innovating

Obviously, all these innovations seek to address at least one symptom or cause of the perceived democratic malaise in consolidated democracies, contribute to the resilience of new democracies, or assist the expansion of democracy. None by itself is the answer to rising illiberalism, populism, or citizens' apparent distrust, disinterest, and disengagement. They rarely involve fundamental reversal and profound discontinuities. Instead, as Smilov notes in his chapter on Eastern Europe, they are typically of a more incremental and gradual nature, trying to fix and improve rather than displace.

Innovations that seem to be taking place on the margins of democratic systems can still have significant consequences. At first glance, automatic voter registration may seem a rather insignificant change, but it could have a strong impact on political inclusion and hence participation, as a higher number of registered voters is likely to result in increased voter turnout, thereby influencing election results. Other seemingly marginal changes include absentee voting and early voting, which increase the potential pool of voters and, like automatic voter registration, might well impact the outcome of important elections.

Many of the democratic innovations in Table 12.1 are unlike more radical reforms of democracy itself. Fundamental changes to current democracies, such as substitution of elections with lotteries and maximisation of citizen access to power through shorter term limits for and increased numbers of offices, are beyond the scope of this Report. In any case, such reforms would have to be implemented with proper regard to parliaments and to the balance with executive power in national and supranational policy-making as well as with the judiciary.

What is more, not all innovations can be considered best practices in terms of replicability over time and portability to other democracies. The chapters in this Report have made clear that challenges to, and innovations in, democratic systems are significantly path dependent and context bound. Strict voter ID requirements may be commonplace in many countries but raise issues of access in the United States due to historical precedent (see Kuo's chapter). Media-based political parties can be considered an innovation in Eastern Europe given the historical and regional context, but did they foster democracy in places such as Italy under Berlusconi? New online forms of political activism (see Hall's chapter) and social movements (see chapter by Della Porta and Felicetti) can broaden access and provide voice, but what if they replicate or even reinforce political fault lines and leave a divided polity and civil society, as seems to be the case in the US?

In other words, even those types of innovations that could indeed be considered best practices cannot necessarily be translated seamlessly into other contexts, as has been the case for participatory budgeting (PB). Developed in Porto Alegre, Brazil as a political strategy that combined social justice aims with a set of administrative reforms, PB-related projects have been undertaken more or less successfully in Brazil and elsewhere in Latin America. As a best practice that has become a politically neutral device to improve governance, its application in Europe has marginalised the social justice principle and the administrative reform goal and has thus had little impact, if any (Pogrebinschi in this Report; Ganuza and Baiocchi 2012). The translation process could, of course, lead to further innovation, as in Latin America, or it could result in disillusionment, as seems to be the case in some parts of Eastern Europe.

More generally, the cross-national analysis in Haber's chapter shows that innovations are relatively independent of the type of democratic regimes as well as the particular set of challenges facing democracies. This underlines the point that innovations depend on the historical and contemporary context in which they are applied. It also shows that finding a remedy to contemporary malaises of democracy is a process of trial and error in which solutions can be sought elsewhere but ultimately require experimentation and adaptation to determine what works.

Thus, democratic innovations, like democratic systems, are highly context bound and path dependent, which makes their generation and adoption very conditional and riddled with externalities and dilemmas as well as opportunities and risks. In this respect, the Report offers guidance for considering the circumstances under which each innovation might be appropriate and the value each innovation might add. Offe, for example, extracts from the chapters a set of analytical variables or design options that innovators of democratic institutions and practices must consider, among them whether the innovation should address only preference formation or also expression and whether representation is to be based on territorial or functional identity. Obviously the design choices must take into account which symptom the innovation is seeking to remedy. In his chapter, Merkel provides a template for assessing innovations that examines the extent to which each type alleviates or compensates for the malaises of participation, representation, and governance as well as the extent to which each is compatible with the institutions and procedures of representative democracy. Though he applies this framework to direct democratic innovations, it can arguably be used to assess the value of other tools and approaches as well.

Managing and caring for democracy require constant questioning and monitoring, a kind of general stewardship to maintain political checks and balances, test the actions of leaders to ensure responsibility and accountability, pay attention to socioeconomic issues such as equity and inequality, and create awareness that sovereignty is limited. Such stewardship has been, and continues to be, in short supply, while the illusion of democracy taken for granted seems all too widespread. But from this dual neglect and the challenges and frictions thus created come the search for innovations and the reminder that the work of democracy is never done.

References

#aufstehn (2016) [website]. *Anstand statt Notstand!* Retrieved from https://actions.aufstehn.at/anstand-statt-notstand (accessed 17 November 2016).

38 Degrees (2016) [website]. *Refugees Welcome.* Retrieved from https://you.38degrees.org.uk/efforts/refugees-welcome (accessed 18 November 2016).

Abers, R. (2003). 'Reflections on What Makes Empowered Participatory Governance Happen', in A. Fung, and E. O. Wright (eds), *Deepening Democracy: Institutional Innovations in Empowered Participatory Governance.* London, New York: Verso, 200–7.

Abromeit, J., Chesterton, B. M., Marotta, G., and Norman, Y. (eds) (2016). *Transformations of Populism in Europe and the Americas: History and Recent Tendencies.* London: Bloomsbury Academic.

ACE (ACE Electoral Knowledge Network) (2016a) [website]. *Comparative Data: What Is the Legal Voting Age in the National Elections?* Retrieved from http://aceproject.org/epic-en?question=VR001 (accessed 16 January 2017).

ACE (ACE Electoral Knowledge Network) (2016b) [website]. *Countries With E-voting Projects.* Retrieved from http://aceproject.org/ace-en/focus/e-voting/countries (accessed 26 January 2017).

Agamben, G. (2005). *State of Exception.* Chicago: University of Chicago Press.

Ahlquist, J. S., Mayer, K. R., and Jackman, S. (2014). 'Alien Abduction and Voter Impersonation in the 2012 U.S. General Election: Evidence From a Survey List Experiment', *Election Law Journal*, 13(4): 460–75.

Allegretti, G. (2003). *L'insegnamento di Porto Alegre: Autoprogettualità come paradigma urbano.* Florence: Alinea.

Alonso, S., Keane, J., and Merkel, W. (eds) (2011). *The Future of Representative Democracy.* Cambridge: Cambridge University Press.

Anheier, H. K. (ed) (2015). Changing the European Debate: A Rollback of Democracy, *Global Policy*, 6(s1).

Anheier, H. K., and Korreck, S. (2013). 'Governance Innovations', in Hertie School of Governance (ed), *The Governance Report 2013.* Oxford: Oxford University Press, 83–116.

Annan, K. (2016). 'Democracy Under Pressure', *The New York Times*, 6 December 2016. Retrieved from https://www.nytimes.com/2016/12/06/opinion/democracy-under-pressure.html (accessed 27 January 2017).

Ansell, C., and Gash, A. (2007). 'Collaborative Governance in Theory and Practice', *Journal of Public Administration Research and Theory*, 18(4): 543–71.

Atkinson, A. B. (2015). *Inequality: What Can Be Done?* Cambridge, MA: Harvard University Press.

Avritzer, L. (2009). *Participatory Institutions in Democratic Brazil.* Baltimore: Johns Hopkins University Press.

Avritzer, L. (2006). 'New Public Spheres in Brazil: Local Democracy and Deliberative Politics', *International Journal of Urban and Regional Research*, 30(3): 623–37.

Avritzer, L. (2002). *Democracy and the Public Space in Latin America*. Princeton: Princeton University Press.

Baiocchi, G. (2003a). 'Participation, Activism, and Politics: The Porto Alegre Experiment', in A. Fung, and E. O. Wright (eds), *Deepening Democracy: Institutional Innovations in Empowered Participatory Governance*. London, New York: Verso, 45–76.

Baiocchi, G. (ed) (2003b). *Radicals in Power: The Workers' Party (PT) and Experiments in Urban Democracy in Brazil*. London: Zed Books.

Baiocchi, G. (2001). 'Participation, Activism, and Politics: The Porto Alegre Experiment and Deliberative Democratic Theory', *Politics & Society*, 29(1): 43–72.

Bani, M. (2012). 'Crowdsourcing Democracy: The Case of Icelandic Social Constitutionalism', *SSRN Electronic Journal*. Retrieved from https://ssrn.com/abstract=2128531 (accessed 4 November 2016).

Barber, L. (2016) [website]. *The Year of the Demagogue: How 2016 Changed Democracy*. Retrieved from https://www.ft.com/content/7e82da50-c184-11e6-9bca-2b93a6856354 (accessed 19 January 2017).

Barber, M. J. (2016). 'Ideological Donors, Contribution Limits, and the Polarization of American Legislatures', *The Journal of Politics*, 78(1): 296–310.

Bartels, L. M. (2008). *Unequal Democracy: The Political Economy of the New Gilded Age*. Princeton: Princeton University Press.

Bauer, R. F., Ginsberg, B. L., Britton, B., Echevarria, J., Grayson, T., Lomax, L., Mayes, M. C., McGeehan, A., Patrick, T., and Thomas, C. (2014). The American Voting Experience. Report and Recommendations of the Presidential Commission on Election Administration. Washington, DC: Presidential Commission on Election Administration.

Bellamy, R., Merkel, W., Bhargave, R., Bidadanure, J., Christiano, T., Felt, U., Hay, C., Lamboy, L., Pogrebinschi, T., Smith, G., Talshir, G., Urbinati, N., and Verloo, M. (2016). 'Chapter 14: Inequality as a Challenge to Democracy', in *Rethinking Society for the 21st Century*. Paris, Princeton: International Panel on Social Progress.

Benkler, Y. (2014). 'A Public Accountability Defense for National Security Leakers and Whistleblowers', *Harvard Law and Policy Review*, 8: 281–325.

Bentele, K. G., and O'Brien, E. E. (2013). 'Jim Crow 2.0? Why States Consider and Adopt Restrictive Voter Access Policies', *Perspectives on Politics*, 11(4): 1088–116.

Berman, A. (2016) [website]. *Ohio Keeps Making It Harder to Vote*. Retrieved from https://www.thenation.com/article/ohio-keeps-making-it-harder-to-vote/ (accessed 2 November 2016).

Bermeo, N. (2016). 'On Democratic Backsliding', *Journal of Democracy*, 27(1): 5–19.

Bernstein, J. (2016) [website]. *Some Democrats Stay Quiet on Voting Reforms*. Retrieved from https://www.bloomberg.com/view/articles/2016-10-05/some-democrats-stay-quiet-on-voting-reforms (accessed 2 November 2016).

Bimber, B., Flanagin, A., and Stohl, C. (2012). *Collective Action in Organizations: Interaction and Engagement in an Era of Technological Change*. Cambridge: Cambridge University Press.

Blackstone, W. (1979 [1768]). *Commentaries on the Laws of England*. Chicago: University of Chicago Press.

Blake, A. (2012) [website]. *Everything You Need to Know About the Pennsylvania Voter ID Fight*. Retrieved from https://www.washingtonpost.com/news/the-fix/wp/2012/10/02/the-pennsylvania-voter-id-fight-explained/ (accessed 2 November 2016).

Blank, G. (2013). 'Who Creates Content? Stratification and Content Creation on the Internet', *Information, Communication & Society*, 16(4): 590–612.

Blokker, P. (2012). 'Grassroots Constitutional Politics in Iceland', *SSRN Electronic Journal*. Retrieved from https://papers.ssrn.com/sol3/papers.cfm?abstract_id=1990463 (accessed 4 November 2016).

Brady, K. (2016) [website]. *Almost Two Thirds of Germans Believe Islam 'Does Not Belong in Germany,' Poll Finds*. Retrieved from http://www.dw.com/en/almost-two-thirds-of-germans-believe-islam-does-not-belong-in-germany-poll-finds/a-19251169 (accessed 4 October 2016).

Brater, J. (2016) [website]. *Update: Oregon Keeps Adding New Voters at Torrid Pace*. Retrieved from https://www.brennancenter.org/analysis/update-oregon-keeps-adding-new-voters-torrid-pace (accessed 2 November 2016).

Brennan Center for Justice (2016) [website]. *Automatic Voter Registration*. Retrieved from https://www.brennancenter.org/analysis/automatic-voter-registration (accessed 2 November 2016).

Burden, B. C. (2007). *Personal Roots of Representation*. Princeton: Princeton University Press.

Burgess, S., and Keating, C. (2013). 'Occupy the Social Contract! Participatory Democracy and Iceland's Crowd-sourced Constitution', *New Political Science*, 35(3): 417–31.

Cabannes, Y. (2004). 'Participatory Budgeting: A Significant Contribution to Participatory Democracy', *Environment and Urbanization*, 16(1): 27–46.

Caiani, M., Della Porta, D., and Wagemann, C. (2012). *Mobilizing on the Extreme Right: Germany, Italy, and the United States*. Oxford: Oxford University Press.

Cain, B. E., Dalton, R. J., and Scarrow, S. E. (eds) (2003). *Democracy Transformed? Expanding Political Opportunities in Advanced Industrial Democracies*. Oxford: Oxford University Press.

Cameron, M. A., Hershberg, E., and Sharpe, K. E. (2012). *New Institutions for Participatory Democracy in Latin America: Voice and Consequence*. New York: Palgrave Macmillan.

Center for Systemic Peace (2016) [website]. *Global Democracy and Autocracy, 1946–2015*. Retrieved from http://www.systemicpeace.org/conflict-trends.html (accessed 27 January 2017).

Chwalisz, C. (2015). *Populist Signal: Why Politics and Democracy Need to Change*. London: Rowman & Littlefield International.

Citrin, J., Green, D. P., and Morris, L. (2014). 'The Effects of Voter ID Notification on Voter Turnout: Results From a Large-scale Field Experiment', *Election Law Journal*, 13(2): 228–42.

Clark, J. R. (1918). *Emergency Legislation Passed Prior to December, 1917, Dealing With the Control and Taking of Private Property for the Public Use, Benefit, or Welfare, Presidential Proclamations and Executive Orders Thereunder, to and Including January 31, 1918, to Which Is Added a Reprint of Analagous Legislation Since 1775*. Washington, DC: Government Printing Office.

Cobb, R. V., Greiner, D. J., and Quinn, K. M. (2010). 'Can Voter ID Laws Be Administered in a Race-neutral Manner? Evidence From the City of Boston in 2008', *Quarterly Journal of Political Science*, 7(1): 1–33.

Commission on Federal Election Reform (2005). Building Confidence in U.S. Elections. Report of the Comission on Federal Election Reform. Washington, DC: Commission on Federal Election Reform.

Connolly, K. (2016) [website]. *Angela Merkel: Internet Search Engines Are 'Distorting Perception'*. Retrieved from https://www.theguardian.com/world/2016/oct/27/angela-merkel-internet-search-engines-are-distorting-our-perception (accessed 21 November 2016).

Coppedge, M., Gerring, J., Lindberg, S. I., Skaaning, S.-E., Teorell, J., Altman, D., Andersson, F., Bernhard, M., Fish, M. S., Glynn, A., Hicken, A., Knutsen, C. H., McMann, K., Mechkova, V., Miri, F., Paxton, P., Pemstein, D., Sigman, R., Staton, J., and Zimmermann, B. (2016). *V-Dem Codebook v6: Varieties of Democracy Project*.

Cross, M. (2008) [website]. *I Vote for the Old-fashioned Way of Balloting in Elections*. Retrieved from https://www.theguardian.com/technology/2008/nov/13/balloting-election (accessed 16 January 2017).

Csink, L., Schanda, B., and Varga, A. Z. (eds) (2012). *The Basic Law of Hungary: A First Commentary*. Dublin: Clarus Press.

Dahl, R. A. (1972). *Polyarchy: Participation and Opposition*. New Haven: Yale University Press.

Dalton, R. J. (2004). *Democratic Challenges, Democratic Choices: The Erosion of Political Support in Advanced Industrial Democracies*. Oxford: Oxford University Press.

Dathan, M. (2015) [website]. *Aylan Kurdi: David Cameron Says He Felt 'Deeply Moved' by Images of Dead Syrian Boy but Gives No Details of Plans to Take in More Refugees*. Retrieved from http://www.independent.co.uk/news/uk/politics/aylan-kurdi-david-cameron-says-he-felt-deeply-moved-by-images-of-dead-syrian-boy-but-gives-no-10484641.html (accessed 4 October 2016).

Della Porta, D. (2015). *Social Movements in Times of Austerity: Bringing Capitalism Back Into Protest Analysis*. Cambridge: Polity Press.

Della Porta, D. (ed) (2009a). *Another Europe: Conceptions and Practices of Democracy in the European Social Forums*. London: Routledge.

Della Porta, D. (2009b). 'Another Europe: An Introduction', in D. Della Porta (ed), *Another Europe: Conceptions and Practices of Democracy in the European Social Forums*. London: Routledge, 3–25.

Della Porta, D. (ed) (2009c). *Democracy in Social Movements*. Basingstoke: Palgrave Macmillan.

Della Porta, D. (ed) (2007). *The Global Justice Movement: Cross-national and Transnational Perspectives*. Boulder: Paradigm Publishers.

Della Porta, D., and Diani, M. (2006). *Social Movements: An Introduction*. 2nd ed. Oxford: Blackwell.

Della Porta, D., and Mattoni, A. (eds) (2014). *Spreading Protest: Social Movements in Times of Crisis*. Colchester: ECPR Press.

Della Porta, D., and Rucht, D. (2013). 'Power and Democracy in Social Movements: An Introduction', in D. Della Porta, and D. Rucht (eds), *Meeting Democracy: Power and Deliberation in Global Justice Movements*. Cambridge: Cambridge University Press, 1–22.

Diamond, L. (2015). 'De-polarizing', *The American Interest*, 11(2). Retrieved from http://www.the-american-interest.com/2015/10/10/de-polarizing/ (accessed 2 November 2016).

Dicey, A. V. (1982 [1915]). *Introduction to the Study of the Law of the Constitution*. Indianapolis: Liberty.

DNC Voting Rights Institute (2005). Democracy at Risk. The 2004 Election in Ohio. Washington, DC: DNC Voting Rights Institute.

Dostal, J. M. (2015). 'The Pegida Movement and German Political Culture: Is Right-wing Populism Here to Stay?', *The Political Quarterly*, 86(4): 523–31.

Dryzek, J. S. (2012). *Foundations and Frontiers of Deliberative Governance*. Oxford: Oxford University Press.

Dryzek, J. S. (2009). 'Democratization as Deliberative Capacity Building', *Comparative Political Studies*, 42(11): 1379–402.

Dunham, J. (2016). The Battle for the Dominant Message. Freedom of the Press 2016. Washington, DC: Freedom House.

Dupré, C. (2003). *Importing the Law in Post-communist Transitions: The Hungarian Constitutional Court and the Right to Human Dignity*. Oxford: Hart.

Eidelson, J. (2016) [website]. *Bucking a Trend, Blue States Pass Laws to Make Voting Easier*. Retrieved from http://www.bloomberg.com/politics/articles/2016-09-01/blue-states-pass-their-own-voter-laws (accessed 2 November 2016).

EIU (The Economist Intelligence Unit) (2016) [website]. *Democracy Index 2015*. Retrieved from http://www.eiu.com/public/topical_report.aspx?campaignid=DemocracyIndex2015 (accessed 26 January 2017).

European Commisson (2015). Eurobarometer 83. Brussels: European Commisson. Retrieved from http://ec.europa.eu/public_opinion/archives/eb/eb83/eb83_en.htm (accessed 2 February 2017).

European Commisson (2011). Eurobarometer 76. Brussels: European Commisson. Retrieved from http://ec.europa.eu/public_opinion/archives/eb/eb76/eb76_en.htm (accessed 2 February 2017).

Farrell, P., Evershed, N., and Davidson, H. (2016) [website]. *The Nauru Files: Cache of 2,000 Leaked Reports Reveal Scale of Abuse of Children in Australian Offshore Detention*. Retrieved from https://www.theguardian.com/australia-news/2016/aug/10/the-nauru-files-2000-leaked-reports-reveal-scale-of-abuse-of-children-in-australian-offshore-detention (accessed 4 October 2016).

Ferejohn, J., and Pasquino, P. (2004). 'The Law of the Exception: A Typology of Emergency Powers', *International Journal of Constitutional Law*, 2(2): 210–39.

File, T., and Crissey, S. (2012). Voting and Registration in the Election of November 2008. Washington, DC: US Census Bureau.

Fischer, F. (2012). 'Participatory Governance: From Theory to Practice', in D. Levi-Faur (ed), *Oxford Handbook of Governance*. Oxford: Oxford University Press, 457–71.

Fishkin, J. S. (2009). *When the People Speak: Deliberative Democracy and Public Consultation*. Oxford: Oxford University Press.

Fishkin, J. S., and Luskin, R. C. (2005). 'Experimenting With a Democratic Ideal: Deliberative Polling and Public Opinion', *Acta Politica*, 40(s3): 284–98.

Foa, R. S., and Mounk, Y. (2017). 'The Signs of Deconsolidation', *Journal of Democracy*, 28(1): 5–15.

Franklin, M. N. (2004). *Voter Turnout and the Dynamics of Electoral Competition in Established Democracies Since 1945*. Cambridge: Cambridge University Press.

Freise, M., Paulsen, F., and Walter, A. (2015). 'Nailing Jello to the Wall: Civil Society and Innovative Public Administration', in M. Freise, F. Paulsen, and A. Walter (eds), *Civil Society and Innovative Public Administration*. Baden-Baden: Nomos, 13–38.

Friedrich, C. J. (1941). *Constitutional Government and Democracy: Theory and Practice in Europe and America*. Boston: Little, Brown and Co.

Fritsch, K., O'Connor, C., and Thompson, A. K. (eds) (2016). *Keywords for Radicals: The Contested Vocabulary of Late-capitalist Struggle*. Chico: AK Press.

Fukuyama, F. (2012). 'The Future of History', *Foreign Affairs*, 91(1): 52–61.

Fung, A. (2011). 'Reinventing Democracy in Latin America', *Perspectives on Politics*, 9(4): 857–71.

Fung, A. (2006). 'Varieties of Participation in Complex Governance', *Public Administration Review*, 66(s1): 66–75.

Fung, A. (2004). *Empowered Participation: Reinventing Urban Democracy*. Princeton: Princeton University Press.

Fung, A. (2003). 'Recipes for Public Spheres: Eight Institutional Design Choices and Their Consequences', *Journal of Political Philosophy*, 11(3): 338–67.

Gallup (2017) [website]. *Congress and the Public*. Retrieved from http://www.gallup.com/poll/1600/congress-public.aspx (accessed 27 January 2017).

Gallup (2016a) [website]. *Confidence in Institutions*. Retrieved from http://www.gallup.com/poll/1597/confidence-institutions.aspx (accessed 27 January 2017).

Gallup (2016b). *Gallup World Poll: Confidence in National Government; Confidence in Honesty of Elections*. Retrieved from http://www.gallup.com/services/170945/world-poll.aspx (accessed 26 January 2017).

Ganuza, E., and Baiocchi, G. (2012). 'The Power of Ambiguity: How Participatory Budgeting Travels the Globe', *Journal of Public Deliberation*, 8(2). Retrieved from http://www.publicdeliberation.net/jpd/vol8/iss2/art8/ (accessed 4 November 2016).

Gaskins, K., and Iyer, S. (2012). The Challenge of Obtaining Voter Identification. New York: Brennan Center for Justice, New York University School of Law.

Geissel, B. (2009). 'How to Improve the Quality of Democracy? Experiences With Participatory Innovations at the Local Level in Germany', *German Politics and Society*, 27(4): 51–71.

Geissel, B., and Joas, M. (2013). *Participatory Democratic Innovations in Europe: Improving the Quality of Democracy?* Opladen: Barbara Budrich.

Geissel, B., and Kern, K. (2000). 'Soziales Kapital und Lokale Agenda 21: Lokale umweltpolitische Initiativen in den USA', in H. Heinelt, and E. Mühlich (eds), *Lokale 'Agenda 21'-Prozesse: Erklärungsansätze, Konzepte und Ergebnisse*. Wiesbaden: VS Verlag für Sozialwissenschaften, 257–76.

Geissel, B., and Newton, K. (eds) (2012). *Evaluating Democratic Innovations: Curing the Democratic Malaise?* New York: Routledge.

Gerbaudo, P. (2012). *Tweets and the Streets: Social Media and Contemporary Activism*. London: Pluto Press.

GetUp! (2015) [website]. *Light the Dark: Australia Welcomes Refugees*. Retrieved from https://www.getup.org.au/campaigns/refugees/light-the-dark-for-aylan/light-the-dark-australia-welcomes-refugees (accessed 10 November 2016).

Gilens, M., and Page, B. I. (2014). 'Testing Theories of American Politics: Elites, Interest Groups, and Average Citizens', *Perspectives on Politics*, 12(3): 564–81.

Giraldo, F. (2011). 'Participación ciudadana en la Toma de Decisiones', in S. Jost (ed), *20 Años de la Constitución colombiana: Logros, Retrocesos y Agenda pendiente*. Bogota: Konrad Adenauer Stiftung, 226–40.

Gladwell, M. (2010) [website]. *Small Change: Why the Revolution Will Not Be Tweeted*. Retrieved from http://www.newyorker.com/magazine/2010/10/04/small-change-malcolm-gladwell (accessed 4 October 2016).

Goodin, R. E. (2006). 'Deliberative Impacts: The Macro-political Uptake of Mini-publics', *Politics & Society*, 34(2): 219–44.

Goodwin, M. (2011). Right Response. Understanding and Countering Populist Extremism in Europe. A Chatham House Report. London: Royal Institute of International Affairs.

Grabbe, H., and Lehne, S. (2016) [website]. *Can the EU Survive Populism?* Retrieved from http://carnegieeurope.eu/2016/06/14/can-eu-survive-populism/j1vb (accessed 2 November 2016).

Graeber, D. (2013). *The Democracy Project: A History, a Crisis, a Movement*. London: Allen Lane.

Grönlund, K., Setälä, M., and Herne, K. (2010). 'Deliberation and Civic Virtue: Lessons From a Citizen Deliberation Experiment', *European Political Science Review*, 2(1): 95–117.

Grose, C. (2016a). Evaluating California's Top-two Primary. Candidates Are More Bipartisan and More Responsive to Independent Voters in Top-two Primaries Than in Closed Primaries. Los Angeles: USC Price School of Public Policy, Schwarzenegger Institute for State and Global Policy.

Grose, C. (2016b). Political Reforms in California Are Associated With Less Ideologically Extreme State Legislators. Los Angeles: USC Price School of Public Policy, Schwarzenegger Institute for State and Global Policy.

Guggenberger, B. (2012). '"Verflüssigung" der Politik—was dann?', *Aus Politik und Zeitgeschichte*, 62(38–9): 10–7.

Gutmann, A. F., and Thompson, D. (1996). *Democracy and Disagreement*. Cambridge, MA: Harvard University Press.

Gylfason, T. (2012). 'Constitutions: Financial Crisis Can Lead to Change', *Challenge*, 55(5): 106–22.

Habermas, J. (1992). *Faktizität und Geltung: Beiträge zur Diskurstheorie des Rechts und des demokratischen Rechtsstaats*. Frankfurt am Main: Suhrkamp.

Haggard, S., and Kaufman, R. R. (1995). *The Political Economy of Democratic Transitions*. Princeton: Princeton University Press.

Hajnal, Z., Lajevardi, N., and Nielson, L. (2016). Voter Identification Laws and the Suppression of Minority Votes. San Diego: University of California.

Hall, N., and Ireland, P. (2016) [website]. *Transforming Activism: Digital Era Advocacy Organizations*. Retrieved from http://ssir.org/articles/entry/transforming_activism_digital_era_advocacy_organizations (accessed 4 October 2016).

Hall, T. (2012). 'Electronic Voting', in N. Kersting (ed), *Electronic Democracy*. Opladen: Barbara Budrich, 153–76.

Halvorsen, S. (2012). 'Beyond the Network? Occupy London and the Global Movement', *Social Movement Studies*, 11(3–4): 427–33.

Hamilton, A. (2001a [1788]). 'The Federalist No. 24', in A. Hamilton, J. Jay, and J. Madison (eds), *The Federalist*. Gideon ed. Indianapolis: Liberty Fund, 117–21.

Hamilton, A. (2001b [1788]). 'The Federalist No. 28', in A. Hamilton, J. Jay, and J. Madison (eds), *The Federalist*. Gideon ed. Indianapolis: Liberty Fund, 136–9.

Hamilton, A., Jay, J., and Madison, J. (eds) (2001 [1788]). *The Federalist*. Gideon ed. Indianapolis: Liberty Fund.

Han, B.-C. (2012). 'Im Schwarm', *Frankfurter Allgemeine Zeitung*, 8 October 2012. Retrieved from http://www.faz.net/-gpf-73bpm (accessed 2 February 2017).

Han, H. (2014). *How Organizations Develop Activists: Civic Associations and Leadership in the 21st Century*. Oxford: Oxford University Press.

Heller, P. (2001). 'Moving the State: The Politics of Democratic Decentralization in Kerala, South Africa, and Porto Alegre', *Politics & Society*, 29(1): 131–63.

Helms, L. (2016). 'Democracy and Innovation: From Institutions to Agency and Leadership', *Democratization*, 23(3): 459–77.

Hicks, W. D., McKee, S. C., Sellers, M. D., and Smith, D. A. (2015). 'A Principle or a Strategy? Voter Identification Laws and Partisan Competition in the American States', *Political Research Quarterly*, 68(1): 18–33.

Hirschman, A. O. (1970). *Exit, Voice, and Loyalty: Responses to Decline in Firms, Organizations, and States*. Cambridge, MA: Harvard University Press.

Holder, K. (2006). Voting and Registration in the Election of November 2004. Washington, DC: US Census Bureau.

Hood, C. (1991). 'A Public Management for All Seasons?', *Public Administration*, 69(1): 3–19.

IDEA (International Institute for Democracy and Electoral Assistance) (2016a) [website]. *Direct Democracy Database*. Retrieved from http://www.idea.int/data-tools/data/direct-democracy (accessed 26 January 2017).

IDEA (International Institute for Democracy and Electoral Assistance) (2016b) [website]. *Gender Quotas Database*. Retrieved from http://www.idea.int/data-tools/data/gender-quotas (accessed 26 January 2017).

IDEA (International Institute for Democracy and Electoral Assistance) (2016c) [website]. *ICTs in Elections Database*. Retrieved from http://www.idea.int/data-tools/data/icts-elections (accessed 26 January 2017).

Inglehart, R. F., and Norris, P. (2016). Trump, Brexit, and the Rise of Populism. Economic Have-nots and Cultural Backlash. Faculty Research Working Paper Series RWP16-026. Cambridge, MA: Harvard University.

International Budget Partnership (2015) [website]. *Open Budget Survey 2015*. Retrieved from http://www.internationalbudget.org/opening-budgets/open-budget-initiative/open-budget-survey/open-budget-survey-data-explorer/ (accessed 26 January 2017).

Investigatory Powers Tribunal (2016). Investigatory Powers Tribunal Report. 2011–2015. London: Investigatory Powers Tribunal.

Júliússon, Á. D., and Helgason, M. S. (2013). 'The Roots of the Saucepan Revolution in Iceland', in C. Flesher Fominaya, and L. Cox (eds), *Understanding European Movements: New Social Movements, Global Justice Struggles, Anti-austerity Protest*. London: Routledge, 189–202.

Juris, J. S. (2012). 'Reflections on #Occupy Everywhere: Social Media, Public Space, and Emerging Logics of Aggregation', *American Ethnologist*, 39(2): 259–79.

Kaase, M., and Newton, K. (1995). *Beliefs in Government*. Oxford: Oxford University Press.

Kaldor, M., and Selchow, S. (2015). *Subterranean Politics in Europe*. Basingstoke: Palgrave Macmillan.

Karpf, D. (2016). *Analytic Activism: Digital Listening and the New Political Strategy*. Oxford: Oxford University Press.

Karpf, D. (2013) [website]. *Netroots Goes Global*. Retrieved from https://www. thenation.com/article/netroots-goes-global/ (accessed 29 November 2016).

Karpf, D. (2012). *The MoveOn Effect: The Unexpected Transformation of American Political Advocacy*. Oxford: Oxford University Press.

Katz, R. S., and Mair, P. (eds) (1994). *How Parties Organize: Change and Adaptation in Party Organizations in Western Democracies*. London: Sage Publications.

Kauffmann, L. A. (2011). 'The Theology of Consensus', in A. Taylor, and K. Gessen (eds), *Occupy! Scenes From Occupied America*. London, New York: Verso, 46–50.

Keane, J. (2011). 'Monitory Democracy?', in S. Alonso, J. Keane, and W. Merkel (eds), *The Future of Representative Democracy*. Cambridge: Cambridge University Press, 212–35.

Keane, J. (2010). *The Life and Death of Democracy*. London: Simon and Schuster.

Kelemen, R. D. (2016) [website]. *A Dark Age for European Democracy?* Retrieved from https://www.foreignaffairs.com/articles/europe/2016-12-07/dark-age-european-democracy (accessed 27 January 2017).

Kissinger, H. (2014). *World Order*. New York: Penguin Press.

Koonings, K. (2004). 'Strengthening Citizenship in Brazil's Democracy: Local Participatory Governance in Porto Alegre', *Bulletin of Latin American Research*, 23(1): 79–99.

Krastev, I. (2017). 'The Rise and Fall of European Meritocracy', *The New York Times*, 18 January 2017. Retrieved from https://www.nytimes. com/2017/01/17/opinion/the-rise-and-fall-of-european-meritocracy. html (accessed 1 February 2017).

Krastev, I. (2016). 'The Specter Haunting Europe: The Unraveling of the Post-1989 Order', *Journal of Democracy*, 27(4): 88–98.

Krastev, I. (2014). 'From Politics to Protest', *Journal of Democracy*, 25(4): 5–19.

Krastev, I. (2012). 'Putinism Under Siege: An Autopsy of a Managed Democracy', *Journal of Democracy*, 23(3): 33–45.

Kriesi, H. (2014a). 'The Political Consequences of the Economic Crises in Europe: Electoral Punishment and Popular Protest', in N. G. Bermeo and L. M. Bartels (eds), *Mass Politics in Tough Times: Opinions, Votes and Protest in the Great Recession*. Oxford: Oxford University Press, 297–333.

Kriesi, H. (2014b). 'The Populist Challenge', *West European Politics*, 37(2): 361–78.

Kriesi, H. (2005). *Direct Democratic Choice: The Swiss Experience*. Lanham: Lexington.

Kriesi, H., and Pappas, T. S. (2015). *European Populism in the Shadow of the Great Recession*. Colchester: ECPR Press.

Krook, M. L. (2006). 'Reforming Representation: The Diffusion of Candidate Gender Quotas Worldwide', *Politics & Gender*, 2(3): 303–27.

Krook, M. L., and O'Brien, D. Z. (2010). 'The Politics of Group Representation: Quotas for Women and Minorities Worldwide', *Comparative Politics*, 42(3): 253–72.

Kuo, D., and McCarty, N. (2015). 'Democracy in America, 2015', in H. K. Anheier (ed), Changing the European Debate: A Rollback of Democracy, *Global Policy*, 6(s1): 49–55.

La Raja, R. J., and Schaffner, B. F. (2015). *Campaign Finance and Political Polarization: When Purists Prevail*. Ann Arbor: University of Michigan Press.

Landemore, H. (2015). 'Inclusive Constitution-making: The Icelandic Experiment', *Journal of Political Philosophy*, 23(2): 166–91.

Lawless, J. L., and Fox, R. L. (2015). *Running From Office: Why Young Americans Are Turned Off to Politics*. Oxford: Oxford University Press.

Lehmann, J.-P. (2014) [website]. *The Democratic Drift: Political Malaise in the Age of Democracy*. Retrieved from https://www.opendemocracy.net/jean-pierre-lehmann/democratic-drift-political-malaise-in-age-of-democracy (accessed 2 November 2016).

Lehmann, P., and Regel, S. (2015). 'Ungleichheit in der politischen Repräsentation: Ist die Unterschicht schlechter repräsentiert?', in W. Merkel (ed), *Demokratie und Krise: Zum schwierigen Verhältnis von Theorie und Empirie*. Wiesbaden: Springer VS, 157–80.

Levitt, J. (2014) [website]. *A Comprehensive Investigation of Voter Impersonation Finds 31 Credible Incidents Out of One Billion Ballots Cast*. Retrieved from https://www.washingtonpost.com/news/wonk/wp/2014/08/06/a-comprehensive-investigation-of-voter-impersonation-finds-31-credible-incidents-out-of-one-billion-ballots-cast/ (accessed 16 November 2016).

Lijphart, A. (1999). *Patterns of Democracy: Government Forms and Performance in Thirty-six Countries*. New Haven: Yale University Press.

Lindner, R., Aichholzer, G., and Hennen, L. (eds) (2016). *Electronic Democracy in Europe: Prospects and Challenges of E-publics, E-participation and E-voting*. Cham: Springer International.

Linz, J. J., and Stepan, A. C. (1996). *Problems of Democratic Transition and Consolidation: Southern Europe, South America, and Post-communist Europe*. Baltimore: Johns Hopkins University Press.

Lipton, E., and Urbina, I. (2007). 'In 5-year Effort, Scant Evidence of Voter Fraud', *The New York Times*, 11 April 2007: A1. Retrieved from http://www.nytimes.com/2007/04/12/washington/12fraud.html (accessed 2 November 2016).

Locke, J. (1988 [1680-1690]). *Two Treatises of Government*. Cambridge: Cambridge University Press.

Lublin, D. (1999). *The Paradox of Representation: Racial Gerrymandering and Minority Interests in Congress*. Princeton: Princeton University Press.

Mair, P. (2013). *Ruling the Void: The Hollowing of Western Democracy*. London, New York: Verso.

Maltezou, R. (2016) [website]. *Greek MPs Approve End to Bonus Seats, Lower Voting Age*. Retrieved from http://www.reuters.com/article/us-eurozone-greece-electoral-bill-idUSKCN1011NS (accessed 16 January 2017).

Manin, B. (2008). 'The Emergency Paradigm and the New Terrorism: What if the End of Terrorism Was Not in Sight?', in S. Baume, and B. Fontana (eds), *Les usages de la séparation des pouvoirs*. Paris: M. Houdiard, 136–71.

Manin, B. (1997). *The Principles of Representative Government*. Cambridge: Cambridge University Press.

Mansbridge, J. J. (2015). 'Deliberative und nicht-deliberative Verhandlungen', in A. Bächtiger, S. Shikano, and E. Linhart (eds), *Jahrbuch für Handlungs- und Entscheidungstheorie. Band 9: Deliberation und Aggregation*. Wiesbaden: Springer VS, 1–39.

Marantz, A. (2016) [website]. *Trolls for Trump*. Retrieved from http://www.new-yorker.com/magazine/2016/10/31/trolls-for-trump (accessed 21 November 2016).

Margetts, H., John, P., Hale, S., and Yasseri, T. (2016). *Political Turbulence: How Social Media Shape Collective Action*. Princeton: Princeton University Press.

McCombs, M. E. (2004). *Setting the Agenda: The Mass Media and Public Opinion*. Cambridge: Polity Press.

McCormick, T. (2016) [website]. *The World's Largest Refugee Camp Is Invited to Please Shut Down*. Retrieved from https://foreignpolicy.com/2016/07/21/the-worlds-largest-refugee-camp-is-invited-to-please-shut-down-kenya-somalia-dadaab/ (accessed 4 October 2016).

McDevitt, M., and Chaffee, S. (2002). 'From Top-down to Trickle-up Influence: Revisiting Assumptions About the Family in Political Socialization', *Political Communication*, 19(3): 281–301.

McGhee, E., and Shor, B. (2016). Has the Top Two Primary Elected More Moderates? CDDRL Working Papers. Stanford: Stanford Center on Democracy, Development, and the Rule of Law.

McLaren, L. (2017). 'Immigration, National Identity and Political Trust in European Democracies', *Journal of Ethnic and Migration Studies*, 43(3): 1–21.

Merkel, W. (ed) (2015a). *Demokratie und Krise: Zum schwierigen Verhältnis von Theorie und Empirie*. Wiesbaden: Springer VS.

Merkel, W. (2015b). *Nur schöner Schein? Demokratische Innovationen in Theorie und Praxis*. Frankfurt: Otto Brenner Stiftung.

Merkel, W., and Ritzi, C. (eds) (2017). *Die Legitimität direkter Demokratie: Wie demokratisch sind Volksabstimmungen?* Wiesbaden: Springer VS.

Michels, A. (2011). 'Innovations in Democratic Governance: How Does Citizen

Participation Contribute to a Better Democracy?', *International Review of Administrative Sciences*, 77(2): 275–93.

Michels, R. (1911). *Zur Soziologie des Parteiwesens in der modernen Demokratie: Untersuchungen über die oligarchischen Tendenzen des Gruppenlebens.* Leipzig: Klinkhardt.

Micklethwait, J. (2014) [website]. *The West's Malaise*. Retrieved from http://www.economist.com/news/21631693-worries-about-democracy-will-resurface-2015-says-john-micklethwait-wests-malaise (accessed 2 November 2016).

Milata KG (2016). Academic Corruption Perception Ranking 2016: Ukraine Becomes 11th Surveyed State. Retrieved from http://milata-kg.de/en/press (accessed 7 February 2017).

Minnite, L. C. (2010). *The Myth of Voter Fraud*. Ithaca: Cornell University Press.

Mogus, J., and Liacas, T. (2016). Networked Change. How Progressive Campaigns Are Won in the 21st Century. Ganges: NetChange Consulting. Retrieved from http://netchange.co/report (accessed 4 October 2016).

Montesquieu, C. d. S. (1989 [1748]). *The Spirit of the Laws*. Cambridge: Cambridge University Press.

Müller, J.-W. (2016). *What Is Populism?* Philadelphia: University of Pennsylvania Press.

Mungiu-Pippidi, A. (2015a). Public Integrity and Trust in Europe. Berlin: ERCAS European Research Centre for Anti-corruption and State-building.

Mungiu-Pippidi, A. (2015b). *The Quest for Good Governance: How Societies Develop Control of Corruption*. Cambridge: Cambridge University Press.

NCSL (National Conference of State Legislatures) (2016) [website]. *Same Day Voter Registration*. Retrieved from http://www.ncsl.org/research/elections-and-campaigns/same-day-registration.aspx (accessed 16 November 2016).

Newton, K. (2012a). 'Curing the Democratic Malaise With Democratic Innovations', in B. Geissel, and K. Newton (eds), *Evaluating Democratic Innovations: Curing the Democratic Malaise?* New York: Routledge, 3–20.

Newton, K. (2012b). 'Making Better Citizens?', in B. Geissel, and K. Newton (eds), *Evaluating Democratic Innovations: Curing the Democratic Malaise?* New York: Routledge, 137–62.

Nez, H. (2012). 'Délibérer au sein d'un mouvement social: Ethnographie des assemblées des Indignés à Madrid', *Participations*, 4(3): 79–102.

Niemeyer, S. (2014). 'A Defence of (Deliberative) Democracy in the Anthropocene', *Ethical Perspectives*, 21(1): 15–45.

Nienaber, M. (2016) [website]. *More Than 10,000 Protest Against Racism in Several German Cities*. Retrieved from http://uk.reuters.com/article/uk-europe-migrants-germany-march-idUKKCN0Z50OO (accessed 4 October 2016).

Norris, P. (2002). *Democratic Phoenix: Reinventing Political Activism*. Cambridge: Cambridge University Press.

Obama, B. (2016) [website]. *Remarks by the President in Address to the Illinois General Assembly*. Retrieved from https://www.whitehouse.gov/the-press-office/2016/02/10/remarks-president-address-illinois-general-assembly (accessed 2 November 2016).

OECD (Organisation for Economic Co-operation and Development) (2015). *Government at a Glance 2015*. Paris: OECD Publishing.

Offe, C. (2011). Crisis and Innovation of Liberal Democracy: Can Deliberation Be Institutionalised? Unpublished Manuscript.

Parkinson, J., and Mansbridge, J. J. (eds) (2012). *Deliberative Systems: Deliberative Democracy at the Large Scale*. Cambridge: Cambridge University Press.

Participedia [website]. *Cases | Participedia*. Retrieved from http://participedia.net/en/browse/cases (accessed 1 January 2017).

Parvin, P. (2015). 'Is Deliberative Democracy Feasible? Political Disengagement and Trust in Liberal Democratic States', *The Monist*, 98(4): 407–23.

Patterson, T. (2009). 'Voter Participation: Records Galore This Time, but What About Next Time?', in S. S. Smith, and M. J. Springer (eds), *Reforming the Presidential Nomination Process*. Washington, DC: Brookings Institution Press, 44–63.

Peruzzotti, E., and Smulovitz, C. (2006). *Enforcing the Rule of Law: Social Accountability in the New Latin American Democracies*. Pittsburgh: University of Pittsburgh Press.

Peters, B. (1993). *Die Integration moderner Gesellschaften*. Frankfurt am Main: Suhrkamp.

Pew Research Center (2015). Beyond Distrust: How Americans View Their Government. Washington, DC: Pew Research Center. Retrieved from http://www.people-press.org/2015/11/23/beyond-distrust-how-americans-view-their-government/ (accessed 16 November 2016).

Pew Research Center (2014). Political Polarization in the American Public. Washington, DC: Pew Research Center. Retrieved from http://www.people-press.org/2014/06/12/political-polarization-in-the-american-public/ (accessed 16 November 2016).

Pew Research Center (2009). End of Communism Cheered but Now With More Reservations. Washington, DC: Pew Research Center. Retrieved from http://www.pewglobal.org/2009/11/02/end-of-communism-cheered-but-now-with-more-reservations/ (accessed 2 February 2017).

Placek, M. A. (2016). '#Democracy: Social Media Use and Democratic Legitimacy in Central and Eastern Europe', *Democratization*. Retrieved from http://www.tandfonline.com/doi/full/10.1080/13510347.2016.1202929 (accessed 2 November 2016): 1–19.

Plattner, M. (2010). 'Populism, Pluralism, and Liberal Democracy', *Journal of Democracy*, 21(1): 81–92.

Pogrebinschi, T. (forthcoming). 'Deliberative Democracy in Latin America', in A. Bächtiger, J. S. Dryzek, J. J. Mansbridge, and M. Warren (eds), *The Oxford Handbook of Deliberative Democracy*. Oxford: Oxford University Press.

Pogrebinschi, T. (2016). Comparing Deliberative Systems: An Assessment of 12 Countries in Latin America. Paper Presented at the American Political Science Association 2016 in Philadelphia, 1–4 September, 2016 and the European Consortium of Political Research 2016 General Conference in Prague, 7–10 September, 2016.

Pogrebinschi, T. (2013a). *The Pragmatic Turn of Democracy in Latin America.* Berlin: Friedrich Ebert Stiftung.

Pogrebinschi, T. (2013b). 'The Squared Circle of Participatory Democracy: Scaling up Deliberation to the National Level', *Critical Policy Studies*, 7(3): 219–41.

Pogrebinschi, T., and Samuels, D. (2014). 'The Impact of Participatory Democracy: Evidence From Brazil's National Public Policy Conferences', *Comparative Politics*, 46(3): 313–32.

Popper, H. (2012) [website]. *Argentina's Senate Passes Bill to Lower Voting Age.* Retrieved from http://www.reuters.com/article/us-argentina-vote-idUS-BRE89H03L20121018 (accessed 16 January 2017).

Refugee Migrant Coalition (2015). Protection, Resettlement and Integration. Ireland's Response to the Refugee and Migration 'Crisis'. Retrieved from http://www.irishrefugeecouncil.ie/campaigns-policy/publications (accessed 19 January 2017).

Reporters Without Borders (2016) [website]. *A 'Deep and Disturbing' Decline in Media Freedom.* Retrieved from https://rsf.org/en/deep-and-disturbing-decline-media-freedom (accessed 27 January 2017).

Riffkin, R. (2014) [website]. *Public Faith in Congress Falls Again, Hits Historic Low.* Retrieved from http://www.gallup.com/poll/171710/public-faith-congress-falls-again-hits-historic-low.aspx (accessed 16 November 2016).

Rosanvallon, P. (2008). *Counter-democracy: Politics in an Age of Distrust.* Cambridge: Cambridge University Press.

Rosner, M. (2016) [website]. *Democracy.* Retrieved from https://ourworldindata.org/democracy/ (accessed 27 January 2017).

Rossiter, C. L. (1950). 'War, Depression, and the Presidency, 1933–50', *Social Research*, 17(4): 417–40.

Rossiter, C. L. (1948). *Constitutional Dictatorship: Crisis Government in the Modern Democracies.* Princeton: Princeton University Press.

Rowland, D. (2012) [website]. *Fight Over Poll Hours Isn't Just Political.* Retrieved from http://www.dispatch.com/content/stories/local/2012/08/19/fight-over-poll-hours-isnt-just-political.html (accessed 2 November 2016).

Ryan, M., and Smith, G. (2012). 'Towards a Comparative Analysis of Democratic Innovations: Lessons From a Small-n fsQCA of Participatory Budgeting', *Revista International de Sociología*, 70(2): 87–120.

Santos, B. d. S. (2007). *Democratizing Democracy: Beyond the Liberal Democratic Canon.* London, New York: Verso.

Santos, B. d. S. (2006). *The Rise of the Global Left: The World Social Forum and Beyond.* London: Zed Books.

Santos, B. d. S. (1998). 'Participatory Budgeting in Porto Alegre: Toward a Redistributive Democracy', *Politics & Society*, 26(4): 461–510.

Sartori, G. (1970). 'Concept Misformation in Comparative Politics', *American Political Science Review*, 64(4): 1033–53.

Schmitt, C. (2014 [1921]). *Dictatorship*. Cambridge: Polity Press.

Schmitt, C. (2007 [1926]). *The Concept of the Political*. Chicago: University of Chicago Press.

Schmitt, C. (2006 [1922]). *Political Theology: Four Chapters on the Concept of Sovereignty*. Chicago: University of Chicago Press.

Schmitter, P., and Trechsel, A. (2004). Green Paper: The Future of Democracy in Europe. Trends, Analyses and Reforms. Strasbourg: Council of Europe. Retrieved from http://www.coe.int/t/dgap/democracy/activities/key-texts/02_Green_Paper/GreenPaper_bookmarked_en.asp (accessed 6 February 2017).

Schönleiter, G. (2003). 'World Social Forum: Making Another World Possible?', in J. Clark (ed), *Globalizing Civic Engagement: Civil Society and Transnational Action*. London: Earthscan, 124–49.

Seibel, W. (2016). *Verwaltung verstehen: Eine theoriegeschichtliche Einführung*. Berlin: Suhrkamp.

Selee, A. D., and Peruzzotti, E. (2009). *Participatory Innovation and Representative Democracy in Latin America*. Washington, DC, Baltimore: Woodrow Wilson Center Press; Johns Hopkins University Press.

Shirky, C. (2008). *Here Comes Everybody: The Power of Organizing Without Organizations*. New York: Penguin Press.

Sintomer, Y., Allegretti, G., Herzberg, C., and Röcke, A. (2009). *I bilanci partecipativi in Europa: Nouvo Esperienze Democratiche Nel Vecchio Continente*. Rome: Ediesse.

Sintomer, Y., Herzberg, C., Allegretti, G., and Röcke, A. (2010). Learning From the South: Participatory Budgeting Worldwide—An Invitation to Global Cooperation. Dialog Global 25. Bonn: InWEnt.

Smilov, D. (2013). 'Populism of Fear: Eastern European Perspectives', in H. Giusto, D. Kitching, and S. Rizzo (eds), *The Changing Faces of Populism: Systemic Challengers in Europe and the U.S.* Brussels, Rome: Foundation for European Progressive Studies; Fondazione Centro per la Riforma dello Stato; Fondazione Italianieuropei, 227–54.

Smilov, D. (2009). 'The Power of Assembled People: The Right to Assembly and Political Representation', in A. Sajó (ed), *Free to Protest: Constituent Power and Street Demonstration*. Utrecht: Eleven International Publishing, 87–104.

Smilov, D., and Smilova, R. (2015). 'Informal Politics and Formal Media Structures', in J. Zielonka (ed), *Media and Politics in New Democracies: Europe in a Comparative Perspective*. Oxford: Oxford University Press, 197–216.

Smith, G. (2009). *Democratic Innovations: Designing Institutions for Citizen Participation*. Cambridge: Cambridge University Press.

Smith, G. (2005). *Beyond the Ballot: 57 Democratic Innovations From Around the World*. London: Power Inquiry.

Smith, G., Richards, R. C., and Gastil, J. (2015). 'The Potential of Participedia as a Crowdsourcing Tool for Comparative Analysis of Democratic Innovations', *Policy & Internet*, 7(2): 243–62.

Sontag, R. (2013). The End of Sovereign Democracy in Russia. What Was It, Why Did It Fail, What Comes Next and What Should the United States Think of This? Rising Experts Task Force Working Paper. Washington, DC: Center on Global Interests.

Stanton, J., Altin, V., Hall, J., Wells, L., and Sinmaz, E. (2015) [website]. *The Final Journey of Tragic Little Boys Washed up on a Turkish Beach: Mother and Sons Who Died in Sea Tragedy Are Taken From Morgue After Heartbroken Father Says Goodbye to the Family He Couldn't Save*. Retrieved from http://www.dailymail.co.uk/news/article-3219553/Terrible-fate-tiny-boy-symbolises-desperation-thousands-Body-drowned-Syrian-refugee-washed-Turkish-beach-family-tried-reach-Europe.html (accessed 21 November 2016).

Talpin, J. (2012). 'When Democratic Innovations Let the People Decide: An Evaluation of Co-governance Experiments', in B. Geissel, and K. Newton (eds), *Evaluating Democratic Innovations: Curing the Democratic Malaise?* New York: Routledge, 184–206.

Talpin, J. (2007). Schools of Democracy: The Construction of Civic Competence in Participatory Governance Institutions. PhD Dissertation. Florence: European University Institute.

The Iraq Inquiry (2016). Statement by Sir John Chilcot: 6 July 2016. London: The Iraq Inquiry. Retrieved from http://www.iraqinquiry.org.uk/the-report/ (accessed 24 November 2016).

Toma la Plaza (2011) [website]. *En las Características del 15M—Inclusividad, Horizontalidad, Inteligencia colectiva y No-violencia—está la Clave que nos permitirá cambiar el Mundo y nuestras Vidas*. Retrieved from http://madrid.tomalaplaza.net/2011/08/12/en-las-caracteristicas-del-15m-in-clusividad-horizontalidad-inteligencia-colectiva-y-no-violencia-esta-la-clave-que-nos-permitira-cambiar-el-mundo-y-nuestras-vidas/ (accessed 9 December 2016).

Torfing, J., Peters, B. G., and Sørensen, E. (2012). *Interactive Governance: Advancing the Paradigm*. Oxford: Oxford University Press.

Touchton, M., and Wampler, B. (2014). 'Improving Social Well-being Through New Democratic Institutions', *Comparative Political Studies*, 47(10): 1442–69.

US Court of Appeals for the Fourth Circuit (2016). *N. Carolina State Conference of NAACP v. McCrory*, No. 16-1468, 2016 WL 4053033, Judgment of 29 July 2016.

van Gelder, S. R. (2011). *This Changes Everything: Occupy Wall Street and the 99% Movement*. San Francisco: Berrett-Koehler.

van Reybrouck, D. (2016). *Against Elections: The Case for Democracy*. London: The Bodley Head.

Vatter, A. (2014). *Das politische System der Schweiz*. Baden-Baden: Nomos.

Venice Commission. Opinion on Act CLXII of 2011 on the Legal Status and Remuneration of Judges and Act CLXI of 2011 on the Organisation and Administration of Courts of Hungary. Strasbourg: Council of Europe. Retrieved from http://www.venice.coe.int/webforms/documents/default.aspx?pdffile=CDL-AD(2012)001-e (accessed 7 February 2017).

Voteview.com (2016) [website]. *Political Polarization*. Retrieved from http://voteview.com/political_polarization_2015.htm (accessed 16 November 2016).

Vowe, G. (2014). 'Digital Citizens und Schweigende Mehrheit: Wie verändert sich die politische Beteiligung der Bürger durch das Internet?', in K. Voss (ed), *Internet und Partizipation: Bottom-up oder Top-down? Politische Beteiligungsmöglichkeiten im Internet*. Wiesbaden: Springer VS, 25–52.

Wagener, V. (2010). *Opinion: Wulff Makes Integration Centerpiece of Unity Day Speech*. Retrieved from http://www.dw.com/en/opinion-wulff-makes-integration-centerpiece-of-unity-day-speech/a-6071079 (accessed 4 October 2016).

Wagner, M., Johann, D., and Kritzinger, S. (2012). 'Voting at 16: Turnout and the Quality of Vote Choice', *Electoral Studies*, 31(2): 372–83.

Wampler, B. (2008). 'When Does Participatory Democracy Deepen the Quality of Democracy? Lessons From Brazil', *Comparative Politics*, 41(1): 61–81.

Wampler, B. (2007). *Participatory Budgeting in Brazil: Contestation, Cooperation, and Accountability*. University Park: Pennsylvania State University Press.

Wampler, B. (2000). *A Guide to Participatory Budgeting*. Retrieved from http://www.participatorybudgeting.org/full-article-library/ (accessed 4 November 2016).

Wampler, B., and Avritzer, L. (2004). 'Participatory Publics: Civil Society and New Institutions in Democratic Brazil', *Comparative Politics*, 36(3): 291–312.

Warren, M. (2012). When, Where and Why Do We Need Deliberation, Voting, and Other Means of Organizing Democracy? A Problem-based Approach to Democratic Systems. Paper Presented at the Annual Meeting of the American Political Science Association 2012 in New Orleans. Retrieved from https://papers.ssrn.com/sol3/papers.cfm?abstract_id=2104566 (accessed 26 January 2017).

Warren, M. (2009). 'Citizen Participation and Democratic Deficits: Considerations From the Perspective of Democratic Theory', in J. DeBardeleben, and J. Pammett (eds), *Activating the Citizen: Dilemmas of Participation in Europe and Canada*. Basingstoke: Palgrave Macmillan, 17–40.

Warren, M., and Pearse, H. (2008). *Designing Deliberative Democracy: The British Columbia Citizens' Assembly*. Cambridge: Cambridge University Press.

Watkins, F. M. (1940). 'The Problem of Constitutional Dictatorship', in C. J. Friedrich, and E. S. Mason (eds), *Public Policy: A Yearbook of the Graduate*

School of Public Administration, Harvard University. Cambridge, MA: Harvard University Press.

Watkins, F. M. (1939). *The Failure of Constitutional Emergency Powers Under the German Republic*. Cambridge, MA: Harvard University Press.

Weber, M. (1919). *Politik als Beruf*. Leipzig: Duncker & Humblot.

Weiser, W., and Opsal, E. (2014). The State of Voting in 2014. Executive Summary. New York: Brennan Center for Justice, New York University School of Law.

Weßels, B. (2015). 'Political Culture, Political Satisfaction and the Rollback of Democracy', in H. K. Anheier (ed), Changing the European Debate: A Rollback of Democracy, *Global Policy*, 6(s1): 93–105.

White, M. (2010) [website]. *Clicktivism Is Ruining Leftist Activism*. Retrieved from https://www.theguardian.com/commentisfree/2010/aug/12/clicktivism-ruining-leftist-activism (accessed 4 October 2016).

White, S., and Hill, R. J. (1996). 'Russia, the Former Soviet Union and Eastern Europe: The Referendum as a Flexible Political Instrument', in M. Gallagher, and P. V. Uleri (eds), *The Referendum Experience in Europe*. Basingstoke: Macmillan, 153–70.

Willoughby, W. W., and Rogers, L. (1921). *An Introduction to the Problem of Government*. Garden City: Doubleday, Page & Company.

Witt, J. (2015). To Save the Country. Unpublished Manuscript. New Haven: Yale Law School.

Zeglovits, E., and Aichholzer, J. (2014). 'Are People More Inclined to Vote at 16 Than at 18? Evidence for the First-time Voting Boost Among 16- to 25-year-olds in Austria', *Journal of Elections, Public Opinion and Parties*, 24(3): 351–61.

About the Contributors

Helmut K. Anheier is President, Dean, and Professor of Sociology at the Hertie School of Governance. He also holds a Chair of Sociology at Heidelberg University and serves as Academic Director of the Centre for Social Investment. His research centres on indicator systems, social innovation, culture, philanthropy, and organisational studies. He is author of over 450 publications and has won several international prizes for his scholarship. His most recent publication is the second edition of the textbook *Nonprofit Organizations: Theory, Management, Policy* (Routledge, 2005 and 2014).

Ewa Atanassow is Junior Professor of Political Thought at Bard College Berlin. Her research centres on the history of liberalism with emphasis on Tocqueville. Her articles and reviews have appeared in the American Political Science Review, Global Policy, Journal of Democracy, and Nations and Nationalism among others. She is the co-editor of *Tocqueville and the Frontiers of Democracy* (Cambridge, 2013) and *Liberal Moments: Liberalism in a Global Perspective* (Bloomsbury Academic, forthcoming).

Donatella Della Porta is Professor of Political Science and Dean at the Institute of Human and Social Sciences at the Scuola Normale Superiore, where she directs the Centre on Social Movement Studies (Cosmos). Among the main topics of her research: social movements, political violence, terrorism, corruption, the police, and protest policing. She holds honorary doctorates from the universities of Lausanne, Bucharest, and Goteborg and is the author of 85 books, 130 journal articles, and 127 contributions in edited volumes.

Andrea Felicetti is Postdoctoral Researcher at the Institute for Humanities and Social Sciences, Scuola Normale Superiore. His academic interests include democratic theory, deliberative democracy, social movements, and comparative politics. He has worked at the Institute for Governance and Policy Analysis, University of Canberra; the Hoover Chair of Social and Economic Ethics, Catholic University of Louvain; University of Lille 3; and the European University Institute.

Matthias Haber is Postdoctoral Research Scientist for the Governance Report at the Hertie School of Governance. He is a political scientist with research interests in party politics, electoral behaviour, machine learning, survey experiments, and measurement problems. He was previously Research Associate at the Collaborative Research Center 'Political Economy of Reforms' at the University of Mannheim. He holds degrees from the University of Mannheim, the University of Essex, and the University of Potsdam.

Nina Hall is Lecturer in Global Governance at the Hertie School of Governance. She researches on transnational advocacy, global refugee and migration governance, and climate change and is currently collaborating with a global network of digital activists. Her book *Displacement, Development and Climate Change: International Organizations Moving Beyond their Mandates* was published by Routledge in 2016. She has a PhD in International Relations from the University of Oxford and previously worked with the New Zealand Ministry of Foreign Affairs and Trade.

Anke Hassel is Academic Director of the Institute of Economic and Social Research (WSI) of the Hans Boeckler Foundation and Professor of Public Policy at the Hertie School of Governance in Berlin. She is also a faculty member of the Berlin Graduate School for Transnational Studies. Her research interests focus on the interplay between modern business and social systems, and she has written extensively about the transformation of the German political economy in a comparative perspective and the role of labour market institutions in the eurozone.

Nicole Helmerich is Post-doctoral Researcher at the Hertie School of Governance. Her work revolves around the role of business in transnational governance, transnational private regulation, corporate responsibility, transnational workers' rights, sustainability, and good corporate governance. Her most recent publication is *Sustainability Politics and Limited Statehood. Contesting the New Modes of Governance* (Palgrave Macmillan, 2017), co-edited with Alejandro Esguerra and Thomas Risse.

Ira Katznelson is Ruggles Professor of Political Science and History at Columbia University and President of the Social Science Research Council. His most recent book, *Fear Itself: The New Deal and the Origins of Our Time* (Liveright, 2013), has been awarded the Bancroft Prize in History and the Woodrow Wilson Foundation Award in Political Science. He has served as President of the American Political Science Association and is Research Associate at Cambridge University's Centre for History and Economics.

Sonja Kaufmann is Associate Editor for the Governance Report and Research Associate at the Hertie School of Governance. Before joining the Hertie School, she worked at the Berlin Social Science Research Center and the Free University's Collaborative Research Center 'Governance in Areas of Limited Statehood', researching on various aspects of new forms of governance.

Olga Kononykhina is a quantitative sociologist and a data scientist at the Hertie School of Governance. Her research focuses on data-driven projects in the fields of culture, civil society, governance, and development. She has previously worked at the Centre for Social Investment in Heidelberg, the Johns Hopkins University, the National Research University Higher School of Economics in Moscow, and CIVICUS. She is currently pursuing a PhD at Heidelberg University.

Didi Kuo is Program Manager at the Program on American Democracy in Comparative Perspective at the Center on Democracy, Development, and the Rule of Law at Stanford University. Her research interests include democratisation, clientelism, and political reform, particularly in advanced democracies. She is working on a book manuscript about patronage, business, and institutional reform in the United States and Britain.

Regina A. List is Managing Editor of the Governance Report project and coordinator and researcher for other governance- and culture-related projects at the Hertie School of Governance. She is also Managing Editor of the *Journal of Civil Society*. She has researched, written, and edited numerous publications on governance, democracy, civil society, and nonprofit organisations. She previously worked at Johns Hopkins University, where she coordinated the Johns Hopkins Comparative Nonprofit Sector Project.

Wolfgang Merkel is Director of the Democracy and Democratization Research Unit at the Berlin Social Science Centre (WZB) and Professor for Political Science at Humboldt University. He has published numerous books and articles on the crisis of democracy, quality of democracy, transition to democracy, social democracy, and social justice. He was previously Professor of Political Science at the Universities of Heidelberg and Mainz.

Alina Mungiu-Pippidi is Professor of Democracy Studies at the Hertie School of Governance. She chairs the European Research Centre for Anti-corruption and State-Building (ERCAS) at the Hertie School, where she manages ANTICORRP, an ongoing research project on anticorruption policy, and DIGIWHIST. She is also chair of the civil society anticorruption coalition in her native country Romania. Her work has been published as journal articles and monographs, most recently *A Quest for Good Governance* (Cambridge University Press, 2015).

Claus Offe was Professor of Political Sociology at the Hertie School of Governance until 2015 and is now Professor Emeritus. Previous positions include professorships at the Humboldt University of Berlin, as well as Universities of Bielefeld and Bremen, where he served as Director of the Center for Social Policy Research. His fields of research include democratic theory, transition studies, EU integration, and welfare state and labour market studies. His most recent book in English is *Europe Entrapped* (Polity, 2014).

Jean Pisani-Ferry is Professor of Economics and Public Management at the Hertie School of Governance. From 2013 to 2017 he served as Commissioner-General for Policy Planning, reporting to the French Prime Minister. Prior to this, he contributed to founding the Brussels-based economic think tank Bruegel in 2005 and served as its Director. He was previously Executive President of the French PM's Council of Economic Analysis; Senior Economic Adviser to the French Minister of Finance; Director of CEPII, the French institute for international economics; and Economic Adviser with the European Commission.

Thamy Pogrebinschi is Senior Researcher at the Berlin Social Science Centre (WZB), a faculty member of the Berlin Graduate School of Social Sciences at the Humboldt University, and Adjunct Professor of Political Science at the State University of Rio de Janeiro. At the WZB she coordinates the project Innovations for Democracy in Latin America (LATINNO). She has published six books on political theory, and her current research on participatory democracy in Latin America has been published in edited volumes in four languages as well as in academic journals.

Andrea Römmele is Professor for Communication in Politics and Civil Society at the Hertie School of Governance. Her research interests are in the field of comparative political communication, political parties, and public affairs. She is co-founder and Editor-in-Chief of the *Journal for Political Consulting and Policy Advice*. She was previously visiting fellow at the Johns Hopkins University and at the Australian National University. Her most recent book, co-edited with Svenja Falk and Michael Silverman, is *Digital Government: Leveraging Innovation to Improve Public Sector Performance and Outcomes for Citizens* (Springer, 2017).

Daniel Smilov is Programme Director at the Centre for Liberal Strategies in Sofia, Recurrent Visiting Professor of Comparative Constitutional Law at Central European University in Budapest, and Associate Professor of Political Theory at the Political Science Department, Sofia University St. Kliment Ohridski. Previously he was Research Fellow at the Centre for Policy Studies at Central European University, Jean Monnet Fellow at the European University Institute in Florence, and a visiting scholar at Boalt Hall School of Law, University of California Berkeley.